The World Beyond Digital Rights Management

The British Computer Society

BCS is the leading professional body for the IT industry. With members in over 100 countries, BCS is the professional and learned Society in the field of computers and information systems.

BCS is responsible for setting standards for the IT profession. It is also leading the change in public perception and appreciation of the economic and social importance of professionally managed IT projects and programmes. In this capacity, the Society advises, informs and persuades industry and government on successful IT implementation.

IT is affecting every part of our lives and that is why BCS is determined to promote IT as the profession of the 21st century.

Joining BCS

BCS qualifications, products and services are designed with your career plans in mind. We not only provide essential recognition through professional qualifications but also offer many other useful benefits to our members at every level.

BCS membership demonstrates your commitment to professional development. It helps to set you apart from other IT practitioners and provides industry recognition of your skills and experience. Employers and customers increasingly require proof of professional qualifications and competence. Professional membership confirms your competence and integrity and sets an independent standard that people can trust. Professional Membership (MBCS) is the pathway to Chartered IT Professional (CITP) status.

www.bcs.org/membership

Further Information

Further information about BCS can be obtained from: BCS, First Floor, Block D, North Star House, North Star Avenue, Swindon, SN2 1FA, UK.

Telephone: 0845 300 4417 (UK only) or + 44 (0)1793 417 424 (overseas)

Email: customerservice@hq.bcs.org.uk

Web: www.bcs.org

The World Beyond Digital Rights Management

Jude C. Umeh

 **BCS**

The British Computer Society
Publishing and Information Products
First Floor, Block D
North Star House
North Star Avenue
Swindon
SN2 1FA
UK

www.bcs.org

ISBN 978-1-902505-87-9

British Cataloguing in Publication Data.
A CIP catalogue record for this book is available at the British Library.

Typeset by Lapiz Digital Services, Chennai, India.
Printed and bound in Great Britain by Antony Rowe Ltd, Chippenham, Wiltshire

To my family

Contents

List of Figures and Tables

Author

Jude C. Umeh is a certified Technical Architect and member of the Sector Consulting Group within Capgemini's global Telecom Media and Entertainment (TME) community. He has over ten years experience in a variety of technical and strategic roles, and his background and areas of expertise include: music, media and e-business consultancy; digital content and rights management; as well as evaluating, recommending and delivering packaged solutions to large organisations.

Jude has worked with key music and media industry organisations to help define the future business processes and technologies that will shape their response to an increasingly challenging digital environment. He has authored several white papers and articles including *Rights Management and the Music Industry* (Capgemini 2006), *Evolving the New Music Business* (Capgemini 2005) and *Mobile Digital Rights Management (mDRM)* in 2004. He also contributes regularly to the thought leadership, development and delivery of solutions and services to the various stakeholders in these fields.

Jude holds a Masters degree in computer science from the University College London and is a chartered member of the BCS where he serves as committee member in the North London Branch. Jude is an experienced conference speaker and moderator, and has contributed his expertise to various international events such as: DRMStrategies Conference 2004 and 2005 in Los Angeles and New York; the IP-Trends Summit 2005 and 2006 in San Francisco and Monaco; as well as several BCS events on Music and Digital Rights Management in London.

Foreword

Who would have thought that the digital content revolution would really be about rights? An ad-hoc collection of academics, technologists, publishers and policy wonks that came together in late 1993 did. The proceedings of a conference in Washington, DC, called Technological Strategies for Protecting Intellectual Property in the Networked Multimedia Environment (still available at http://www.cni.org/docs/ima.ip-workshop) show – in 20/20 hindsight – a bunch of blind men attempting to describe the elephant that they know is in the room.

The world has changed a lot since then, and yet with respect to the problems of rights management, it has not changed all that much: the essential problems that content owners face when distributing their content in digital form persist. Bits are still easy to copy, the internet is still essentially an open architecture and many types of content rights are still tracked with blunt instruments such as statistical sampling and blanket licensing.

By the time I co-wrote *Digital Rights Management: Business and Technology* in 2001 (Rosenblatt et al 2002), the mouthful used for the conference noted above had condensed to the simpler term digital rights management (DRM). There was some idea that the technology could be used to create new types of business models for content, such as subscription music services, but the internal machinery of media companies turned out to be as ill-equipped to handle these new models as consumers were ill-equipped to appreciate them. Therefore much of the emphasis in DRM – particularly now that the internet bubble was bursting – was on media companies' attempts to use it to emulate old physical media models rather than invent new ones.

As Jude Umeh shows in this book, there is still a vast wealth of untapped possibilities in DRM. The collective understanding of rights management has certainly increased: much more is understood than in 2001 about how rights underlie commerce in intellectual property and how those processes can be automated. The subtle relationships between copyright law and DRM technology are being explored instead of ignored. Digital devices other than personal computers (PCs) are being used to consume and produce content in quantities never previously imagined.

At the same time, controversy around DRM has also increased, especially in recent years. The most popular licensed internet content service in the world, Apple's iTunes, uses a DRM technology (FairPlay) that some call too restrictive while others call it too lax. DRM has become, relatively speaking, a sensationalist topic for business and technology journalists. It is the subject of frequent governmental lobbying efforts as well as organised protests, and it is now a perennial topic of discussion at the European Commission and other exalted forums.

Indeed, the term DRM has become a sort of shorthand for the constant three-way tug-of-war among consumers, technology vendors and the media industry that pervades the digital media world today.

Unfortunately, readers who would like to make sense of this world have their work cut out for them; for some of us, it's a full-time job. Understanding digital rights management requires that one understands security and ecommerce technologies, law and public policy issues (across different national boundaries), economics and the arcana of the media business – all of which are in constant states of flux.

Luckily, this book now exists to guide those who wish to understand DRM. Jude Umeh has laid out a rich context for DRM that encompasses the broad issues of technology, stakeholders, content models and system integration that need to be understood in order to have a complete picture of DRM. Some parts of this book may inevitably be obsolete over time, but Umeh has taken great care to isolate them and to leave the reader with concepts and contexts that should apply to the digital media world for a good while.

Long after all of the specific technical solutions discussed here disappear, the same challenges will remain. It will still be trivially easy to copy bits. Yet there will still be differences of opinion about whether or not certain uses of content should be allowed, there will still be challenges in integrating DRM with media companies' back-office systems and content pirates will continue to find ways of distributing content without authorisation that slip past whatever obstacles legal systems can lob at them. In other words, there will still be a need for this book to give people seeking to understand these issues a framework for doing so.

Bill Rosenblatt
New York City
March 2007

Acknowledgements

This book was written as a result of a flippant remark I made to Matthew Flynn, BCS Commissioning Editor, in autumn 2005. I carelessly said to him that I could write a book on DRM that would look great among his growing collection of BCS books and he said 'Why don't you?'; this is the outcome (thanks Matthew). I would also like to acknowledge the following people for their contributions, large and small, to the writing of this book.

First and foremost, my profound thanks go to Bill Rosenblatt for his many contributions to this work such as the Foreword, and for his invaluable comments, feedback and topic insight, as well as for the opportunity to participate in JupiterMedia's DRM Strategies Conferences in 2004 and 2005. These events proved to be the perfect forum for interaction and immersion in all things DRM. I would also like to thank Charles Brown at the University of Westminster and Jonathan Cornthwaite at Wedlake Bell for reviewing and providing constructive feedback on the early chapters of this book. My thanks also go to Farokh Billimoria, Rajan Samtani and Joshua Duhl for their feedback and insight into the relevant enabler industries in the content economy. Thanks are also due to Edyta Kilian at IMS Conferences for the opportunity to participate in the IP-Trends Summits in 2005 and 2006.

I would like to express my gratitude to some of my mentors and role models (whether they know it or not), including: Andy Mulholland (FBCS), author and global CTO at Capgemini; Rene Carayol for challenging my presumptions about this topic back in 2004; Richard Boulderstone, Director of eStrategy at the British Library; and Dr C. C. Umeh, prize-winning playwright, educationist and University Don at Caritas University, Nigeria, as well as being the father of one Jude Umeh.

I also wish to acknowledge the great encouragement from my colleagues in the BCS North London Branch committee especially: Dalim Basu (FBCS), Stephen Cameron (soon to be BCS author), Patrick Roberts, Richard Tandoh, Rebecca King, Celeste Rush, John Ryan and others past and present. My thanks also to my colleagues in Capgemini, especially those in the global TME sector, and the UK's Sector Consulting Group, who have made it a great environment in which to work and develop professionally.

Finally, this book is dedicated to my family for all their love, support and encouragement throughout its writing, especially to my parents, Dr and Mrs Umeh; to my loving wife Yvonne; and to my USA family (UK, Sabina, Kese, Valentine and Vincent); thanks for all the moral support guys. Peace.

Glossary

AACS The copy protection scheme for next-generation video discs. http://www.aacsla.com/

Advanced Encryption Standard (AES) Standard for symmetric cryptography endorsed by the National Institute of Standards and Technology in the USA.

Algorithm An algorithm is a well-defined computational procedure that takes a variable input and generates a corresponding output (Oppliger 2005).

Analogue A continuously variable quantitative value. Analogue copies degrade through each generation of copies made.

Application programming interface (API) A logical connection through which one software component talks to another.

Authentication The art and science of detecting exactly what person – or what physical or logical device or entity – you are dealing with in a specific interaction.

Bandwidth A measure of capacity in an electronic communications channel. Higher bandwidth implies greater throughput of information hence faster speed of transmission.

Biometrics An authentication technology that is used to identify individuals based on unique physical characteristics such as fingerprints, retina patterns or voice prints.

Blog (also weblog) A web log, or web-based journal, of short dated entries in reverse chronological order that usually focuses on a specific topic, is frequently updated by the author and commented upon by the readers.

Business model Refers to the revenue generation strategy and tactics of content businesses. It involves all of the parties in a business transaction within the content value chain.

Chat/instant messaging The process of communicating with other internet users in real time.

Conditional access (CA) The term used to describe the systems for controlling the viewing of television signals in a broadcast (e.g. satellite or set-top cable) television system.

Content management system (CMS)   A server-based repository that offers library services at a minimum, with many extended and related technologies (also applies to document management systems).

Content Scrambling System (CSS)   The encryption scheme for DVD video discs, which was famously cracked by Jon Lech Johansen's DeCSS program in 1999.

Copy protection   The use of technology to prevent the copying of analogue or digital data. This is not the same as DRM, which is geared more towards controlling how the copied content may be used.

Copyright   An intellectual property right (IPR) based on cultural expectations and laws that aim to strike a balance between the ability of a creative person to get paid for their efforts and the long-term needs of society.

Creative commons   A website, technology or concept, designed to sensibly apply the copyright system and rules in a manner that is both suitable and practical for the internet age.

Cryptography   This is the discipline of keeping and selectively sharing   secrets, which is a key component of DRM systems.

Customer relationship management (CRM)   A system for managing and integrating all of an enterprise's interactions with customers to provide consistency and effectiveness.

Data mining   The process of transforming raw data into higher-level constructs, such as predictive models, explanatory models, filters or summaries by using algorithms from fields such as artificial intelligence and statistics.

Digital   The representation of information by discrete values such as 1 and 0, as opposed to the continuously varying values of the analogue domain.

Digital asset management (DAM)   Provides a repository for data types such as images, audio and video, and typically includes the functionality to search and manipulate these objects.

Digital certificate   A digital document that uses cryptography to create a mathematically unique association between some data and an entity that certifies that data.

Digital Millennium Copyright Act (DMCA)   A piece of US legislation that is designed to bring copyright legislation into the internet age.

Digital rights management (DRM)   Technology or technologies that enable the secure distribution, promotion and sale of digital media content.

Disintermediation This occurs when simplifications in technology, economic forces or other factors cause the displacement of someone, usually an intermediary, from a customary role in a process.

Disruptive technologies New products or distribution processes superior to those that they replace. They effectively change the basis of competition in an entire industry.

DivX A video codec with great compression efficiency. Also refers to the now dead company that was built around this codec.

Ebooks Digital or electronic books, including text, digital images and digital audio books.

Ecommerce The general exchange of goods and services electronically. Ecommerce can occur between businesses and consumers (B2C), business-to-business (B2B) or even consumer-to-consumer (C2C).

Ecosystem (DRM ecosystem) A collection of systems that deliver managed content distribution using a consistent technology base including DRM.

Email A form of electronic messaging where a user creates a text message (that may have a number of attachments) and sends it to a recipient.

Encryption The process of obscuring information to make it unreadable without a reverse process of decryption.

Enterprise DRM Refers to solutions built around the application of DRM technologies in a corporate environment.

EZ-D A disposable DVD-Video-compatible optical disk developed by a company called Flexplay.

Fair use/Fair dealing A copyright exception that explicitly allows copyrighted goods to be copied under specific circumstances.

Fingerprint Specific term of art for technology that recognises commercial content (specifically music) 'on-the-fly', even when that content has no inherent DRM or metadata.

File format The layout of a digital asset such as physical media (CD/DVD) or of files containing video or music.

File Transfer Protocol (FTP) An internet protocol that is used for the transfer of large files.

Hacker A person with both the skills and inclination to learn about – and possibly circumvent – various forms of computer security, for example network security and DRM.

High definition (HD) Refers to the next generation of high-density video formats and media (e.g. HD-DVD and Blu-Ray discs) as well as the recording and transmission mechanisms.

Identity management (IDM) A broad administrative area that deals with identifying individuals in a system (a network, a country, an enterprise) in order to control their access to resources within that system.

Intellectual property This refers to creations of the mind: inventions, literary and artistic works, symbols, names, images and designs used in commerce (WIPO 2006a).

Internet Interconnected network of computing resources based on the TCP/IP protocols.

Internet Protocol (IP) The Internet Protocol is a method for creating a unique address for resources on the internet. An IP address is used to route data to and from the computers on the network, and is made up of two parts that identify the network (network identifier) and the particular or host machine (host identifier) within that network.

Interoperability The ability of different types of computers, networks, operating systems and applications to work together effectively, without prior communication, in order to exchange information in a useful and meaningful manner.

iPod The dominant portable music player device created by Apple Computers and used globally.

IPTV TV content delivered over the internet using the Internet Protocol.

IPv6 IPv6 is the next incarnation of the Internet Protocol that is aimed at rectifying various issues and limitations of the current IP addressing format (i.e. <nnn.nnn.nnn.nnn>).

iTunes Apple Computers online music store and music management software that works together with the iPod music player.

J2EE (Java 2, Enterprise Edition) Widely used platform for building, deploying and managing web services.

License The right to legitimately use or resell intellectual property.

Long tail This term is used to describe the economics of low-volume, niche product exploitation facilitated by the 'infinite shelf space' of the web and ecommerce.

Mash-up A combination of two or more business models, processes, technologies, products or services to create a new one.

Micropayments (or microtransaction) A spontaneous financial transaction for small goods or services, involving very small amounts of money.

Mind share A market research term that broadly refers to the consumer's complete familiarity, and buy-in, to a product, service or brand name.

MP3 MP3 is both an audio codec and an associated file format used for the storage and transmission of high-quality compressed music.

MPEG2-TS A high definition formal of MPEG2 video.

Napster The original program that started the peer-to-peer file-sharing craze.

Open source Commonly used to refer to software that is released with its source code. The term is sometimes used interchangeably with 'free software'. The Open Source Initiative (OSI; http://www.opensource.org/) website states that the term should be used only to describe software that has been certified by OSI.

Patent A monopoly on the creation or sale of an invention granted through an institution like the UK Patent Office.

Peer-to-peer (P2P) network A networked communications model wherein there is no 'hierarchy' and substantially all of the participants have the same capabilities, for example, both providing and obtaining content.

Personal digital assistant (PDA) Refers to a class of portable electronic devices that include several productivity, communication and media-playing functionalities.

Personal video recorder (PVR) A consumer electronics device that uses a hard-disk drive for recording content.

Platform This term generically describes a closely related family of products, technologies or computer systems.

Portal This term refers to companies or electronic systems that provide a portal service to resources and content (both internal and external).

Reverse engineering Analysing a product to determine how it functions. This is often performed by researchers, competing organisations and hackers to determine how protection mechanisms work.

Rights Data Dictionary A set of clear, consistent, structured, integrated and uniquely identified terms.

Rights Expression Language A machine-readable language for expressing what rights are available for certain items of content and certain users.

Royalty The percentage of the price of an IP-based product that is paid to the rights owner of the intellectual property for its use.

Search engine A service that scans content on the internet based on specific keywords and returns a list of content in which they were found.

Social networking and online communities A self-selecting, peer-to-peer group that connects people by interest, skills and practices.

Streaming media Technology for rendering audio or video from a remote source over an IP connection. The content is resident on a server and the client machine renders the content without having complete or permanent copies of it locally.

Superdistribution The wilful uncontrolled distribution of digital goods that generate revenue based on controlling their use, not controlling copying.

Time shifting Watching or listening to some media programming at a time other than when it was originally broadcast.

Transmission Control Protocol (TCP) The protocol that controls the transmission of data between peers or clients and servers on the internet.

Watermark Watermarking, a type of steganography, is the insertion of (usually) hidden data such as copyright information into visible data such as a JPEG image.

Wrapper Digital content protection, in which a digital asset is 'wrapped' using cryptography so that it can only be accessed with the help of an 'unwrapping' agent that knows the key.

Video-on-Demand (VOD) A service that allows users to view video content as and when they desire. It may be over the internet or satellite/cable channels.

Web 2.0 This refers to the newer applications, services and online usage practices that centre around collaboration on the web. Most Web 2.0 services are based on the ability to contribute and share content.

Weltanschauung German term meaning 'worldview'. Often used by systems analysts to refer to a subjective point of view.

Wi-Fi   Wireless Fidelity refers to wireless local area networks that use one of several 802.11 standards (e.g. 802.11a, 802.11g, 802.11b and 802.11n).

Workflow   The process whereby items of work move from one person or process to another in an organisation.

XML   A language designed to identify document elements and attributes in a text stream for application processing in multiple domains.

Note on glossary sources

Except where stated otherwise, all of the terms and definitions above were taken or adapted from two excellent sources:

* The OCLC glossary. http://www.oclc.org/reports/escan/appendices/glossary.htm
* Gord Larose's DRM Dictionary. http://www.info-mech.com/drm_dictionary.html

Introduction

WHAT IS DIGITAL RIGHTS MANAGEMENT

Digital rights management (DRM) is a term that is used to describe the technologies and systems that deliver the capability to control and specify the rights associated with digital content. It is primarily concerned with the management of intellectual property rights (IPRs), specifically those related to copyright, in an electronic environment. DRM can also be defined as the technology that protects content against unauthorised access and usage and which enforces the restrictions on what users can do with it. The term DRM was coined in the 1990s to represent the emerging technologies that were used to enforce the rights of content owners at the dawn of the internet revolution. Like most things DRM did not emerge out of nothing, but has been developed over many years through the efforts of various people in the technology, media, electronics and other industries.

DRM is also concerned with managing content rights outside the digital domain, and it deals with some of the issues encountered by content at the boundary of the electronic and physical realms. A good way to understand this might be to consider the fact that a creative idea is only a figment of someone's imagination, which has no intrinsic value on its own until it is expressed in one form or another. However, even the expression is of limited value unless it has been captured or recorded in a form that can be shared with others; at this point it can be made into a product or distributed in various tangible or non-physical forms to consumers that may (or may not) be willing to pay for it. It is important to recognise that the values placed on these expressed ideas are typically only a reflection of the perception of its worth by the market and consumers at large. The demand for these idea-based products is exploited by content providers who generate revenue by exchanging these goods for money. DRM touches on all of these aspects of the content-based economic systems that evolved through the basic journey from idea to product, in both digital and physical environments, and as such it is clearly and intimately connected with the dynamics of the rapidly evolving new content economy.

The ultimate end-point for the progression of events described in this book looks set to be the provision of content as a service. It involves the creation of new architectures that enable the use of digital content across various layers in a service hierarchy that may be described as a service-oriented content architecture. The concept of service orientation is not new and many industries now have the opportunity to try and realise the business benefits inherent in a coherent architected business and operational environment. This book is not about service-oriented architectures, but it touches on some of the ways that the evolving content economy can be developed to engage with, and evolve alongside, the whole ethos of service orientation. A system, or business enterprise, that uses or supplies content can be viewed either as a service consumer or service provider. Most systems or businesses will produce and use content to various degrees in their daily operations; therefore the flow of that content both within and outside the enterprise boundaries needs to be managed and this is where DRM can be most effective.

WHY THIS BOOK

The primary aim of this book is to provide an understanding of the basic concepts of DRM, its context and historical background, the technologies involved and the industries and people affected by it. It serves as a solid and comprehensive introduction for those new to the field, but can also be used by experts as the launching pad for further research into the more advanced aspects of the relationship between technology, intellectual property and the various stakeholders. The intended audience for this book includes all consumers of content in its various forms, as well as the end-users of the channels and products that are used to disseminate and consume content. This applies to virtually everyone, but particularly to those in the media and entertainment industry, the legal profession, government, technology (i.e. computing and consumer electronics), academia and corporate enterprises. For these people, and others, it should prove a useful grounding tool for those aspects of the digital intellectual property ecosystem that may perhaps be unfamiliar.

Secondly, the first decade of the 21st century is proving to be a time in which many of the promises and much of the hype of the information age are finally being proved (or disproved, as the case may be). DRM is turning out to be a particularly tough and contentious solution to an issue that affects a large swathe of the content-consuming public in general, and the creative content-based industries in particular. Events that unfold on a daily basis help to highlight the fact that digital technology, telecommunications and the internet are all slowly becoming part of the fabric of everyday life; they hint at the enormous potential of these technologies to enrich the life of future generations. However, there is a unique opportunity at this point in time for most people to get involved in the debate over the widespread availability of 'free' information and content versus the socio-economic concept of IPRs. This book should help to stimulate that debate and offer an insight or two as to the best way forward for all parties concerned.

Finally, although there are several other books and theses on this topic that do an excellent job of covering specific areas such as the technology, business and socio-political aspects of DRM, it is still difficult to find one that also addresses the specific stakeholders of the DRM landscape in a holistic manner. This book identifies five key stakeholder domains to which all parties affected by DRM and the content economy belong. These are: the creative stakeholders; the commercial stakeholders; the technology stakeholders; the governance (i.e. legal/legislative) stakeholders; and the consumer or end-user stakeholder group. Most people belong to one or more of these domains, at one time or another, in their personal and professional lives (e.g. the author belongs to four out of five stakeholder groups) and can therefore appreciate the unique perspective from those domains, but there still needs to be more complete awareness and understanding of all stakeholder domains in order to fully grasp the issues at stake. Therefore this book brings together all of the stakeholders (representing all of the entities at play in the evolving content economy) and examines their motivations and contributions to the current situation, as well as its potential solution in the long run.

HOW DOES IT COVER DRM?

This book addresses the confluence of technology, communication, intellectual property, and social developments that have combined to create the need for DRM and other mechanisms for preserving the rights of content owners in the 21st century. It is organised into four distinct parts as shown in Figure 0.1, and the scope is primarily focused at the United Kingdom, the European Union and the larger worldwide audience, in that order.

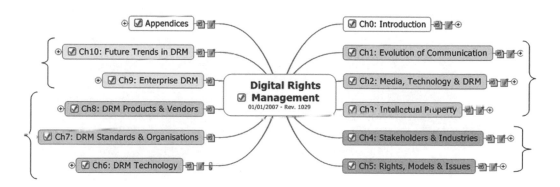

FIGURE 0.1 *Organisation and mind map of the book*

This introduction is followed by multiple chapters, which can be grouped together into four parts, which are briefly outlined as follows.

- **Chapters 1, 2 and 3.** These make up the first part of the book and provide a richly detailed context for DRM. They cover the historical background and context of DRM with an exploration of the evolution of human communication in Chapter 1, the evolution of information technologies and DRM in Chapter 2 and an overview of the concept of IPRs, and copyright in particular, in Chapter 3.
- **Chapters 4 and 5.** The second part covers the economic context of DRM. It provides an overview of the stakeholder domains and industries affected by DRM in Chapter 4. This is followed, in Chapter 5, by an introduction to the digital rights, models and issues that make up the transactional landscape of the digital content economy and DRM.
- **Chapters 6, 7 and 8.** The third part describes the technology of DRM, with a look, in Chapter 6, at the components, reference architecture and external environment that make up the DRM ecosystem. Chapter 7 examines the various standards related to DRM and some of the organisations that help govern the digital ecosystem. Finally, Chapter 8 briefly describes some of the major DRM products and vendors that exist in the market today.
- **Chapters 9 and 10.** This final part provides an overview of the possible progression of DRM technology by discussing the DRM offshoot called enterprise DRM in Chapter 9, followed by a sneak peek at the likely future trends in DRM in Chapter 10.

The book concludes with references and recommended further reading.

1 Evolution of Communication

In its rightful context, DRM occupies only a very small niche in the whole media, technology and communications universe. However, this niche occurs at a significant intersection of these worlds, and as a result the impacts and implications of DRM are widely reflected in a variety of areas in our present day life. This book presents the development of DRM from its earliest forms and uses, such as in software encryption, to the most sophisticated of present day offerings. However, in order to fully appreciate the complexity of the issues that surround DRM, it is necessary to explore some of the factors that came together to necessitate the development of these DRM technologies and applications in the first place.

This chapter starts out by exploring the development of various communication methods and their associated transmission channels. It also touches on the fact that virtually every major innovation, in the evolution of communications technology, has had a disproportionate impact on new and existing media channels. Furthermore the development of the internet as a major communication channel underscores this point, not least because of the challenges and opportunities it presents to the content industries.

Finally, it is necessary to point out that this chapter dwells mainly on the significant events and milestones that occurred along the evolutionary timeline of communication. It is designed to provide a historical context for the human and social aspects of DRM; therefore each sub-topic is concluded with a brief look at the relationship with, and impact on, information control and rights management over the years. These end-notes form the linking threads that bind the historical context with the current need to control information, and as a result also provide a contextual reason for the existence of DRM.

OVERVIEW

The evolution of human communication, and the tools that are used to facilitate it, is a fascinating topic and one that rightly stands within the discipline of mass communication in any university curriculum. This section will highlight major milestones in the evolution of human communication and media, especially in relation to information rights and control.

Major milestones in the evolution of human communication

Figure 1.1 illustrates the major milestones in the evolution of communication, from prehistory and the dawn of symbolic expression, to the current multi-format and multichannel means of communication available to us today. It is interesting to note that as time progresses the gap between significant milestones also tends to decrease. This may be attributable to the fact that the more recent events have greater resonance with us and directly impact our current existence, as opposed to the events that occurred many centuries ago and are now taken for granted as part of normal everyday life. This is worth keeping in mind, especially in the final chapter where we discuss future trends and examine relevant aspects of the ongoing communication evolution. Figure 1.1 illustrates the following major communication categories, as discussed in the remainder of this chapter:

- **basic communication** – covering signs, symbols and the spoken and written words;
- **mass communication** – covering print, audio, visual and audiovisual channels;
- **hyper-communication** – dealing with the telecommunication and internet-enabled media channels.

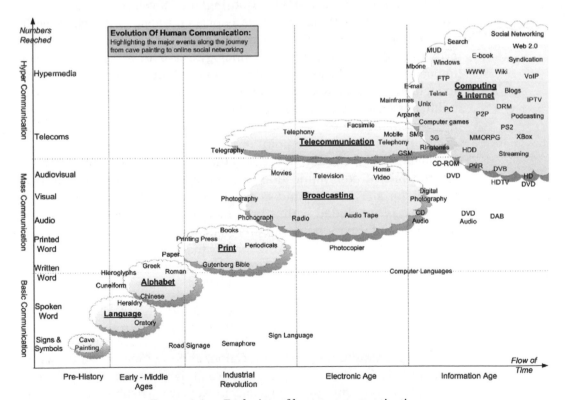

FIGURE 1.1. *Evolution of human communication*

BASIC COMMUNICATION

Signs and symbols

Some of the earliest and most accessible forms of communication are visual in nature, and include the use of symbols with specific meanings. The following list outlines the major forms:

- **Cave drawings.** This was used by prehistoric cave dwellers to communicate and record events in their lives. A modern parallel would be urban street art or graffiti.
- **Drums.** Drums used by some early societies (and some present day ones) to communicate with each other over short distances or at social events.
- **Heraldry.** This is a system of symbols (e.g. coat of arms) used to represent individuals, families, countries and such institutions as churches and universities.
- **Semaphores.** This is a method of communication by using hand flags in different positions (also could be by means of light flashes). It is a precursor to the telegraph and is still used today by air traffic ground control and railway semaphores.
- **Pre-electric telegraph.** Similar to semaphores, the early telegraphy systems were mostly visual in nature and consisted of relays for transmitting information in various forms (e.g. smoke or fire signals, visual symbols and codes) over a distance. The invention of the telescope made it possible to do this over even greater distances.
- **Sign language.** This is a system of hand (and facial and body) gestures developed for communication with and by deaf people. There are several types of sign language with variations on the meaning and types of gestures used. Other uses of sign language can be very potent, for example, the insulting 'up yours' finger gesture, the 'V' for victory sign or the 'W' hand signature of Western Los Angeles street gangs.
- **Traffic signs.** These were developed, with the increasing use of road vehicles, to control the movement of people and vehicles on the roads.

SIGNS AND SYMBOLS – IMPLICATIONS FOR INFORMATION CONTROL AND RIGHTS MANAGEMENT

This is generally not applicable to the above medium of signs and symbols when used for their basic communication purposes, although it could be argued that the symbols, which are images, fall under the copyright of the owner or creator as we shall see later in Chapter 3.

Oral communication (the spoken word)

Speech and language are a fundamental to human communication. We use language to communicate in written or spoken form, and it is a strong social bonding mechanism in human societies across the world. It is still unclear whether the origin of human language is a biological, cultural or spontaneous evolutionary phenomenon. In fact it could well have developed through some combination of some or all of these factors and more besides. However, it is commonly accepted that the human brain and physiology are designed to support language and speech from an early stage in our development. According to an online dictionary website (http://www.yourdictionary.com/) there are over 6,700 known languages spoken in the world. Some 2,261 of these have writing systems and the others are only spoken. Therefore oral communication is a very powerful method for conveying concepts and ideas to others, especially as it also delivers an immediate emotional impact when used in certain contexts such as the following:

- **Oration.** This has been used for centuries as a means of motivating groups of people towards a common cause or purpose. Oratorical skills are highly prized in the fields of religion, politics or sales, where it may be used to achieve various goals including conversion, election, commerce, warfare and rebellion.

- **Education.** The use of oral communication for education is still a core part of learning even today. Lecture halls and classrooms are filled with teachers and students, right across the globe, engaged in learning through this most direct means of imparting knowledge. Many early societies also passed on their history and culture to the next generation via the time-honoured oral tradition of story telling.

- **Artistic performance.** The most potent form of oral communication, outside its basic use for interpersonal exchange of information, is in the artistic performance of song, poetry and prose. In this context, the information and ideas conveyed are intimately intertwined with the method of delivery. The words themselves become part of the idea conveyed and not just a means of transmitting a concept.

Based on this, it would be fair to surmise that the spoken word, as a means of communication, delivers on the much-touted goal of modern media to inform, educate and entertain the audience.

THE SPOKEN WORD – IMPLICATIONS FOR INFORMATION CONTROL AND RIGHTS MANAGEMENT

Spoken words on their own do not have much significant implication for information control and rights management, except within legal constructs such as confidentiality, secrecy and privacy over which the speaker has some influence. However, once the words are recorded they also fall under copyright and become subject to all of the rights and restrictions accordable to the creator or owner of the recorded work.

Written communication (the written word)

The history of the written word is fascinating, both because of its intimate link with our past and present civilisations, and its close ties to the origin of the concept of copyright. This section presents an overview of the timeline that traces the development of the written word, from early forms of writing to the modern day textual information media.

Early writing

Cuneiform
The earliest primitive 'writing', or marks made on an object, is as old as humanity itself, but the first fully fledged writing system was developed circa 3500 BC, by the ancient Sumerians who used a form of cuneiform, or wedge-shaped characters written on clay, metal, stone or other materials, to communicate with each other.

Hieroglyphics
At around 3000 BC, the ancient Egyptians developed a form of writing based on pictorial symbols, or hieroglyphs, which were carved on stone or drawn on papyrus scrolls.

Chinese calligraphy
Chinese calligraphy was probably developed around 1500 BC, and is still considered one of the most advanced forms of writing with up to 50,000 characters.

Alphabetic writing

The alphabet is the basis of modern written communication and it differs from pictorial systems by using letters in the alphabet to form the words. The development of modern alphabetic writing can be traced through some ancient civilisations as follows:

- **The Phoenician alphabet.** Widely regarded as the origin of the alphabetic system of writing, the Phoenician alphabet came into existence circa 1500 BC. It was developed by adapting and simplifying Egyptian hieroglyphs. This early writing system also gave rise to Hebrew, Aramaic (which led to Arabic and many Indian scripts) and the Greek alphabetic writing systems.
- **The Greek alphabet.** This improved on the Phoenician alphabet by including vowels and thus created the first truly modern alphabet.
- **The Roman alphabet.** This was borrowed from the Greek alphabet and is widely used, with minor modification, by many languages (including English) to this day.

Writing sits next to speech as the second most important early step in the evolution of human communication. It enables the exchange of messages and information over long distances and vast periods of time, thus making it the original version of today's concept of place shifting and time shifting in the broadcasting worlds.

One of the most important developments to evolve directly as a result of writing is the use of written messages to convey information from person to person in the form of letters. This practice later gave rise to the idea of postage, and postal services, which are still very much with us today. The modern postal service in the UK was established as far back as 1635, by royal proclamation of Charles I, according to the postal heritage website (Postalheritage 2006).

THE WRITTEN WORD – IMPLICATIONS FOR INFORMATION CONTROL AND RIGHTS MANAGEMENT

The spread of the written word certainly brought with it several implications for information control, but it was not until the advent of the printing press, which made it much easier to reproduce copies of existing works, that it became much more of a concern to the owners of those works. However, even before the printing press was invented, there were already some misgivings about writing. For example, Plato the Greek philosopher was known to have expressed the view that writing would adversely impact people's ability to remember details and that written messages could be open to misinterpretation or could fall into the wrong hands (much like email messages today). In many ways these thoughts are not dissimilar to the arguments posed by some people today about the effect of computing on handwriting or the internet on illegal file sharing.

Computer languages

Computer languages are primarily used to instruct computers in the numeric binary language of ones and zeros (1s and 0s). They are a special type of written communication and have become the new languages of the late 20th and early 21st centuries. They may well be the next step in the evolution of languages and writing, and the significant events in their evolution are traced as follows.

First-generation languages (1GLs)

These languages (also known as machine language) are very low-level numeric codes that pass instructions used by the logic components of the computer (e.g. central processing unit (CPU) and memory) to perform a specific command.

Second-generation languages (2GLs)

These languages (also called symbolic languages) were introduced to make it easier and faster to program computers by using a single keyboard character to represent specific commands such as 'read' or 'write'. These symbols are then translated into machine language by a program called an assembler. These languages were usually specific to a particular processor family and environment.

Third-generation languages (3GLs)

These are high-level languages developed to solve particular types of problems. They are mostly independent of the hardware or environment, and are largely algorithmic or procedural in nature. 3GLs may be used between different machines because they are translated into machine language by a compiler specific to each machine type. Some examples of 3GLs include:

- **FORTRAN** (FORmula TRANslation) – mainly for scientific calculations;
- **COBOL** (COmmon Business Oriented Language) – for business applications;
- **ALGOL** (Algorithmic Language) – for mathematical and scientific applications;
- **Pascal** – an imperative programming language based on ALGOL;
- **BASIC** (Beginners All-purpose Symbolic Instruction Code) – developed as a teaching language for use in personal computers, several dialects of this language have subsequently evolved over the years;
- **C** – was introduced in 1972 to implement the UNIX operating system;
- **C++** – was developed as the object-oriented extension of the C language;
- **JAVA** – was developed by Sun Microsystems, in the mid-1990s, as a fully object-oriented programming language.

Fourth-generation languages (4GLs)

Unlike previous generations, these non-procedural languages are used to specify what needs to be done without saying exactly how it must be accomplished. All 4GLs are designed to reduce programming effort, as well as the time and cost associated with software development. Different types of 4GLs are designed for specific purposes such as report and form generation, data manipulation, design and even system generation (e.g. computer-aided software engineering or 'CASE' tools). Examples of 4GLs include Oracle PL/SQL, Progress 4GL, Postscript, ABAP, SAS, SQL, Ab Initio, Mathematica, Visual Basic Form Editor and Windows™ Forms.

Fifth-generation languages (5GLs)

These languages are all about solving problems by using constraints given to the program, rather than using an algorithm written by a programmer. Some examples of 5GLs derived from artificial intelligence research include:

- **PROLOG** (Programming LOGic) – used for logical processes and automatic deductions;
- **LISP** (LISt Processing) – used for pattern matching and list processing;
- **LOGO**;
- **PILOT**;
- **Occam**.

The future of computer languages will most likely include the results of ongoing works and research in the fields of natural language commands and autonomous systems, but even these advancements will still ultimately rely on the translation of ever-more complex commands into the simple numeric code that machines will understand.

COMPUTER LANGUAGES – IMPLICATIONS FOR INFORMATION CONTROL AND RIGHTS MANAGEMENT

This is highly relevant because the systems that implement DRM are usually developed using one or several computer programming languages. Therefore these systems, as well as the language they are written in, are very much exposed to information control and rights management since they also fall under copyright law.

MASS COMMUNICATION

Mass media is a term that encompasses television, radio, cinema, newspapers, books and magazines, as well as telephony and the internet. These channels are often used as a major means of driving social cohesion and a source of popular culture. Mass media is mainly used to inform, entertain and educate audiences of any size: from a global scale (e.g. the FIFA World Cup) to small community-based or niche specialist groups (e.g. DRM enthusiasts). This section explores the history of major traditional forms of mass media as a background to the newer 'hypermedia' of the internet, which is examined in the next section.

Print and publishing

The mass reproduction of words and images on paper, or other materials, is known as printing, and it is one of the most important means of mass communication today. The following sections briefly describe some of the significant milestones in the history of the print and publishing industries.

The printing press

The art of printing using wooden blocks was invented in China during the Tang dynasty (i.e. between the 4th and 7th century AD). Wood block printing was expensive and inflexible, but the invention of the movable type by Pi Sheng in the 11th century helped to make it affordable to print and sell books to a larger readership. In the 15th century, a German by the name of Johannes Gutenberg, perhaps inspired by Chinese printing techniques, invented the first European printing press. Prior to this, books were created by the laborious process of hand-copying existing works, often by illiterate monks, in monasteries across Europe. The advent of printing during the renaissance period, circa 1300–1600, ushered in a period of great intellectual activity and the Gutenberg press made it relatively inexpensive to produce printed materials with which to feed the demand. This had a significant impact on European society, by and large, including an increase in literacy, the ready availability of mass information via newspapers, leaflets and pamphlets, as well as the growth of advertisement. The printing press and process, as invented by Gutenberg, remained largely unchanged until the 19th century with the introduction of more advanced printing methods such as lithography and stereotyping, as well as the invention of the rotary press. Modern print technology is now mostly electronic.

Paper

The earliest paper-like writing material was derived from the papyrus plant, and was used by the ancient Egyptians as far back as 3000 BC. The word 'paper' is derived from papyrus. In 105 AD, the Chinese court official T'sai Lun described a process for making paper from mulberry tree bark. This practice spread to Korea and Japan circa 600 AD, and on to Tibet and India thereafter. From here it slowly filtered into the Middle East via the Turks, and then into 13th century Europe via the Italians who made their paper from hemp and linen rags. The invention, in the 19th century, of steam-powered paper-making machines, which used wood pulp to make cheaper paper, enabled the widespread adoption of paper-based products and publications.

Publishing

The main difference between print and publishing is that printing is mainly concerned with the replication of written content, but publishing is a business superset that also deals with commissioning works, negotiating deals, editing, production (i.e. printing), distribution and sale of the written work. The global publishing industry is huge and it produces a sizeable amount of revenue in the modern knowledge and information economy. According to the *Encyclopaedia Britannica*, modern publishing is based on three major inventions, i.e. writing, paper and printing, and on one crucial social development, the spread of literacy. Interestingly, all three inventions are directly responsible for the spread of literacy, thus illustrating the transformative powers of mass communication on society as a whole.

There are two broad categories of publications, periodicals (or regular publications such as newspapers) and non-periodicals or single publications such as books. These categories are illustrated as follows.

Periodicals

Newspapers are by far the most widely read publication ever since ancient times (the Roman '*Acta Diurna*' is considered to be one of the earliest newspapers). Magazines cover more specialised topics targeted at specific groups and have longer circulation intervals (e.g. weekly, monthly, quarterly or longer).

Non-periodicals

Books are the oldest of all publications and have served as the repository of man's knowledge, as well as the societal or cultural archives, for many civilisations. Books are designed to serve as a means of circulating lengthy messages in a portable and permanent form.

Other types of publishing include maps and atlases, music sheets, calendars, diaries, timetables, instruction guides, pamphlets, postcards and greeting cards.

PRINT AND PUBLISHING – IMPLICATIONS FOR INFORMATION CONTROL AND RIGHTS MANAGEMENT

The implications are self-evident in an industry that exists solely to supply and distribute the written word (and images) to a wide audience. The advent of print technologies made it more attractive and economically feasible for people to engage in the commercial piracy of published works. As a direct consequence of this, the first copyright laws and statutes were introduced to establish just who has the rights to make copies of a work.

Broadcast communication

Broadcasting forms a major part of today's mass media landscape, and it covers various technologies and processes that have evolved to take advantage of each new media and innovation over the years. Entire industries with different business models have evolved in the areas of mass communication and broadcasting including the radio, television and film industries, and they all use the incredible power of media to influence society by informing, educating and entertaining people everywhere. This section presents a brief historical and contextual overview of broadcast media and some other communication technologies such as telephony.

Radio

Radio is the wireless transmission of sound signals that are used to deliver programmed audio content (i.e. speech and music) to a diverse group of people over great distances. While this may not fully convey the power of the medium that it describes, it is fair to say that radio ushered in the age of broadcasting as well as the growth of the massive global broadcast industry that developed alongside it. A brief timeline of major milestones in the development of radio is as follows:

- In 1893, Nikola Tesla demonstrated the principles of radio, and successfully transmitted some long-distance signals.
- Frequency-modulated (FM) radio was invented by Edwin H. Robinson (and patented in 1933) to create clearer audio signals with less static.
- Regency introduced the pocket transistor radio, the TR-1, in 1954.
- The first (radio) communication satellite, TELSTAR, was launched in the early 1960s. The late 1990s saw the dawn of digital transmissions and broadcasting.

RADIO – IMPLICATIONS FOR INFORMATION CONTROL AND RIGHTS MANAGEMENT

During the early development of radio, there was a large amount of legal wrangling over the various patents and claims to inventions related to radio. To this day, it is still somewhat difficult to wholly attribute the invention of radio to any one person or group of individuals. It would appear that the birth of this media and technology also coincided with a rise in intellectual property awareness and litigation, and that the significance of the invention was not lost on the various parties, or vested interests, present at the time.

Television

Television is derived from Greek and Roman words that roughly translate to 'far seeing', and is a system for broadcasting and receiving moving pictures and sound over distance. The origin of modern television can be traced back as follows.

Analogue TV

Constantine Perskyi coined the term 'television' in a paper at the Paris World Exhibition in 1900. In 1925, inventor John Logie Baird demonstrated televised silhouette images in London and, in 1928, Baird's company broadcast the first transatlantic television signal between London and New York. The British Broadcasting Corporation (BBC) started regular TV broadcasts from Alexandra palace between 1932 and 1936 and, in 1967, BBC2 began the first regular colour broadcasts in Europe. Teletext was invented by BBC and Independent TV (ITV) engineers in the 1970s. By the 1980s, many advanced nations proposed adopting digital television services and they created timelines to complete digital switchover in the early 21st century.

Digital TV

Digital television (DTV) and high-definition television (HDTV) are two major recent developments that should go a long way to enhance the TV experience for viewers. The main features of DTV include:

- support for high-definition (HD) image transmission with unprecedented picture clarity;
- support for widescreen (16:9 aspect ratio) formats for added visual impact;
- enhanced audio capability with Dolby Digital/AC3 and 5.1 channel surround sound;
- ability to multicast up to four versions of the same program in standard definition;
- MPEG-2 compression increases the amount of information that can be transmitted;
- DTV can simultaneously transmit data, such as an enhanced electronic program guide (EPG), alongside video and audio, thereby enabling viewer interactivity

DTV standards developed along different lines, not unlike the analogue TV standards of the past, and these digital standards include:

- **ATSC** – developed by USA's Advanced Television Systems Committee (ATSC);
- **DVB** – Digital Video Broadcast (DVB) was developed in Europe and has several variants (e.g. Terrestrial DVB-T, Satellite DVB-S, Cable DVB-C and Handheld/Mobile DVB-H);
- **ISDB** – developed and used in Japan (also uses analogue HD transmission).

TELEVISION – IMPLICATIONS FOR INFORMATION CONTROL AND RIGHTS MANAGEMENT

The invention of television and its rise to a prominent position in the lives of many people today is a testament to the power of the media. The fact that it engages users with both sound and vision, two of the most developed senses for communication, is probably very significant. Also, and perhaps because of this, it has many implications for information control and rights management including the need for music and image rights as well as geographical or territorial rights. Other factors include language translation issues, programme viewer ratings and censorship, among many others.

Cable and satellite

The development of cable and satellite was based on the widespread demand for, and penetration of, television into homes across the globe, especially in places where signal reception was weakest. The following timeline traces the origins of cable and satellite to the present day.

1940s

Cable TV began in 1948 as a community access television (CATV) system used by John Walson to provide TV signals to people in the mountains of Pennsylvania USA.

1950s

In 1957, Russia launched Sputnik 1, the first man-made satellite with radio signals.

1960s

Syncom, the world's first geosynchronous communications satellite, was launched in 1963. Syncom 3 transmitted live television coverage of the 1964 Olympic Games in Tokyo. In 1969 Apollo 11 transmitted live TV pictures from the surface of the moon.

1970s

Home Box Office (HBO), a leading US cable channel, was launched in 1972. By 1975 Radio Corporation of America (RCA) launched the first US satellite designed exclusively for three major national television networks. HBO also used this system to transmit premium television content (e.g. Muhammad Ali's 'Thrilla in Manila' heavyweight boxing match) to cable TV.

1980s

In 1986, HBO began to scramble its signal, requiring Direct to Home (DTH) customers to purchase a decoder box and subscription. Also the Satellite Broadcasting and Communications Association (SBCA) was created to promote the VideoCipher II encoding method to protect satellite broadcasters from piracy. UK cable services emerged in the mid-1980s.

1990s

UK's Sky Television and British Satellite Broadcasting (BSB) merged to form British Sky Broadcasting (BSkyB) in 1990. In 1991, the UK cable companies were granted the right to offer telephony alongside their TV services in an early example of convergence.

2000s

In 2006, BSkyB and the BBC started offering HDTV content. Also BSkyB purchased internet service provider (ISP) EasyNet and began offering broadband services. Between 2006 and 2007 UK cable operator NTL: Telewest (formed by the merger of Telewest and NTL in 2005) bought Virgin Mobile and rebranded as VirginMedia to offer multiple services (i.e. television, telephony, mobile and broadband) in a 'quadruple play' of converged services as it is known in the industry jargon.

> ## CABLE AND SATELLITE – IMPLICATIONS FOR INFORMATION CONTROL AND RIGHTS MANAGEMENT
>
> These are the same as for terrestrial broadcasting and generally relate to copyright law, which we discuss in Chapter 3. One major point about cable and satellite TV systems is that they helped to usher in the concept of pay TV, which involves the use of a decoder or set-top box (STB) to unscramble the encrypted TV content and signals. This is also commonly known as conditional access (CA), and it was one of the earliest ways to directly monetise TV content at the point of consumption.

Telecommunications

Telecommunication involves the transmission of signals over a distance for the purpose of communication. This process may involve the use of wires, optical fibres or the transmission of electromagnetic waves by electronic transmitters. We describe the basic elements of a telecommunication system as:

- a transmitter that takes information and converts it to a signal for transmission;
- a transmission medium over which the signal is transmitted;
- a receiver that receives and converts the signal back into usable information.

Modern telecommunication is widespread and supported by many devices and a vast array of networks that connect them, including computer, public telephone, radio and television networks. This complex system needs extensive laws and regulations to govern them and in the UK the Wireless Telegraphy Act of 1904 (and subsequent versions) is the foundation of all communication laws. The Act originated from the early invention of electric telegraphy and wireless transmission, but it has since evolved to include most modern forms of telecommunication and broadcasting. This section examines some of the major inventions and events in the timeline of telecommunication starting from early telegraphy to modern mobile telephony.

Electric telegraphy

The electric telegraph was invented by Samuel Morse in the early 19th century as a long-distance rapid communication system. The Morse code alphabet (also invented by Samuel Morse) was used to encode messages for transmission over a wire to the recipient system. Later developments include the invention of a duplex circuit that could transmit and receive messages at the same time, as well as the introduction of time division multiplexer by Baudot, in 1872, which increased the number of channels that could be used simultaneously. Telegraphy systems improved throughout the 20th century, with the use of special radio links to carry multiple channels in a single circuit. These wireless radiotelegraphs with their expanded bandwidth were made possible by major innovations such as microwave radio, waveguides, satellites and lasers.

Telephony

Telephony is the two-way transmission of speech by electrical signals over wires or radio between two devices, called telephones, over a distance. It also includes the systems, accessories, and operating methods used for this purpose. The telephone device itself sends and receives voice messages by converting them into electrical signals to be transported great distances. The following timeline describes the milestones in the development of telephony.

Birth of the telephone

Alexander Graham Bell, a famous Scottish inventor, is widely considered to have invented the telephone, which he patented in 1876. The early history of the telephone was fraught with litigious claims over its invention, and other contenders include one Elisha Gray (who also developed a telephone device, but submitted his patent application just a few hours later than Bell) and an Italian by the name of Anthony Meucci who invented and demonstrated an earlier device in 1860, but did not file for a patent. In 1892, Thomas Edison was awarded the US patent for the telephone over Bell and other applicants.

Early days of telephony

Initially, each telephone had to be connected directly to another telephone in order to communicate; however, in 1877 the introduction of the switchboard enabled multiple devices to connect to each other through an operator.

Telephone networks

The widespread use of telephones went very much hand-in-hand with the proliferation of telephone networks from the late 19th century onwards. According to www.connected-earth.com:

> It was one of many 'chicken and egg' situations in the history of telecommunications – which comes first, the network or service? (Connected Earth 2006)

Without a network, the telephone is redundant, and without pre-existing users to call, it is difficult to sell telephones to new ones. Breaking through this barrier represents a classic example of the network effect, whereby the value of a system or product increases with the number of people that use it.

Digital networks

Digital telephone networks are slowly replacing the original public switched telephone network (PSTN), and improving the capacity and quality of the network. Long-distance transmission networks now use fibre-optic technology, which provides greater multiplexing capability, that is, the ability to carry multiple digital switched circuits on a single transmission line. The use of digital fibre connectivity has steadily crept towards the consumer, and the quest is on to completely digitise the 'last mile' of connectivity, right to the end-user device. Other recent developments include: Internet Protocol (IP) telephony or 'voice over IP' (VOIP); higher capacity connections such as ISDN and digital subscriber line (DSL); and cordless telephones and mobile or cellular phone systems (discussed separately below).

TELEPHONY – IMPLICATIONS FOR INFORMATION CONTROL AND RIGHTS MANAGEMENT

The impact of telephony can be felt in many ways today, but this was not always the case and it took some time before people fully engaged with its potential as a social mechanism. This was due to a shift in the perception and use of telephony from being seen as a tool for urgent business or emergency purposes only, to its more common use as a social and personal communication tool. Media law professor Susan Crawford observed in her weblog that the original perception was fostered by the first generation of telephony service managers (mostly ex-telegraphy managers) who associated telephony with urgent business and emergencies just like the telegraph. Crawford then drew some significant parallels with the early ISPs and described how they also viewed the internet as just another network 'like the telephone' and sought to impose the same models, but the resistance this time has been far more fierce and immediate (Crawford 2005).

Facsimile (fax)

The fax machine is a device that can scan a physical document and convert its content into a compressed electronic format that is then transmitted over a telecommunication network to a receiving system that translates and replicates the electronic image back into a physical document via a printer. Early fax machines were both expensive and difficult to operate, but in 1966 the Xerox Company introduced a smaller version that could also send transmissions over existing telephone lines. The modern fax machines gained popularity during the 1970s and 1980s, especially in Japan where they became the preferred tool for transmitting handwritten Kanji characters. Today, fax machines are in global use everyday by individuals and businesses, but the development of internet applications such as email has started to erode the use of fax technology.

Mobile telephony

Mobile telephony is a more recent development with roots in the advent of wireless radio communication. It consists of a portable handset that can send and receive signals from a base station located in a cell (i.e. a small geographical area of coverage). The technology allows the transfer of connectivity from one cell to another as the user travels, and this is the key feature of the mobility service. Wireless communities exist in three categories that developed chronologically as follows:

(i) **Fixed user base**. These use devices located on or in buildings, homes, offices, other fixtures such as a ham shack, or attached to posts or trees.

(ii) **Mobile user base**. These use devices that are vehicle based, for example, wireless systems in trucks, vans, cars, boats or motorcycles.

(iii) **Portable user base**. These are systems and devices that are worn or carried upon the human body. Also covers implantable wireless communication devices.

The last two categories are of particular importance because they are associated with the popular concept of mobility, and they have evolved from continuous improvements in and the miniaturisation of mobile components and devices. A brief timeline of mobile telephony milestones is given as follows.

The dawn of mobile telephony

Radiophones were available in the USA as far back as the 1940s and were used heavily during the Second World War. However, those phones were more closely related to two-way radios than true mobile telephony. The first true commercial public mobile telephone networks were launched in Finland in the early 1970s.

First generation (1G)

In the mid-1970s, first-generation mobile communications leveraged the invention of the microprocessor, and digitisation of the control link between the mobile phone and the cell site. The first mobile telephone devices were bulky briefcase sized units with very short battery life.

Second generation (2G)

The introduction of digital 2G mobile phone systems in the early 1990s brought better quality and higher capacity at lower cost to consumers. It also saw the emergence of smaller handheld devices, which led to their increased uptake and the spread of cellular sites. Other interesting developments saw the introduction of certain disruptive technologies and user behaviour that led to the rapid growth of hitherto unknown and unplanned services. These technology-led innovations include the following:

• **Short message service (SMS).** This is a service for sending short messages between mobile phones. It was originally developed as a

Global System for Mobile (GSM) communications, and probably only intended as a way to alert the mobile user of a specific event (e.g. received voice mail) or for more sophisticated applications such as telemetry. SMS has since evolved to become a significant method for sending text messages from one mobile user to another. The SMS service is now available on a wide range of networks, including 3G, and has caused subtle but interesting changes in society and language since it became immensely popular.

- **Ring tones.** The mobile phone ring tone has created significant revenue for its providers. A ring tone is the customisable sound made by a telephone to indicate an incoming call. Later mobile phones allowed users to associate different ring tones to different phonebook entries and to create their own ring tones either on the phone itself or from other external sources. Commercial ring tone services provide downloadable ring tones in what has become a lucrative mobile music industry.

2.5 generation (2.5G)
The 2.5G systems were developed as an extension to existing 2G networks. They provided some of the features of the next generation (3G) systems.

Third generation (3G)
3G mobile phone technologies, as described in the International Telecommunications Union's (ITU) IMT-2000 family, are designed to deliver faster communications services, including voice, fax and internet, anytime and anywhere with seamless global roaming. It also enables innovative applications and services such as multimedia entertainment and location-based services.

Future generations (3.5G and 4G)
These next-generation technologies, which are still under development, aim to provide even faster speeds and greater bandwidth as the technologies improve.

In conclusion, mobile telephony has had a huge impact, and mobile-phone subscriptions now outnumber fixed-line subscriptions in many markets. This phenomenal market penetration in such a short space of time means that one in six of the world's population now own a mobile phone or two (it is now commonplace for people to have one phone for work and another for personal use). According to OFCOM (2006) the following key observations also serve to further illustrate the point:

- There are over 65 million mobile phone subscriptions in the UK.
- 31% of all UK voice calls originated from mobiles.
- Some 31% of consumers surveyed now consider their mobile to be their main telephone, up from 21% in 2004.

- As many UK households now have a mobile phone as have a landline phone and, for the first time, the proportion of households relying on mobile phones exclusively (10%) is the same as the proportion who only use landline phones.

MOBILE TELEPHONY – IMPLICATIONS FOR INFORMATION CONTROL AND RIGHTS MANAGEMENT

The future of mobile telephony looks likely to be around the convergence of telephony, broadcasting and internet connectivity. This is typical of the aforementioned trend of service combinations commonly referred to as 'N-play' (where N stands for the multiple numbers of combined services offered, e.g. mobile and fixed telephony, broadband internet, cable or satellite television etc.). In any case, the mobile phone (or similar personal device) will still play a key part in the way we communicate, but will most likely be in connection with other convergent capabilities such as mobile computing, gaming, music consumption, digital photography, switchable fixed-line telephony, digital television and so on. Other possible uses may also include security, identification and micropayments for goods and services, which are all key to the whole concept of DRM as we shall see in later chapters.

Others – photography and motion pictures

Photography and motion pictures (also known as films, movies or cinema) are not strictly broadcast media, but are a bona-fide communications media that developed alongside the other broadcast technologies that they contribute to and complement. For example, the motion picture was used as a news media format (e.g. movie tone newsreels), and photographic images are a staple of the print media industry. This section briefly outlines the development of photography and motion picture technology.

Photography

A very brief outline of major milestones in photography, starting from its birth in the early 19th century, is as follows.

Dawn of photography

In 1826 Nicéphore Niépce took the first permanent photograph and in 1839 Louis Daguerre patented the daguerreotype. In 1840 William F. Talbot invented the positive and negative photographic process.

Early innovations

The mid-to-late 19th century saw the introduction of the first colour photograph, the invention of nitrate celluloid film and the creation of the

Kodak camera by George Eastman. In the early 20th century, the xenon flash lamp and strobe photography was invented, as was the 35 mm format and 135 film cartridges. The Polaroid instant image camera was created in 1948, and the first fully automatic cameras appeared in 1959.

Digital photography

In 1973 Fairchild Semiconductor released the first large image forming charge coupled device (CCD) chip and in 1986 Kodak scientists invented the first megapixel sensor, which heralded the birth of digital photography.

Motion pictures (filmed entertainment or film)

Motion pictures are produced by recording people and objects with cameras or by using animation, special effects or computer-generated images. Traditional celluloid-based films are made of a progressive series of individual frames, which produce the illusion of moving images when shown rapidly in succession. This is only possible because the human eye briefly retains an image after the source has been removed, an effect commonly known as 'persistence of vision'. The history of film is very closely intertwined with that of photography and other significant inventions such as the light bulb, flexible film (or celluloid), the motion picture camera and the film projector. The history and study of the motion picture and its industry is a vast area in which much research and publications already exist; therefore this section will only outline the major events in the development of this media format. The excellent website Filmsite.org (2006) was a primary source for most of the information contained here.

Pre-cinema history

Early philosophers such as Aristotle, Lucretius and Ptolemy described the phenomenon of persistence of vision (brief afterimages retained in human vision) as far back as 300 BC.

Early innovations

Between 1832 and 1877, devices such as the phantasmagoria, phenakistoscope, zoetrope and praxinoscope were developed and used to create two-dimensional images in motion. They were the precursors of modern animation. The first motion-picture camera and projector, the Kinetograph and Kinetoscope, were invented by Thomas Edison and William Dickson in the period 1890–1893.

Silent era

In 1895, Auguste and Louis Lumière invented and patented the Cinématographe, a combination movie camera and projector. By the early 1900s, US film theatres were flourishing, Hollywood became a municipality and film companies started to buy screen rights to books and plays (mostly because, in 1909, an American court had ruled that unauthorised films infringed on copyrights). This period also witnessed the formation of several important studios such as Fox, Universal, Paramount and Warner Brothers.

Sound and the golden age of Hollywood
The 1920s saw the introduction of sound and dialogue into hitherto 'silent' films. Several versions of sound technology were introduced including Phonofilm, Vitaphone (by Warner) and Movietone (by General Electric and Fox). Walt Disney introduced the first animated cartoons with sound and a new studio, Metro–Goldwyn–Mayer (MGM), dubbed the famous lion's roar into its logo and signature. The Motion Picture Association of America (MPAA) was created around this time to provide self-policing for Hollywood, and the 1930s and 1940s became known as the 'golden age' of Hollywood.

The challenge of television and video
The 1950s brought a decline in cinema audience numbers due to the rise of television, but the film industry countered with the widespread use of colour and widescreen formats such as CinemaScope, Techniscope, Cinerama, VistaVision, as well as three-dimensional (3D) film formats. However the early 1960s also saw the launch of the consumer Video Tape Recorder (VTR) by Ampex and by Sony, who also introduced the Video Cassette Recorder (VCR). In the 1970s, Sony's Betamax and JVC's VHS (Video Home Systems) appeared in the consumer market, but the VHS became dominant in the 1980s.

Computer-aided film
The 1990s brought increased use of computer special effects in film and animation production. It also brought the introduction of computer-based editing, the rise of the Digital Versatile Disc (DVD) format and the realisation of the internet as an advertising and viral-marketing medium when it helped propel a low-budget, pseudo-documentary cult film called *The Blair Witch Project* (1999) into one of the most profitable films in Hollywood history. The early 21st century Hollywood studio system is dominated by six global entertainment companies (i.e. Time Warner, Viacom, Fox, Sony, NBC Universal and Disney), and computer animated or enhanced blockbuster films such as *Finding Nemo* (2003), *Shrek 2* (2004) and *Pirates of the Caribbean 2: Dead Man's Chest* (2006) are becoming the norm.

Films can be used to inform and educate the people, but its most powerful impact has been to entertain audiences in a social setting. The visual component of motion pictures grant it an immediate and universal power of communication, but the inclusion of music, translated dialogues and subtitles really extends it to other cultures. Motion pictures help to reflect the time, society and culture in which they are made, and can also influence them in several ways (e.g. fashion, language and social behaviour).

> ## MOTION PICTURES – IMPLICATIONS FOR INFORMATION CONTROL AND RIGHTS MANAGEMENT
>
> The motion picture is a composite media format that uses both original and derived components of sound, pictures and animation, to express an idea or narrate a story. This makes it important, but sometimes very difficult, to ensure that the appropriate permissions have been secured from various rights owners before the film is released into general circulation. This also applies to other audiovisual media like broadcast TV.

HYPER-COMMUNICATION (ONLINE MEDIA AND INTERACTIVITY)

The next stage in the evolution of communication arrived with the dawn of computing and the internet. This area is in a state of hyperactive and dynamic development, with the constant discovery and application of new paradigms that only fuel the expansion of this new communication platform. This section presents an overview of the evolution of online communication tools and examines the ways in which it has adopted and extended the other communication media. There is no attempt here to make an explicit connection with information control and rights management, because it is the same issues raised by this medium that have given rise to the need for tools such as DRM.

Online communication

The power and impact of internet technology, as a disruptive innovation, cannot be over emphasised, especially in relation to communication methods. This is because, in most instances, the internet provides an equivalent or parallel version of the existing and established communication media and channels. The term 'hyper-communication', as used here, refers to this overlay and is not to be confused with the increasingly popular concept that describes a system of cell-based biological communication (although some interesting parallels exist there too).

According to an eMarketer report, worldwide internet access became available to over 1 billion people in late 2005 (eMarketer 2006). This is a significant milestone considering the fact that the internet has only been around in the last half century. The internet has several remarkable qualities, but by far the most astonishing has been the rapid rate of adoption as well as the new technologies, applications and behaviours that have since emerged. Figure 1.2 shows the adoption rate for various media formats over time in comparison with the internet.

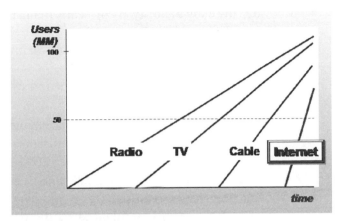

FIGURE 1.2   *Rate of media adoption (source: Morgan Stanley (2003))*

Diffusion theory (for innovation)

This precipitous rise in internet adoption may be explained by the famous theory on the 'diffusion of innovation', which was first used by Ryan and Gross, in 1943, to research rural sociology (Yates 2004). The theory was subsequently applied to communications research by Everett M. Rogers, who viewed diffusion as the process by which an innovation is adopted by members of a certain community (Rogers 1995). He claimed that the four main factors that influence adoption of an innovation are:

(i)   **the innovation itself** – for example, nature and general applicability;
(ii) **the communication channels** – used to propagate it;
(iii) **the time taken** – to propagate the information;
(iv) **the user community** – to which the innovation is communicated.

Rogers went on further to explain the four major theories that deal with the diffusion of innovation, and these are briefly summarised as follows:

(i) **The innovation-decision process**. This is based on time and five distinct stages of:
   (a) persuasion of the merits of the innovation;
   (b) knowledge, or awareness, of the innovation;
   (c) decision to adopt the innovation;
   (d) implementation of the innovation;
   (e) confirmation and validation of the derived benefits.

(ii) **The individual innovativeness**. This is based on the type of people to adopt an innovation and when they do so. It may be represented by a bell curve of the percentage distribution of individuals that adopt the innovation, as follows:
   (a) the innovators [2.5%] – includes the risk-takers and pioneers;
   (b) early adopters [13.5%] – help to spread the word about the innovation;

(c) the early majority [34%] – early mainstream adopters convinced by the above;

(d) the late majority [34%] – later mainstream adopters that are more cautious;

(e) the laggards [16%] – sceptics and cynics that adopt as a last resort.

(iii) **The rate of adoption**. This is typically represented by an S-curve graph, which traces the rate of innovation adoption; it grows slowly and gradually in the beginning, then accelerates to a plateau of stable growth, before tapering off finally into its eventual decline.

(iv) **The perceived attributes**. This is based on the notion that adoption of an innovation is influenced by the perception of the following attributes in that innovation:

(a) relative advantage – over an existing innovation or the status quo;

(b) compatibility – with existing values and practices;

(c) simplicity – the innovation must not be too complex;

(d) trial period – allow an initial trial without commitment to adopt;

(e) results – must offer observable results and outcomes for comparison.

New media categories

So how exactly does diffusion theory apply to the very rapid adoption of internet technologies and new media as shown in Figure 1.2? The answer may be found in the fact that, as observed earlier, the new internet communication formats have some close parallels with (and in some cases are inspired by) existing traditional media formats. Therefore the same, albeit exaggerated, rules of diffusion may be applicable to them. These new media applications and formats may be grouped into one of three categories as follows.

Category 1: written language inspired formats

Electronic mail (email). Considered to be the 'killer application' of the internet, and with good reason, as it has become a staple format for electronic communication between people across the world. It is characterised by its rapid transmission, global reach, ubiquity of content type (via attachments) and low cost of use.

Traditional media parallels include letters or 'snail mail', telegrams and fax.

Web pages. The web also achieved widespread use over a relatively short period of time. It consists of vast amounts of hyperlinked documents and information organised together as web pages, and which may be grouped together as a website. The components of a web page include text, audio, video, graphics, animation, executable code and hyperlinks. A web browser is normally required to view a web page.

Traditional media parallels include catalogues, brochures, magazines, newsletters and journals, advertisements and notice boards.

Weblogs (or blogs). Blogs are a form of online diary or journal that has become very popular with people as a means of documenting and communicating their thoughts and opinions on any topic of interest to them and their audience. Some blogs have provision for contributed content and comments.

Traditional media parallels include journals and diaries.

Wiki. A wiki is a collaborative web application that enables anybody to contribute content to a web page. A prime example is the online web encyclopaedia or Wikipedia (http://www.wikipedia.org).

Traditional media parallels include opinion boards, collaborative research papers and anthologies.

Online web chat and instant messaging. Instant messaging is an internet application that enables the exchange of real-time messages between users. The online version could be embedded in a web page and used for various purposes including customer service or opinion polls.

Traditional media parallels include telex and telegraphs.

Content syndication and news feeds. This provides the ability for publishers of online content (e.g. newsletters, blogs), which is regularly updated, to deliver a feed of their content to others via a subscription mechanism that refreshes the subscriber's reader application with updates as they are published. The technology used includes XML feeds such as RSS (Really Simple Syndication) or Atom.

Traditional media parallels include newswires.

Category 2: broadcast media inspired formats

Internet radio. This involves the use of streaming media technology to transmit audio content over the internet to a potential global audience. It is relatively cheap and easy to set up and start broadcasting content with minimal technical knowledge, as there are many established services and online frequently asked questions (FAQ) sheets to start with. The websites http://www.live365.com and http://www.shoutcast.com are examples of internet radio.

Traditional media parallels include the radio.

Internet TV (IPTV). This is the transmission of TV programs over the internet, using streaming media protocols. It is also known as IPTV, which alludes to the use of IP to deliver the TV content. The relative low-cost setup and operational requirements make it attractive to both new and established players in the TV industry.

Traditional media parallels would include the television.

Podcasts. This is a method of distributing audio or video content over the internet using syndication feeds for playback on mobile devices and personal computers. Podcasts are similar to blogs and may focus on a particular topic that is regularly updated by the publisher or 'podcaster'.

Traditional media parallels include the radio.

Video-on-Demand (VOD). Internet VOD refers to the ability to obtain and view video content as and when required over the internet. The term can be used to describe any number of services including IPTV, podcasts and other download services that make content available to recognised users on demand.

Traditional media parallels include video and DVD rental shops, videos and DVDs.

Category 3: telephony inspired format

VOIP. VOIP (also known as IP telephony or internet telephony) refers to the routing of voice conversations over the internet or through any other IP-based network. VOIP traffic can be carried on any IP network, even those not connected to the rest of the internet. This technology makes it very cheap to place and receive calls to and from anyone with the appropriate tools in any part of the world.

Traditional media parallels include the telephone.

The above three categories, and the preceding section on diffusion theory, help to reinforce the points that innovation is rarely self-emergent and rarely occurs in total isolation. This is because it can be difficult to judge the real value of an innovation without a frame of reference or a means of comparison. Therefore it makes more sense to view the so-called 'new media' formats as an evolution of existing communication paradigms. However, the novel uses and behaviours that arise from the adoption of these new media formats are not necessarily constrained by this fact, and may well qualify to be considered truly emergent, disruptive and revolutionary. This is an extremely poignant issue for established content industries and business models, as we shall see in Chapter 5.

CONCLUSION

In summary, in this chapter we have explored various factors in cultural and technological evolution that contributed to the need and development of DRM. We also highlighted the implications of these factors from the perspective of information control and rights management. We looked briefly at historical milestones in the evolution of human communications, from basic signs and symbols to the spoken and written words, then we examined the birth of mass communication including print and publishing, broadcast with radio, TV and satellite, as well as the growth of telecommunication tools such as telegraphy, facsimile, telephony and mobile telephony. Finally, we concluded this chapter by touching on diffusion theory and the rapid advent and adoption of internet communication tools such as the web, email, weblogs, internet telephony and news feeds. In the next chapter we look at the development of mass media storage, computers and networking technologies, as well as the history of DRM technologies and their application.

2 Media, Technology and DRM

This chapter starts with a look at the evolution of media storage and replication technologies, followed by the development of computing and internet technologies, which helped to spawn the knowledge and information economy of today. It finally explores the evolution of DRM technologies, from the earliest forms to the current and perhaps more controversial incarnations. One major caveat is that the development of internet and web applications is happening so fast that what might be considered 'state of the art' at the time of writing may have become outdated, or even obsolete, by the time it is read. So the approach adopted here, as in the rest of the book, has been to cover the major developmental trends in DRM technology, only using specific technology examples to highlight major shifts and events in the timeline.

STORAGE AND REPLICATION MEDIA

The previous chapter explored the evolution of communication and media in its various forms; it also highlighted the abundance of information sources and hinted at the phenomenal amount of information that is generated every day. This latter aspect essentially sets the ground for our discussion of the evolution of media storage, replication and other relevant technologies in this section. The history of storage media runs parallel to major developments in communication technology and in some cases it even helped emphasise their capabilities thereby influencing their uptake and usage to some extent.

The main types of digital storage and replication technology that exist today include both magnetic and optical media formats. Together they hold the bulk of new and recent information generated through various channels and mass communication technologies. They are relatively cheap, in terms of cost per quantity of data held, in comparison with other media storage formats. However, two critical factors need to be considered as follows:

(i) The longevity of data held – neither media format can be guaranteed over a certain period of time, which depends on the storage conditions and environment. The actual material that makes up the media is often subject to degradation over time.

(ii) Obsolescence of the hardware and software used to access the information held in the media is a very real issue, especially given the fast changing nature of technology and formats.

Table 2.1, which is taken from the UK's Digital Preservation Coalition's (DPC) website, shows an indicative longevity chart for data held in magnetic and optical storage media at different temperatures (DPC 2002). Several organisations devoted to the preservation of digital media have been formed across the world; in the UK, the DPC serves just such a purpose.

TABLE 2.1   *Generic sample figures for the lifetimes of media (source: DPC (2002))*

Device	25RH 10°C	30RH 15°C	40RH 20°C	50RH 25°C	50RH 28°C
D3 magnetic tape	50 years	25 years	15 years	3 years	1 year
DLT magnetic tape cartridge	75 years	40 years	15 years	3 years	1 year
CD/DVD	75 years	40 years	20 years	10 years	2 years
CD-ROM	30 years	15 years	3 years	9 months	3 months

Important milestones in the development of these magnetic and optical media storage formats are presented in the rest of this section.

Magnetic media

This includes magnetic tapes (e.g. reels, cartridges and cassettes) and magnetic disks (e.g. hard disks and floppy disks). They all use the magnetic properties of metallic materials suspended in a non-magnetic mixture on a substrate to provide versatile and cheap storage. The storage capacity and magnetic charge retention that holds the data have improved significantly over the years. The major considerations in using magnetic media include:

- storage away from strong magnetic fields (e.g. in electrical equipment and motors) as they may affect the media and lead to data loss;
- maintaining a clean operating environment and minimal handling or use of the media in order reduce wear and tear or the risk of damage, from particles, to the media and devices;
- optimised storage conditions in order to reduce risk of oxidation of the ferromagnetic material or similar problems with the substrate materials.

Magnetic tape (audio and video)

In the following we outline some major milestones in the development of magnetic media. The source of this information and much more can be found at the excellent BBC hosted H2G2 website (H2G2 2004).

Audio tape

In 1928, Fritz Pfleumer patented the application of magnetic powders to a strip of paper or film for recording audio, and 'tape recording' was born. With further improvement and lower prices, home tape recording started in early 1950, and was followed by the introduction of stereo and multi-track systems. The 1960s saw the introduction of the smaller eight-track cartridge and compact cassette, which along with lower prices and Dolby noise-reduction technology made audio tape the most popular recording technology until the late 1980s. The digital revolution and computer technology led to the introduction, circa 1987, of the Digital Audio Tape (DAT), which is also used in computer storage and audio mastering.

Video tape

In the 1950s, early video systems used fast moving tape over stationary multi-track heads to cater for the huge bandwidth demanded by video recording. By mid-1956, Ampex developed the system of rotating heads that read video tapes at slower speeds and went on to create the first practical VTR used by major TV studios. The advent of home video recording began in the 1960s and became fully established with the introduction of the video cassette by Sony in the early 1970s. However, a format war between Sony's Betamax and JVC's VHS cassettes led to the domination of the market by the VHS format in the 1980s. The introduction of the consumer video camera recorder (camcorder) led to the development of smaller 8 mm tapes, which also aided portability. The digital revolution ushered in digital tape formats such as Digital8, Mini-DV and Micro-DV in the late 1980s.

Magnetic disks (computer storage)

The use of magnetic media is quite well established in the field of computing, and ever since its early beginnings, the use of electromagnetic devices for storage (or as memory) has been fundamental to the development of the computer. The three classes of computer memory are given as follows:

- **Primary memory**. This is mainly used to execute programs and store transient information between the CPU and the secondary memory. This type of memory is usually in the form of volatile random access memory (RAM) modules.
- **Secondary memory**. This is usually the mass storage memory device that holds the bulk of the computer's data, programs and the operating system (OS). This type of storage is non-volatile, but is optimised for easy access and data retrieval. Examples of this memory class include disk-based devices such as internal and external hard-disk drives (HDDs).
- **Backup archives**. This class of memory is used to store data for archive or backup purposes. It usually holds a large amount of data and may be stored away from the computer. Access and speed of retrieval are not as important here as the ability to retain and preserve the data for lengthy periods. An example of this memory class is the tape archive (using digital tape media similar to DAT).

Some significant events in the development of magnetism-based computer storage, taken from the H2G2 website (H2G2 2004), are outlined as follows:

- In 1951, the use of magnetic tape for data storage was introduced and initially based on low-density steel tape, but it later evolved into Mylar-based oxide tape with higher data density. These tape devices could be used in all three classes of memory, that is, to execute programs, store data and archive information, but the performance of tape-based memory is limited by the need to access data in a linear fashion (to fast forward or rewind to get at specific data).
- The magnetic data hard disk was introduced in 1955 by IBM's 350 Disk File device. Disk access is much faster, as the disk spins at a high speed, and the magnetic read–write heads can get at data anywhere on the disk surface. The use of multiple platters also helped to increase data density.
- In 1971 IBM introduced the cheap floppy disk by enclosing a thin eight-inch magnetic disk platter in an envelope and in 1973 they sealed several platters in a single disk assembly, which gave rise to the HDD used by most computers today.

Optical media

Optical storage media primarily uses laser light to read information from a data layer embedded in a transparent and protective material. The optical media formats can be grouped into three main families according to their recording capability as follows:

- **Read only**. This includes commercial and mass-produced discs with pre-recorded audio, video, data or a mixture of these content types.
- **Recordable**. Represents the write once, read many times (WORM) format, which provides users with the ability to record content once onto a blank disc.
- **Rewriteable**. This extends the above capability to enable multiple recordings and reuse of the same disc.

There are several types of optical media available today, and they mostly came into mainstream usage towards the end of the 20th century. The earliest to appear was the LV (Laser Vision) disc with the capacity to store an hour of video on each side. This was followed by the compact disc read only memory (CD-ROM), which used a series of pits and plateaux in a metallic coating as the data layer. The recordable disc formats (e.g. CD-R) employ a light sensitive dye as their data layer and are thus less stable than CD-ROMs. The rewritable disc formats (e.g. CD-RW) use magneto-optical or phase-change technology to enable the reuse of the same disc. Another optical format introduced is the MiniDisc, which featured a small magneto-optical disc protected by a cartridge and came in read-only, rewritable or data only versions.

The introduction of the DVD format brought increased data capacity (e.g. up to 4.7 GB) and it had equivalent read only (DVD-ROM), recordable (DVD-R) and rewriteable (DVD-RW) variants. The next stage has a trend of very high-capacity DVD formats such as the HD-DVD and Blu-Ray discs, which cater for HD video content. This higher capacity was achieved by using lasers with shorter wavelengths that can read–write more in the media. Other significant developments in optical storage include early stage holographic storage technologies, which promise to deliver a step change in storage capacity by recording, storing and retrieving data throughout the material of the media, instead of just on the surface. Table 2.2, which is adapted from the International Federation of Library Associations website (IFLA 2000), shows various optical media formats in chronological order.

TABLE 2.2   *Timeline for optical media (source: IFLA (2000))*

Media	Year of launch	Type and media	Capacity	Record and replay method
LV (Laser Vision) Disc	1982	Analogue – video and still image	Up to 2 hours of video	Mechanically pressed and optically read by laser
CD-ROM	1981	Digital – all media (except CD-V or analogue video)	Up to 77 min audio or 650 MB of data	Mechanically pressed and optically read by laser
CD-R	1992	Digital – all media	Up to 77 min audio or 650 MB of data. Later versions can hold over 80 min audio or 700 MB of data	Thermally written by laser and optically read by laser
CD-RW	1996	Digital – all media	Up to 77 min audio or 650 MB of data. Later versions can hold over 80 min audio or 700 MB of data	Phase-change written by laser and optically read by laser
DVD	1997	Digital – all media	4.7–18 GB of data or 4 hours of audio and video depending on quality	Mechanically pressed and optically read by laser
DVD-R	1997	Digital – all media	4.7–18 GB of data or 4 hours of audio and video depending on quality	Thermally written by laser and optically read by laser

(continued)

TABLE 2.2   *(continued)*

Media	Year of launch	Type and media	Capacity	Record and replay method
DVD-RW	1998	Digital – all media	4.7–18 GB of data or 4 hours of audio and video depending on quality	Phase-change written by laser and optically read by laser
MD MiniDisc	1992	Digital – sound	80 min audio	Mechanically pressed and optically read by laser
MD MiniDisc Recordable	1992	Digital – sound	80 min audio	Magnetically written by laser and optically read by laser
MD MiniDisc Data	1993	Digital – data	Over 600 MB of data	Magnetically written by laser and optically read by laser
HD DVD	2006	Digital – all media	15 GB single-layer or 30 GB dual-layer disc	Shorter wavelength (405 nm) blue–violet laser
Blu-Ray	2006	Digital – all media	25 GB single-layer or 50 GB dual-layer disc	Shorter wavelength (405 nm) blue–violet laser
Holographic storage (HVD)	2005	Digital – all media	Over 300 GB initially (1 GB s^{-1} data speed, see http://computer.howstuff.works.com)	Intersecting signal and reference lasers for read–write

Optical discs are an increasingly popular method of storage and because the device reader is not in physical contact with the disc there is less likelihood for mechanical failure leading to data loss. However, there is the issue of damage to the disc through poor handling or storage.

Other storage media

Alternatives to magnetic and optical media exist in the form of electronic storage formats such as solid-state non-volatile random access memory (NVRAM) systems. These come in various forms such as compact flash (CF) and secure digital (SD) cards, which use flash RAM and are commonly used in devices such as mobile phones, digital cameras, personal digital assistant (PDAs) and MP3 players. While these electronic storage systems are versatile and convenient, they have limited capacity (only a few gigabytes) and are relatively more expensive (per megabyte of storage) than other mass storage media. There are also limits on the number of times that data can be written and read, and they have a finite shelf life of about 10 years. These factors make them great for short-term storage and data transfer, but they will require huge improvements in technology, capacity and durability to compete with the other storage media described previously.

Statistical observations on information and storage

According to a University of California report in 2003,

> newly created information is stored in four physical media of print, film, magnetic and optical; and is seen or heard in four information flows through the electronic channels of telephone, radio, TV, and the Internet (Lyman and Varian 2003)

The report also made some significant observations based on their findings as shown in Table 2.3 and some of which are listed as follows:

- Print, film, magnetic and optical storage media produced about 5,000,000 TB of new information in 2002. Ninety-two per cent of new information was stored on magnetic media, mostly on hard disks.
- Information flow through electronic channels (i.e. telephone, radio, TV and the internet) contained almost 18,000,000 TB of new information in 2002.
- Ninety-eight per cent of the above total was sent and received in telephone calls. Worldwide telephone calls contained 17,300,000 TB of new information.
- Worldwide TV produced about 31 million hours of original programming (70,000 TB) out of 123 million total hours of broadcasting.
- The web contains about 170 TB of information on its surface and emails generate about 400,000 TB of new information each year worldwide.
- Peer-to-peer (P2P) file exchange on the internet is growing rapidly. The majority of P2P users only download files. The largest files exchanged are video files larger than 100 MB, but the most frequently exchanged files contain music (e.g. MP3 audio).

TABLE 2.3   *Worldwide production of original information in 2002 (source: Lyman and Varian (2003))*

Storage medium	2002 Upper estimate (TB)	2002 Lower estimate (TB)	1999–2000 Upper estimate (TB)	1999–2000 Lower estimate (TB)	Per cent change in upper estimates
Paper	1,634	327	1,200	240	36%
Film	420,254	76,69	431,690	58,209	–3%
Magnetic	5,187,130	3,416,230	2,779,760	2,073,760	87%
Optical	103	51	81	29	28%
TOTAL	**5,609,121**	**3,416,281**	**3,212,731**	**2,132,238**	**74.5%**

In conclusion, the above observations are really not that surprising given that we live in an increasingly connected world. Therefore it may perhaps be more sensible, and expedient, to apply information control and rights management at the content creation stage, rather than at the later stages of transportation and storage. However, because it is infinitely more difficult to control another person's intention than it is to manage their access to content, it seems that the latter course of action is more practical, hence the current need for solutions such as DRM to manage the tide of information unleashed by digital technology.

DIGITAL TECHNOLOGY AND THE INTERNET

The historical timeline of digital technology traces the life of computing from its birth and distant analogue past to the current proliferation of internet technologies and their associated applications. This section describes the development of digital and internet technology with a view to setting the context for the later chapters in this book. It is also directly related to the theme of information control and rights management, as these technologies are all part and parcel of DRM.

History of computing technology

There are many books and other sources of information that deal with this subject, which in itself is a vast and interesting topic to explore. However, the purpose of this section will be to mark the major milestones in the development of computing technology, hence it has been kept at a relatively high level. Some recommendations for further reading are made in the appendices and can be used as a starting point for further research.

Preamble

The whole idea of computing is inextricably linked with digits, numbers and the manipulation of numbers by calculation. The first calculation tools were almost certainly man's own fingers, hence the word 'digit', which refers to a finger or toe, is also used to describe a numeric value. The term 'calculate' derives from the Latin word for pebble and these were used early on to represent larger numeric values and could also store/represent intermediate values in calculation.

Early calculation and calculators

One of the earliest calculating machines in recorded history is the abacus, a device that used beads on a frame (or even symbols drawn on sand) to represent and manipulate numerical values. The introduction of Arabic numerals into Europe, during the 8th and 9th centuries AD, also brought the concept of 'zero' and the fixed places for decimals (e.g. 10s, 100s, 1000s etc.), which helped to simplify mathematical calculations. Professor Wilhelm Schickard built the first mechanical calculator in 1623 and, in the early 1820s, Charles Babbage created the Analytical Engine, a mechanical computer that could solve any mathematical problem and which could perform simple conditional operations by using punch cards. The countess of Lovelace, Lady Augusta Ada Byron, published a description of Babbage's Analytical Engine and in it she outlined the fundamentals of computer programming, including data analysis, looping and memory addressing.

Logic and logic machines

The concept of logic and the use of logic diagrams have been around for a long time; the Greek philosopher Aristotle is thought to have used a logical tree diagram (or 'porphyry tree') to represent the relationships between different species. In the 1890s, John Venn introduced the use of overlapping circles or ellipses in the eponymous Venn diagram and this complemented the popular Boolean algebra that was, and is still, used in computation and logic. Charles Stanhope invented one of the earliest usable logic machines in the early 1800s and in 1936 Benjamin Burack constructed an electrical version using light bulbs to display logical relationships between switches.

Early computers

The first-generation computers used vacuum tube technology and were rather large and cumbersome. In 1941, Konrad Zuse created the first general-purpose programmable calculator and also pioneered the use of binary math and Boolean logic in electronic calculation. In 1943, Alan Turing and his colleagues developed the Colossus, a British code-breaking computer that was used in the Second World War. Other notable early computers, which are usually recognisable by their arcane sounding acronyms, include: the ENIAC (1945), the EDSAC (1949), the UNIVAC (1951), the LEO (1951) and the EDVAC (1952). By 1959, the integrated circuit was introduced and quickly became a core component of comput-ers. In 1962, the ATLAS computer, built by a team from the University of Manchester, introduced many modern architectural concepts such as spooling, interrupts, pipelining, interleaved memory, virtual memory and paging. In 1964, the IBM 360 mainframe computer was introduced and soon became the standard for institutional mainframe computing.

The mini, micro and personal computer revolution

By 1965 the cost of an integrated circuit had fallen to about US$10 (from almost US$1,000 in 1959) and Gordon Moore made the famous prediction (now known as Moore's Law) that the number of components in an inte-grated circuit will double every year. These developments helped bring about the use of computers for personal and general business purposes. Other notable milestones include the following:

- Doug Engelbart developed the mouse, word processor and early hypertext and collaborative tools between 1963 and 1968.

- In the early 1970s, the introduction of RAM chips and the micro-processor enabled the creation and uptake of more affordable mini computers.
- The first personal computer (PC) was the 1975 MITS Altair 8800. Other early PC products include the Apple II PC (1977) and the Commodore PET, but many of the early computers did not have many programs apart from those written by the users themselves.
- In 1979, VisiCalc, a spreadsheet program, became the first success-ful software to drive the sale of PCs.
- In the 1980s, the next generation of PCs, the IBM PC (1981), the BBC Micro Computer, Sinclair ZX Spectrum, Commodore 64 (circa 1982) and Apple's Macintosh PC (1984), all made for a more com-petitive market and helped to spread the adoption of PCs in small businesses, schools and homes.

Current offerings

From the early 1990s, Microsoft's Windows operating system began to dominate the desktop PC market. Other major milestones in software that have been the catalyst of change in the field of computing include the Linux operating system, the Netscape browser, Google's search engine and various P2P networks and applications. These applications run on the multi-gigahertz processors of the fast evolving PC systems that exist today.

The main turning point of the computing era is widely considered to have been the advent of the general-purpose microprocessor, which ushered in desktop systems that had more processing power than the monsters of a decade before. Today the processing power available to games consoles, PDAs and mobile phones are in the zone of what were considered supercomputers just a few decades ago. These ongoing developments seem to provide support for Moore's law, but not only with regard to integrated circuits; instead they seem to apply to various degrees to other developments in computing technologies, applications and miniaturisation. Even the speed of innovation is itself increasing at such a pace that some futurists predict we may well reach a point of technological singularity (or big bang), which would lead into a future filled with technological wonders as yet unimagined. A possible early indication of this is the birth and extremely rapid expansion of the internet, as we discuss next.

Internet technology

The impact of the internet on society has been likened to the renaissance and the industrial revolution. In a 2006 *Fortune Magazine* article, Microsoft's Gary Flake claimed that traditional barriers to participation across domains are dropping partly because of the enhanced ability to exchange knowledge, information and concepts. Also because new value is created in those exchanges, it helps to further reduce the barrier to participation in a virtuous cycle of value creation and innovation, and this he surmises is evidence of the evolution of innovation itself (Flake 2006)

The evolution of the internet is well documented on the web, as well as in many books and articles, therefore this section focuses primarily on significant events in the development of this technology. Zakon (2006) is a notable source of information for the following timeline.

1950s

In 1957 the launch of the first artificial Earth satellite, Sputnik, by the Union of Soviet Socialist Republics (USSR) helped to spark the space race and the formation of the Advanced Research Projects Agency (ARPA) by the US Department of Defence.

1960s

In 1962 Paul Baran created the concept of distributed, packet-switching networks and in 1964 J. C. R. Licklider, an early pioneer of the internet, started a project to connect several remote terminals to a central computer using a timesharing mechanism. By 1965 packet switching had been developed by ARPA to enable reliable computer networking and the result was the resilient military ARPA Network (ARPANET), which was designed during the Cold War to withstand a nuclear attack. The first civil computer-to-computer login (between US universities Stanford and UCLA) occurred on 21 November 1969 and heralded the birth of the internet. The first Request for Comments (RFC) was also published in 1969 by Steve Crocker. RFCs are used by the Network Working Group to define and develop networking standards and protocols. They now apply to all aspects of the internet and essentially document everything about the way the internet and computers on it should behave.

1970s

In 1973, Bob Kahn and Vinton Cerf developed the basic ideas of the internet, which included the Transmission Control Protocol (TCP) and IP (or 'TCP/IP' protocol) suite. The first international connection to the ARPANET was also made in 1973 from the University College London via Norway.

1980s

In 1982, TCP/IP became established as the standard protocols for ARPANET and by 1983 the Domain Name System (DNS) was introduced to the internet, which at the time consisted of 1,000 hosts. DNS entries make it possible to use meaningful and human-readable addresses (e.g. bcs.org) for accessing resources on the internet. In 1984 the Joint Academic Network (JANET) was established in the UK for use by academic institutions. By 1987, the number of hosts on the internet had grown to over 10,000 and within two years this had risen to over 100,000.

1990s

In the early 1990s Tim Berners-Lee, a researcher in the European Particle Physics Laboratory (CERN) in Switzerland, developed the World Wide Web. The web was made up of hypertext-linked resources that reside on various host computers across the internet. The resultant 'hyperlinked' pages provided both web-based information and transparent access to older internet facilities such as the File Transfer Protocol (FTP), Telnet, Gopher and Usenet. The web started life with a text-only interface, but in 1992 the National Centre for Supercomputing Applications (NCSA) developed the first graphical web browser called Mosaic and this led to the subsequent popularity of the web as it became accessible to ordinary home users. By this time the number of internet hosts had reached over 1 million and it has grown almost exponentially since then as shown in Figure 2.1.

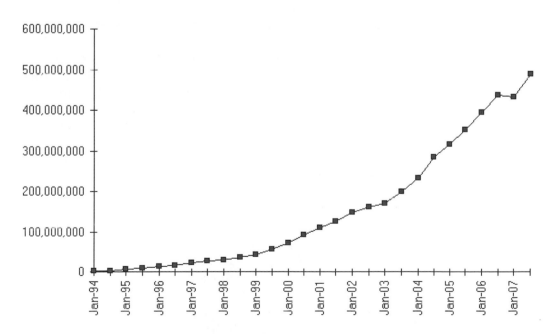

FIGURE 2.1   *Growth in the number of internet hosts over time
(source: Internet Systems Consortium, www.isc.org (2007))*

In 1993, commercial providers started selling internet connections to individuals and in 1994 Mark Andreseen started developing the Netscape web browser, which quickly became market leader over NCSA's Mosaic. By 1995 search engines were using various programs (e.g. worms, spiders, wanderers, crawlers and snakes) to index the web and to provide the facility for users to find resources and information quickly. One such company founded in 1995 by Stanford University students Jerry Yang and David Filo was the extremely successful Yahoo! Other significant events included the launch of the free web-based email service Hotmail in 1996, the transfer of internet governance from US Government agencies to the Internet Corporation for Assigned Numbers (ICANN), internet registrar Network Solutions registering its two-millionth domain name in 1998 and the soon-to-be dominant search engine 'Google' answering over 500,000 queries a day in 1999. SETI@Home was launched in May 1999 as a distributed computing application designed to help with the 'Search for Extra Terrestrial Intelligence' and within a few weeks its distributed internet clients provided more computing power than the most powerful supercomputer of the day.

2000s

Some significant events and milestones that occurred at the dawn of the new millennium include the rise of Napster, a P2P file-sharing network application that came to prominence in 2000, and Wikipedia, a collaborative free online encyclopaedia launched in January 2001, the emergence of major community-based social networking sites such as MySpace.com in 2002 and major denial of service attacks in 2003 (e.g. the SQL Slammer worm, the Sobig.F virus and the Blaster worm). By 2005, spam (or unsolicited emails) containing pornography, viruses, worms and other malevolent content had become a major headache for internet users as shown in Figure 2.2 and by 2006 spam had intensified to about 96% of all emails.

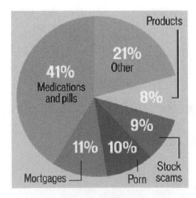

FIGURE 2.2 *Spam content (source: THOCP (2006))*

The future of the internet

Susannah Fox and her colleagues at PEW Internet conducted a survey that evaluated the opinions of various experts as to what the future holds for the internet, and they reached several conclusions, which are summarised as follows (Fox et al. 2005):

- This broad-ranging survey of technology leaders, scholars, industry officials and interested members of the public found that most experts expect serious attacks on the infrastructure of the internet in the coming decade. Some argue that these assaults will become a regular part of life.

- The internet will be more deeply integrated in our physical environment and high-speed connections will proliferate – with mixed results.

- In this era of the blog, experts believe that the internet will bring yet more dramatic change to the news and publishing worlds. They predict the least amount of change to religion.

- Experts are both in awe and in frustration about the state of the internet. They celebrate search technology, P2P networks and blogs, but bemoan the fact that many institutions have been slow to change.

It will be fascinating to watch out for these predictions and observe which, if any, come to pass (and perhaps surpass or fail to meet the expectations). However, it will be even more interesting to observe the emergence of new trends and otherwise unpredictable events, technologies and usage practices that are sure to arise as has happened in the not too distant past.

Mobile computing and gaming platforms

Mobile devices and game technology are the direct offspring or, in some cases, close siblings of digital computer technologies. This section looks at a high-level timeline of the origin and development of computer gaming platforms and mobile computing devices. It also acknowledges the emerging trends of communication and technology convergence in these mobile devices.

Computer games

The computer games industry has rapidly grown into a huge business that even dwarfs the film industry in size, considering that it has only been in existence for a relatively short period of time. The major milestones in this industry are charted as follows.

1950s
Although the first game designed to be played on a cathode ray tube was created in 1947, it was not until 1952 that first game appeared on a computer

when A. S. Douglas created a version of noughts and crosses for the EDSAC computer at the University of Cambridge. It was used as a tool to study human and computer interactions.

1960s

In 1962 the first computer game called *Spacewar!* was developed by student Steve Russell at the Massachusetts Institute of Technology (MIT). In 1968 Ralph Baer, an early computer games pioneer, created a TV-based game for table tennis and target shooting and filed a patent for a 'Television Gaming Apparatus and Method' in 1969.

1970s

In 1972 Nolan Bushnell released the popular arcade video game *Pong*. In 1978 the release of the game *Space Invaders* helped to start the video game craze.

1980s

The classic arcade game *Pac-Man* was released in 1980. The popular game *Tetris* was written by Russian Alexey Pazhitnov in 1985 and was later released onto other game platforms such as the handheld Nintendo Game Boy in 1989. The original home gaming consoles were released in the mid-1980s and include the NES from Nintendo (in 1985) and Sega Master System (in 1986).

1990s

The period leading up to the mid-1990s saw the introduction of further consumer game consoles from companies such as Nintendo and Sega as well as the PlayStation from Sony. In 1993, the release of a game entitled *Doom* took PC gaming to new heights. Similar PC games such as *Quake* (released in 1996) helped to showcase dramatic improvements in PC software and hardware technology.

2000s

Sony released the PlayStation 2 games console in 2000, followed by Microsoft's Xbox and Nintendo's GameCube in 2001. These consoles had become almost as powerful as PCs in processor and graphic capabilities, and yet further innovations were introduced by later consoles such as the Xbox360 and PlayStation 3 (i.e. HD and Blu-Ray gaming) and Nintendo Wii and DS. By 2005 computer games were showing comparable income to the movie industry and the higher returns from games compared to films can be illustrated by the following quote:

> The game Halo 2 for the Xbox console system sold 2.4 million units in its first 24 hours of sales and made $125 million in gross receipts – in
>
> *(continued)*

(continued)

addition, Microsoft was in negotiations with Universal and Fox to turn the game into a movie. In comparison, the all-time record for a film's opening weekend to that point belonged to Spider-Man 2 (2004), which grossed almost $116 million (in July, 2004). Close behind were Shrek 2 (2004) that earned $108 million during its opening weekend (in May, 2004), and Pixar's 'The Incredibles' which drew a $70.5 million gross in its opening weekend (in November, 2004) (Filmsite.org 2006)

This again illustrates the pervasive creep of convergence into yet another mix of technology, entertainment and communication. It was perhaps relatively easier in the past to employ separate measures for information control and rights management in these three areas; however, with increasing convergence it is proving very difficult to put the genie back in the bottle. DRM in the games world, although similar to other software and audiovisual content protection measures, may not work well across these domains, and it also comes with different degrees of protection and usability.

Mobile computing devices

Any computing device that can change location while maintaining functionality even in transit can be classified as mobile. This terminology describes both the capability and functionality of the device, because that is usually a main requirement for purchasing it. Other differentiators, as a result of the above requirements, include the use of batteries to power the device, use of lightweight, energy saving components and design to conserve battery life and the miniaturisation of various components in order to maintain the small form factor that is crucial for portability. They may also include multi-purpose, or swappable, components that provide full-featured functionality to the mobile user and the later incarnations now come with some form of connectivity feature as standard. Devices that fall under the mobile computer category include the following:

- **Laptop or notebook computers** – debuted in the late 1970s and early 1980s with the introduction of models such as the GRiD Compass 1101, the Epson HX-20 and the Gavilan SC, which was the first to be marketed as a 'laptop'. The mid-to-late 1980s saw the entry of major players such as IBM, Compaq, Toshiba, NEC and Apple. The 1990s and 2000s have brought major improvements in processing power and battery life, smaller and lighter hard disks with higher capacities, OS-based power management (e.g. Windows 95), the use of CD-ROMS and DVD drives, better display technology such as thin-film transistor (TFT) screens, power-saving processor technology (e.g. Intel Centrino processors) and greater connectivity with modems, Ethernet/broadband connections, USB, Bluetooth and Wireless Tidelity (Wi-Fi). The latest trend in this area is the development of 'hundred dollar' notebooks, which are intended to help provide for the educational needs of 'every child' in the world.

- **PDAs** – these are usually in the form of handheld devices with some limited computing functionality. They originally started out as personal organisers or digital diary devices, but have since become much more powerful and versatile and now include features such as calculators, clocks, calendars, address books, internet access and email functionality. They can be used to record and playback audio and video and may also incorporate computer games, radio, telephony and even mobile TV features. These devices come complete with cut-down OSs and office suite applications such as spreadsheets and word processing (e.g. Windows Pocket PC). PDAs can also access the internet, intranets or extranets via Wi-Fi. Early examples of handhelds include the Apple Newton, for which the term PDA was first coined, as well as other later offerings by Psion, Palm and Compaq.

- **Smartphones** – a recent development from the mobile phone industry brought on by the numerous technological innovations that make it possible to pack yet more features into smaller electronic devices. The trend is for smaller, better, faster components or devices at cheaper prices for consumers. The smartphone, a combination telephone and PDA, is evidence of the continuous convergence of technology and communication. Just like PDAs, smartphones incorporate several other features such as cameras and videophones, and may even use OSs such as Windows Pocket PC. The major mobile telephone manufacturers such as Nokia, Ericsson and Samsung all have products offerings in this field.

Regardless of origin or type, mobile computing devices now offer versatile connectivity capabilities and have become very powerful communication tools especially in line with the trend for convergence as mentioned above. This brings them into focus with regards to information control and rights management, because their ability to connect with the internet along with powerful multimedia rendering facilities make them a natural medium for the distribution and consumption of digital content. DRM systems have had to take this into account and, as we shall see in later chapters, some efforts have been made to address this field with various Mobile DRM standards and products already in the market. In any case, this has not been plain sailing because mobile functionality presents a particular challenge to internet connectivity. The main issue is basically the fact that mobile devices are, well, mobile, and do not necessarily remain attached to the same network as they move from place to place. Hence, they encounter one of the limitations of the IP addressing method, the use of static network identifiers to route data to the various networks that make up the internet. The solution to this is the inclusion of new mobility support in the current generation of IP with an initiative called Mobility for IPv4 (MIPv4) or Mobile IP. This works by forwarding the data packages from a mobile device's home network to its new location when on the move. Special services are used to identify the device's new location to the home network and the protocol is also backwards compatible with the current IPv4, therefore the sending device does not need to change anything to access the mobile device (IETF 2007).

In so many ways, the true potential of mobility is being realised around us everyday by enabling certain activities that we may take for granted. For example, the author was able to unplug his laptop, relocate to another part of the premises and continue working without losing internet connection thanks to wireless broadband connectivity. The remarkable thing is that this would not have been an option just a mere five years ago. Therefore in light of the rapid rate of innovation and evolution, most measures that enforce information control and rights management will have their work cut out just trying to keep pace. It is only a matter of time before most devices are always connected to a network or the internet regardless of their location.

LEGAL AND LEGISLATIVE DEVELOPMENTS

The legal aspect of the evolution of DRM has tended to be reactionary and based on the immediate need to address certain developments that challenge the status quo in the creative industry and other influential stakeholders. These developments more often than not also challenge existing laws by altering the hitherto accepted landscape and effectively creating new opportunities with advantages and disadvantages that did not necessarily exist, or were sufficiently marginal to be considered insignificant, in the past. With this understanding in place, it may be a simple matter to correlate the significant legal milestones that have occurred in response to trigger events in the evolution of DRM and digital technology. However, that would be too simplistic a view especially given that the legal responses are usually couched in the laws that govern intellectual property (e.g. copyright and patents), thereby making it necessary to understand these constructs before attempting to relate them to DRM. To this end, the next chapter will set the context by covering various aspects of intellectual property and also provide a brief background of the copyright laws that helped give rise to the need for DRM in the first place. In any case, it is important to bear in mind that the intellectual property concept has existed for much longer than the issues raised by the advent of digital content, DRM or indeed electronics and digital technology as a whole.

EVOLUTION OF DRM TECHNOLOGY

DRM technology may be more accurately described as a suite of technology components and applications that work together to enable the effective management of IPRs (e.g. copyright) in the digital domain. However, because content does not exist solely in the digital domain, the scope of the DRM concept also extends to the non-digital world or analogue domain. This latter aspect in itself is a very tall order, for several reasons that will become clear later in this book, but even the core idea of controlling information and rights for every action and intention (including those not yet conceived) is perhaps even more formidable. In a technological context, it is not impossible to implement the necessary controls required to uphold these rules, but a major issue is that the controls can themselves be broken by other technologies in turn. This conundrum may perhaps be best understood by examining the objectives and origins of the DRM technology. To this end, the goal of most DRM systems can be summed up as the ability to provide, to varying degrees, the following capabilities:

- **Rights definition.** Content creators and providers use this capability to help define, organise and manage the rights that can be applied to their works.
- **Content distribution and control.** This addresses the need to protect and manage the content delivery process in order to ensure that the content is accessible only to legitimate end-users. This applies to most commercial media content, hence the public perception of DRM systems in this context only.
- **Access and usage control.** This applies to the ability to control the use of content in various contexts within a specific domain.
- **License and reuse control.** These are systems that implement the rights and licensing on content for use by other publishers, resellers and distributors.
- **Usage tracking and intelligence.** These systems provide data on the usage, distribution and reach of content once it has been published. The information gathered can be used to enforce rights or enhance the services provided.

The need for DRM technology arose as a direct result of the development of digital computer technology and the internet. The former brought with it the ability to create an exact replica of a piece of content, and the latter greatly enhanced the ability to quickly distribute those copies throughout the world. The other often-overlooked aspect of this situation is the low cost (in effort and monetary terms) of using these two technological developments to actually copy and distribute content. In the pre-digital world, it was certainly possible to create high-quality copies of content and distribute them to a large area, but it was also very costly and required intense effort to accomplish in any large-scale way. These barriers have been effectively removed by digital and internet technologies, hence the need for systems that can provide some level of protection for the economic investments of content owners and industries alike. The prevention of unlawful digital replication was already an issue before the rise of the internet and digital media, but it was mostly related to the software industry, which delivered its products in the form of digital computer code and executable programs.

As previously discussed, the early days of computing involved the use of large mainframe machines that supported multiple users. Sometimes these users were able to maintain their own files on the computer and they could set various permissions as to who else could read, change, execute or delete their files on the system. They could also apply these rights to specific groups or types of users on the system (e.g. workgroup, system administrators or all users). This was the beginning of the concept of rights models in the computing world and was also the basis of the rights models used in many modern computer platforms and even in the DRM systems of today. The real and widespread need for rights management and copy protection mechanisms did not arise, in the software industry, until the advent of the PC in the late 1970s. This is because the use of disk-based software distribution methods also made it easy to copy and transfer these files from computer to computer using the same disk technology. Some examples of the disk-based or portable media formats used thus include floppy disks, CD-ROMs, DVDs, memory sticks and portable HDDs. The response to this was the introduction of various key-based software licence techniques that made it necessary to unlock the program before it could be installed or run on the PC. Other methods include the use of hardware dongles, which needed to be attached to a port on the PC before the software would operate as intended.

In the late 1980s, the advent of networking technologies made it even easier to copy and move digital files and programs across the network without physical intervention. This coincided with the introduction of encryption technologies that could be used to control access to the files. Encryption is the process of obscuring information to make it unreadable without a reverse process of decryption, and its use for protecting software as well as other types of information and content has been well documented over the years. For example, in 1991 Phil Zimmermann released the PGP (Pretty Good Privacy) encryption program along with its source code, which quickly appeared on the internet. According to PGP's website at http://www.pgp.com, this public-key encryption tool was so good that US government even filed an export violation case (which was later dropped).

Other early applications of encryption included the protection of programs and other early content such as typefonts on CD-ROMs or on a shared server. According to Rosenblatt et al.:

> between 1994 to 1996, the rise of the Internet as a viable commercial and distribution medium made it imperative for publishers and vendors to appreciate the very real threat of digital piracy (Rosenblatt et al. 2002)

and this led to some significant developments, which gave rise to the paradigm we now know as DRM. These key events include the following:

(i) IBM developed an early incarnation of a DRM product called InfoMarket, which consisted of an encryption-based protection mechanism called Cryptolope and a suite of software to build ecommerce websites for the protected content.

(ii) EPR (Electronic Publishing Resources), another commercial vendor, also created an early DRM system that consisted of a protected end-to-end system for delivering digital content and included a hardware client at the consumer end of the chain. The various patents for EPR technology have survived in the current incarnation of that company, now called Intertrust, which has become one of the biggest names in the DRM space.

(iii) Dr Mark Stefik, a researcher working at the Xerox Palo Alto Research Center (PARC), published a seminal paper (Stefik 1996) that defined the technologist's view of DRM. The paper proposed that, in a completely digital environment, it would be possible to implement a trusted system that enabled the application of precise information control and rights management on any piece of content or data in that system. Stefik also defined a rights language called DPRL (Digital Property Rights Language) for use in creating the rights models that would be used in such a system. The result of this effort was the creation of a division within Xerox to develop software based on DPRL. This division was eventually spun off and renamed ContentGuard Inc., which has since become another big name in DRM, and developed a commercial version of DPRL called the eXtensible Rights Management Language (XrML).

DRM solutions usually come in the form of software-based systems that interact with the client or player device to enforce the applicable rights to the content it renders. These systems have met with various levels of success and adoption by content distributors, equipment manufacturers and the consuming public. The later chapters on DRM technology, products and vendors will explore these topics in some detail, but some immediate examples of these systems include the following:

- **CSS (Content Scrambling System).** This was an early example of a DRM system introduced by the movie industry's DVD Forum around 1996. It used a simple encryption algorithm and also required device manufacturers to restrict or disable digital copy features in their products. This was fairly effective until the 1999 release of a CSS decryption (DeCSS) program created by Norwegian Jon Lech Johansen.

- **SafeCast.** This software copy protection system, developed by Macrovision, was the subject of some controversy because it could potentially cause problems with the OS of a host computer by writing to the boot track of the local disk. SafeCast works by product activation, which is a method of restricting the functionality of a product until a valid licence key is used to register and activate it with the vendor. Intuit and Adobe are companies that have used SafeCast to protect some of their products.

- **Apple's iTunes FairPlay DRM system.** This is one of the success stories of DRM and usability, mostly because it is a relatively non-intrusive protection mechanism that provides a level of confidence to content owners. However, because of its popularity several people including Jon Lech Johansen, the author of DeCSS, have written circumvention programs (e.g. PlayFair and HYMN) to get around the encryption used.

- **Sony compact disc (CD) copy protection.** In 2005 SonyBMG Music Entertainment included the Extended Copy Protection (XCP) and MediaMax CD-3 copy protection software (created by UK-based First4Internet Ltd) on some 100 different albums in an attempt to control unauthorised ripping and distribution of their content. However, the software used a form of rootkit technology that automatically installed on a user's PC when they tried to play the CD. The problem with this approach was exposed in Mark Russinovich's blog article in October 2005, which made known the fact that the rootkit opened security holes on the systems that could be exploited by computer viruses and worms (Russinovich 2005). The upshot was a number of lawsuits filed against SonyBMG and their subsequent recall of the affected CDs.

- **Enterprise DRM (E-DRM or ERM).** This is the use of DRM technology in the corporate or business domain to provide persistent protection of corporate information and data. The technology is usually focused at enterprise documentation in various formats (e.g. Word, PDF, AutoCAD, Tiff etc.) and requires the use of a policy server and identity management (IDM) components to authenticate users and apply the appropriate levels of access rights to the files. The main difference between enterprise and media DRM is that E-DRM is primarily aimed at enforcing enterprise information policies such as regulatory compliance requirements, protecting enterprise intellectual property and trade secrets etc., and it is not overly concerned with consumer issues and media DRM bug-bears such as 'fair use' or privacy.

In conclusion, we can see that the main objective and origin of DRM has to do with information control and rights management, which is an issue that has been around for a very long time, and which has become exacerbated by the development of digital and internet technologies. The future of this technology is very much in the hands of the major stake-holder groups (which we examine in Chapter 4), and will be affected by the emergence of new business models and usage practices that can take advantage of the evolution of communications and technology.

CONCLUSION

In this chapter we have looked at the evolution of storage media from analogue tape to digital formats such as CDs, DVDs and NVRAMs. We have also made some observations about the growth of information storage and throughput in recent years. We also looked at the development of computer and network technology, from early mainframes to desktop PCs, mobile and gaming platforms, as well as the latest trends in convergence and the potential to access your content anywhere, anytime and on any device. This final aspect obviously led directly to the need for and development of DRM technology. Interestingly enough it seems that because DRM has evolved mostly as a reaction to external trends and events that adversely affect the knowledge and creative economy, at best it may only be a cure for the symptom and not the disease itself, hence the difficulty it faces in trying to be all things to all people. In the next chapter, which deals with the concept of intellectual property and copyright, we give some context and shed some light on the legal constructs that have been devised over the years to encourage creativity and provide protection for creative works and the industry it feeds. These statutes, laws and international treaties have all contributed immensely to the justification for the DRM technology we have today.

3 Intellectual Property

According to the World Intellectual Property Organisation (WIPO):

> Intellectual Property refers to creations of the mind: inventions, literary and artistic works, and symbols, names, images, and designs used in commerce (WIPO 2006a)

It goes on to further categorise the various types of intellectual property under two headings:

- **Industrial property.** This includes patents (on inventions), trade marks, industrial designs and geographic indications of source.
- **Copyright.** This covers literary works (e.g. novels, poems, plays, films, musical works), artistic works (e.g. drawings, paintings, photographs and sculptures) and architectural designs. It also includes the related rights of performing artistes, record producers and broadcasters in the expression of the concept or work.

As mentioned at the end of the last chapter, this section is mainly concerned with the concept of intellectual property (especially copyright) and how it relates to DRM. It also delves into how one affects the other in a constantly evolving milieu of technology and society, law and ethics, economics and the basic moral entitlement to the rewards of creative endeavour. The latter aspect of creative artistic expression and the rights to benefit thereof is of particular interest, as it has a direct bearing on the evolution of DRM technology and the laws and doctrines that have developed over many years to support them.

As a purely human construct, intellectual property is almost by necessity an inexact proposition, with some fuzzy areas that are open to interpretation depending on individual circumstances, the property in question, and the country of origin or jurisdiction of the intellectual property system. Therefore in order to keep things simple we shall focus on the concept of intellectual property and copyright as it applies to the UK, the European Union and the rest of the world in that order of priority. Specific examples are derived from certain developments in other countries, such as the USA, that may have addressed some of the recent challenges to established and generally accepted views on copyright.

Finally, in order to grasp the full extent and subtleties of intellectual property (and copyright), it is necessary to understand the origin of these constructs; therefore a brief overview of the various types of intellectual property as well as a brief timeline of the major events in the evolution of copyright is provided in the text. This is followed by a more detailed look at the different aspects of copyright and their relation to digital technology, including the challenges raised by this technology. A brief overview of some of the organisations and treaties that have been introduced to address intellectual property issues at both national and international levels is included, as well as some of the more interesting legal trials and decisions that have been reached in attempting to deal with the effects of the internet and digital technology.

AN OVERVIEW OF INTELLECTUAL PROPERTY

In the UK, the intellectual property system is made up of a small number of the flexible instruments mentioned above including copyright, patents, designs and trade marks. These are broadly adapted for artistic creations, inventions, designs and product identification respectively. IPRs are those rights granted to the creators and owners of works that result from human intellectual creativity. These works may be in the industrial, scientific, literary and artistic domains. They may be in the form of an invention, a manuscript, a suite of software, a product design, a business name or brand identifier (Madhavan 2006). According to the UK Patent Office (UKPO) website the four main types of intellectual property are patents, designs, trade marks and copyright (UKPO 2006), each of which is described in the following.

Patents

A patent is a type of intellectual property that grants an inventor, for a limited period of time, the rights to control the use of their invention. These rights include the ability to stop other people from making, using or selling that invention without the permission of the creator. This effectively provides the inventor with a temporary monopoly on the economic rewards that can accrue from that invention. Patents can be used to protect functional and technical aspects of a product or process, and may be applied to relatively minor or simple improvements on an existing product or process. In order to be granted a patent, however, the invention must fulfil certain conditions such as:

- **novelty** – the invention must be discernibly different from the 'state of the art', which means that it must not have been made available to the public in any form or description prior to the application for patent;
- **innovation** – the invention must show evidence of an inventive step, above and beyond the state of the art, and which is not immediately obvious to a skilled subject matter expert in that area;
- **industrial application** – the invention must be applicable in industry to qualify for a patent.

A patented invention is recorded in a patent document, which contains a description of the invention including drawings and schematics, as well as the claims that define the scope of the protection. In the UK, patent rights last up to 20 years after which they expire and becomes available to the public to use freely. The rights granted by a patent are highly territorial, therefore an inventor would need to cover an invention as many times and in as many regions as he wants for comprehensive protection.

Just like any other property, a patent and other IPRs can be bought, sold, mortgaged or licensed to others. In fact, this has led to the existence of some companies that have no product other than the intellectual property of their patents, which they license to various manufacturers and which forms their main source of income. Examples include companies such as Intertrust and ContentGuard, which hold some of the more significant patents for DRM technology. The downside to this is that some of these patent companies, commonly referred to as 'patent trolls', have made it a standard operating policy to buy up patents in the open market with the express purpose of threatening product manufacturers with costly litigation on the grounds of patent infringement.

Designs

The design (of a product) is the intellectual property of the creator or owner and it covers the appearance of the product or a specific part of it, especially features such as lines, contours, colours, shape, texture, materials or decorations on the product. Design rights in the UK can exist in the following forms:

- **Registered designs.** Registration provides the owner of a design with a monopoly, for a limited time, which stops others from using the design without their express permission.
- **Unregistered design right.** In the UK this protects original and non-commonplace designs that have not been registered from deliberate copying, and it lasts for up to 10–15 years from the time of creation. This right can also be bought, sold or licensed like any other property. There is also a separate system for Community Unregistered Design Right that applies in the UK.
- **Artistic copyright.** This applies to original artwork borne from independent creative effort. The degree of originality required may be open to interpretation in a court of law, but suffice to say that there must be substantial evidence to support the claim to originality.

Trade marks

The UK intellectual property website defines a trade mark as any sign that can distinguish the goods and services of one trader from those of another. The signs may include words, logos, colours, slogans, three-dimensional shapes and sometimes sounds and gestures. Trade marks are used to promote brand recognition and are invaluable as a marketing tool that helps associate an organisation and its product with a certain level of quality or consistent experience for their customers. In the UK a trade mark must be capable of graphical representation (i.e. words and pictures).

A trade mark can be registered in the UK by application to the UKPO, or if the mark has been used long enough to have acquired local distinction, then it may be legally recognised as a trade mark due to its prior rights. Trade mark infringement (such as in 'passing off' a product or service as a well-known brand) can result in legal action by the owner of that trade mark, and the decision is often dependent on the similarity of the marks involved, the similarity of the products and services and an established proof of distinctiveness. UK trade mark registration provides protection for 10 years, but can be renewed by the owner or allowed to lapse.

The current UK trade mark legislation is the Trade Marks Act 1994, which is the UK implementation of the European Trade Marks Directive. In 2004 this act was extended to include under infringement any product or service, even if dissimilar from an established brand, that takes unfair advantage of, or is detrimental to, the registered trade mark of well-known brands.

Copyright

Copyright provides the opportunity for creators to reap economic rewards from a wide group of creative works such as literary works of prose and poetry, art, music, sound recordings, films and broadcast content. It enables the owners of these works to control the use of their material in several ways such as making copies (hence the term copyright), distribution, public performance, broadcast and online usage. Interestingly, this sequence of copyright coverage is identical to and emerged in tandem with the technologies that are used to reproduce and disseminate these works. As we shall see later on, this is not by coincidence. Copyright also grants the moral right to be identified as the creator of a work, as well as the right to object to its distortion or mutilation.

Copyright protection is automatic and exists as soon as there is a record, in any fixed form, of the material that has been created. It is important to note that copyright does not protect the ideas that gave rise to the work, only the expression or manifestation of that idea in some fixed form (i.e. the work itself). Also copyright may not be applied to certain identifiers such as names or titles. A core characteristic of copyright is that the use of copyright material requires the express permission of the copyright owner. However, there are several exceptions to this rule (as we shall see later in this chapter) and as a result certain prohibited uses of a copy-protected work may not infringe copyright. We deal with the significance of copyright exceptions in a later section, but they are mostly related to the main purpose of copyright, which is to enable creators to gain economic benefit and encourage future creativity. It does not purport to hinder the use of creative works except where this may affect the above goals.

Other forms of intellectual property

Apart from the main four types mentioned above, some other types of intellectual property exist, which we describe here for completeness. They include some IPRs that relate to the above properties or are regarded as *sui generis* IPRs (i.e. 'without genre' or 'independent'), which relate only to specialist applications such as databases, integrated circuits or plant varieties. A brief description has been included for some of these rights as follows:

- **Performance rights.** These are granted to performers and those making recordings of their performances to derive some reward from their work. This group includes musicians, singers, actors and other types of performers. In the world of music, performing rights are granted by licence to cover the public performance of musical works. It is part of copyright law and helps to ensure that appropriate payment is made to the composer, lyricist and publisher for the public performance of their music. Examples include broadcasts, concerts, nightclubs, restaurants, shops and other public venues.
- **Related rights.** Also known as neighbouring rights, these refer to the rights of sound recording producers and broadcasters in their works. This distinction is only applicable in some countries. For example, in the UK producers and broadcasters get copyright protection for their material. The rights of this group are internationally protected by the Rome Convention for the Protection of Performers, Producers of Phonograms and Broadcasting Organisations (which was in signed in 1961). In the European Union, the rights of film producers and database creators are also protected by related rights.
- **Moral rights.** This is not an economic right, but instead it provides the content creator with the right to be acknowledged as the creator of the work and the ability to legally challenge any adaptation of the work that may harm their reputation.
- **Trade secrets.** This form of intellectual property applies to different types of information (e.g. formulae, processes, designs, instruments patterns or compilations of information) used by a business to gain a competitive advantage over its rivals in the same field. The main characteristic of this intellectual property is that the information

must be kept and held in secret from any public disclosure whatsoever and, as long as this is the case, it could remain protected in perpetuity (e.g. the formula for Coca-Cola), unlike patents.

- **Geographical indication.** This right restricts the use of a geographical indicator name to products that come from particular region or area and, in some cases, have met certain quality standards. The use these systems are prevalent in Europe and can be often seen on food or wine (e.g. the name 'Champagne' or 'Bordeaux' is strictly controlled by the French *appellation d'origine contrôlée* (AOC) system).

- **Database rights.** Introduced by the European Union in 1996, it applies to the structure and information held in a database. The protection is automatic on the creation of the database and lasts for 15 years with the option to extend. Database rights are designed to prevent the copying of substantial parts of a database (including frequent extraction of insubstantial parts). The UK implementation of this is 'The Copyright and Rights in Databases Regulations 1997', which came into force on 1 January 1998.

- **Publication right.** This provides some degree of protection for works on which copyright has expired only on the condition that it had not previously been made public during the term of copyright. The publication right is automatically granted to the first person to make this work publicly available regardless of current or previous claims of ownership on the work. The publication right is applicable within the European Union and it is similar in scope and characteristic to copyright, but only lasts for 25 years from date of publication.

- **Semiconductor topography protection.** Also known as mask work, this is the IPR granted for the two- or three-dimensional layout of an integrated circuit including the arrangement of the transistors, resistors interconnects and other elements. The photomask used to etch the components cannot be effectively protected under copyright or patents, hence the temporary exclusive reproductive rights granted under mask works.

- **Plant breeders' rights.** Also referred to as plant variety rights, these are the IPRs attached to new plant varieties developed by a plant breeder. They provide the breeder with control of the use of the seeds in the new plant variety, as well as the right to collect a royalty (included in the purchase price paid by buyers) on the variety for several years as an economic return on the effort and incentive to develop other varieties.

- **Supplementary protection rights.** In the European Union a supplementary protection certificate (SPC) can be used to extend the life of a patent for up to five years after it expires. This certificate is usually applicable to medicinal and plant protection methods (e.g. herbicides) that may need to undergo a lengthy regulatory approval process before they can be made widely available. However, the term of extended protection is not the same as the original patent and it cannot be used to extend the overall term for more than 15 years in total.

- **Traditional knowledge.** Refers to the indigenous, local or long-standing traditions particular to specific societies and communities around the world. It is usually integrated into their culture and forms a part of their identity, which may be passed on via oral tradition, stories, legends, folklore, dance, ceremonies and other traditional rituals and practices. The protection comes in the form of defensive actions (e.g. preventing others from patenting traditional knowledge) and proactive measures that involve securing legal protection over the communities' traditional knowledge. Needless to say, there is a healthy amount of debate (among international bodies such as the World Trade Organisation (WTO), WIPO, the Creative Commons and others) over the extent and scope of this form of intellectual property.

- **Passing off.** This is a common law tort (or civil wrong) that provides protection against unfair competition for unregistered trade marks under 'passing off' law. Essentially passing off relates to the situation where a product or service is wrongly associated with or passed off as a known brand in order to gain a competitive advantage, and (often by the same process) damages the goodwill or reputation of that brand or trade mark. Under this law the owner of the brand can take legal action against the infringer.

- **Anti-circumvention.** This is not strictly an IPR, but more of a statute that restricts certain uses of technology. It provides protection against circumvention of copy protection devices, by making it illegal to produce or distribute any tools or methods of circumventing any technological measures taken to protect copyright. This concept was introduced by the WIPO Copyright Treaty (WCT) in 1996 along with other measures to address the need for additional protection for copyright protected works in order to cater for the rapid developments in information technology. Many jurisdictions are starting to implement this treaty, especially anti-circumvention. Examples include the European Union's Copyright Directive (EUCD) and the USA's DMCA (Digital Millennium Copyright Act).

As can be seen from the above examples, intellectual property may come in many forms and formats, which are not necessarily exclusive, but its primary objective is both to protect and encourage creative innovation by enabling the creators and implementers of ideas to get some economic reward for their efforts and thereby benefit society as a whole. However, the concept of protecting intellectual property and its expression is a very contentious issue that has provoked years of debate and discourse among the literati all over the world. For example, in 1851 *The Economist*, a well-respected publication, published the following opinion:

> The public will learn that patents are artificial stimuli to improvident exertions; that they cheat people by promising what they cannot perform; that they rarely give security to really good inventions, and elevate into importance a number of trifles... no possible good can ever come of a Patent Law, however admirably it may be framed. (*The Economist* 1851)

The main thrust of the argument here was that patents were perceived to hinder economic growth by restricting the free use of other people's ideas and hence were antagonistic to free trade. This position is somewhat similar to the sentiment of today's free speech, free software and freedom of information activists. They would have it recognised that 'information wants to be free' on the internet and they make very good arguments in support of this; however, history has shown that other technological challenges in the past have been overcome by a more or less balanced approach that evolved from the various conflicts between stakeholders at any one time. This makes it very likely that, given enough time, a similar conclusion will be reached over the issue of intellectual property on the internet. The area of intellectual property that is arguably most affected by the internet and which is in the process of being addressed by various mechanisms including DRM is that of copyright.

COPYRIGHT

As we stated earlier, copyright is a type of intellectual property that specifically focuses on protecting the expression of an idea, as opposed to the concept or idea itself. This distinction is very important, because it defines the scope of copyright to be largely around the replication and transmission of an expressed idea, and this often puts it in direct conflict with the new technologies that evolve and improve the capability to copy and distribute content. However, copyright is a flexible instrument and it has often had to make adaptations to accommodate the effects of changing times and technologies, mostly by means of certain inbuilt exceptions to its rules (as we show later). Figure 3.1 illustrates the journey from idea to expression, instantiation and distribution, as well as the related scope and boundary of copyright.

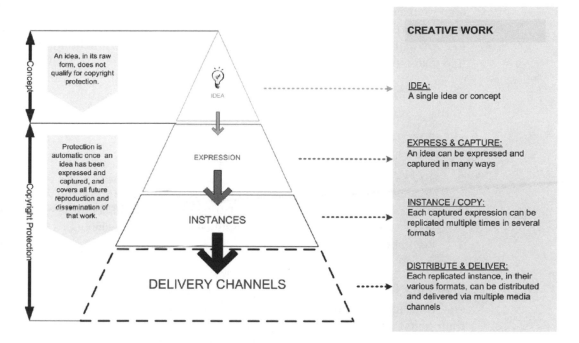

FIGURE 3.1   *The scope of copyright (from idea to instance)*

From this figure, it is clear that copyright covers a vast area in relation to the overall path from an idea to the end-user copy of a work. As a result the rules of copyright have, in one way or another, had an impact on most of the enabling technologies in this route.

The top of Figure 3.1 represents an idea or concept that usually originates from and resides in the mind of the creator. In the copyright domain, this idea may be completely original, partially inspired by or based totally on an existing work, and once it is expressed in some fixed form (e.g. demo recording, draft manuscript or screenplay) it then becomes vested with automatic copyright protection from that moment on. However, from an economic point of view the expressed idea is of limited interest until someone decides to invest time and effort to further develop and reproduce the content for commercial distribution and sale. At this juncture, the end product and copies thereof become the basis for remuneration and financial compensation to all of the people and organisations in the value chain for that product, including the creator. Since copyright is concerned with ensuring the rights of the owner to derive economic benefit from their works, it becomes quite relevant at this stage and influences the structure of the deals that are made in the latter stages of the route to consumer. A typical deal would specify that for each unit or copy of the work sold, a certain percentage of the retail price would be paid to the copyright owner (which may not be the creator), usually after production and retail costs have been deducted. The remainder of this section explores the concept of copyright in more detail by tracing its history from the beginning to its present form, and by examining the various amendments and exceptions to copyright that have helped it to remain relevant, practical and adaptable in a changing environment.

The concept of rights

COPYRIGHT AND THE LAW

The rights of creators of literary, dramatic, musical and artistic works are covered by copyright under the common law system. They are also covered by author's rights under the civil law system. The rights of performers, producers, broadcasters and other entities that disseminate these works to consumers can be described as related, or neighbouring, rights (Sterling 2003)

According to WIPO's copyright pages at http://www.wipo.int/copyright/en/, the idea of copyright 'empowers the creator of a work (and their heirs) with the exclusive right to use, or authorise others, to use the work on agreed terms'. The following points describe the key aspects of copyright:

- **The rights.** The creator of a work can prohibit or authorise several activities on their work including reproduction, public performance, recordings, broadcasting, translation and adaptation.
- **Royalties.** The above activities often require significant investment and may best be undertaken by other parties that are better equipped to replicate, market and distribute the work. The creator would often sell these rights in return for a fee or royalty based on the actual usage of the work.
- **Term.** The economic rights to benefit from these works are limited to a period of 50 years after the death of the author. Some countries may extend this limit above 50 years, for example Table 3.1 contains the duration of copyright for several types of work in the UK.
- **Moral rights.** As stated earlier, this is the right retained by the creator to claim ownership of a work and to object to changes that damage the author's reputation
- **Enforcement.** The copyright owner can enforce their legal rights, through the courts, by inspecting premises for signs of piracy and illegal copies or derivatives of their work. They can also apply for a 'cease and desist' order as well as to seek compensation and damages.
- **Scope.** Copyright only covers the expression of an idea, and not the actual idea itself. This is confirmed by the WTO Agreement on

Trade-Related Aspects of Intellectual Property Rights (or TRIPS Agreement).

- **Mechanism.** Copyright is automatically vested with the creation of a work in some fixed format such as an audio recording or written forms etc. It does not have to be registered and in fact WIPO's website has a disclaimer that reiterates this fact, and is aimed at those organisations that may issue certificates that claim to grant copyright protection.
- **Related rights.** Developed over the past half century around copyrights and provides similar but shorter-lived protection for others such as performing artistes, sound producers and broadcasters.

Duration of copyright

Table 3.1, which is derived from the University of Cambridge Centre for Applied Research in Educational Technologies (CARET) website, shows the duration of copyright protection for several different types of works in the UK.

The question of copyright ownership can often trap the unwary, because even though copyright is automatically vested in a work, the creator is not necessarily the copyright owner. For example, if the work was created in the course of employment, the employer may have prior claim to the copyright depending on their contract with the employee. Table 3.2 lists the ownership of copyright in the several types of works.

TABLE 3.1 *Duration of copyright (source: CARET (2005))*

Type of work	Copyright duration
Literary, dramatic, musical or artistic works	70 years from the end of the calendar year in which the author dies.
Works of unknown authorship	70 years from the end of the calendar year in which the work is made. However, if the work is made available to the public during that time then copyright expires 70 years from the end of the calendar year in which it is first made publicly available.
Computer-generated works	50 years from the end of the calendar year in which the work is made.
Sound recordings	50 years from the end of the calendar year in which the recording is made. If, however, during that period the recording is published (or otherwise communicated to the public), then copyright expires 50 years from the end of the calendar year in which it is first published or communicated.

(continued)

TABLE 3.1 *(continued)*

Type of work	Copyright duration
Films	70 years from the end of the calendar year of the death of the last to die of the following persons: the principal director, the author of the screenplay, the author of the dialogue and the composer of music specifically created and used in the film.
Broadcasts and cable programmes	50 years from the end of the calendar year in which the broadcast is delivered.
Typographical arrangements of published editions	25 years from the end of the calendar year in which the edition is first published.
Crown copyright literary, dramatic, musical or artistic works	125 years from the end of the calendar year in which the work is made; or if published commercially within 75 years from the end of the calendar year it is made; or 50 years from the end of the calendar year in which it is first so published, whichever period is shorter.
Photographs	In general terms it is the year of the photographer's death plus 70 years; or, if anonymous, it lasts 70 years from creation; but, if made publicly available, then it lasts 70 years from the end of the year of publication. More information and subtleties can be found at the UKPO website. http://www.ipo.gov.uk/copy/c-applies/c-photo.htm

TABLE 3.2 *Ownership of copyright (source: CARET (2005))*

Type of work	Initial owner of copyright
Literary, dramatic, musical or artistic work	The person who creates it (e.g. the writer, songwriter, lyricist, artiste).
Photographs	Between July 1912 and August 1989, the owner of the film or negative is the 'author', unless the photograph was commissioned in which case the commissioner is the copyright owner. Copyright on photographs made before or after this period belongs to the photographer, unless under employment in which case the copyright belongs to the employer.
Sound recording	The producer owns the copyright.
Film	Copyright on films made after July 1994 belong to the producer and main director. Copyright on films made before this period belong only to the producer.
The typographical arrangement of a published edition	The publisher owns the copyright.
Computer-generated literary, dramatic, musical or artistic work without a human author	Copyright belongs to the person by whom the arrangements necessary for the creation of the work are undertaken.

The essence of copyright, as touched on before, is that it provides creators with certain incentives such as recognition and economic rewards for their efforts. The copyright system is also designed to provide assurance that the works can be disseminated without fear of piracy, thereby encouraging further creativity and helping to increase access to creative works that can be enjoyed by anyone around the world. The tension between maintaining a structured and organised protection system and the need to ensure full accessibility to protected content often presents the prevailing copyright system with difficult choices. The evolution of copyright in the next section provides an overview of how copyright originated, evolved and adapted itself to meet the tough challenges thrown by significant technological and social developments in its timeline.

The evolution of copyright

As we have seen from the previous section, copyright is closely connected with the economics of replicating and distributing works to a wide audience; it is therefore not surprising that the early beginnings of copyright should coincide with the rise of the printing press in Europe. The following list, adapted from Bill Thompson's (2006) online timeline, highlights some of the more significant events, treaties and organisations that emerged in the evolution of copyright.

Advent of printing technology – the Gutenberg press (1400s–1500s)

In Europe between the 15th and 16th centuries the widespread use of the Gutenberg printing press began to make it much easier for ordinary people to gain access to literary works that hitherto had been the preserve of the clergy and the educated middle and upper classes. However, this also brought with it the issue of increased 'piracy' as it also became more profitable to produce and sell illegal copies of existing printed material; so much so that the printers of the day had to act to try and preserve their livelihood and this resulted in licensing.

Early licensing (1557)

The London Stationer's Company received a Royal Charter from Queen Mary that empowered the printing profession alone to pursue the art and 'mystery' of printing, and which also made it their statutory responsibility to stamp out the publications of 'scandalous, malicious, schismatical and heretical persons'. This brought about the introduction of a system of licensing or pre-publication censorship by printers in order to secure their property rights and to censor controversial works (Thompson 2006).

The Statute of Anne (1710)

Widely considered to be the earliest known copyright law, the Statute of Anne was enacted by the British Parliament in 1710. (The British

Library holds a copy of this statute, which is headlined: '*An Act for the Encouragement of Learning, by Vesting the Copies of Printed Books in the Authors or Purchasers of such Copies, during the Times therein mentioned*'.) The act was a response to the extensive lobbying by booksellers for a new copyright system, based on landed property rights, which would grant them perpetual ownership of the rights to the works. However, the Statute of Anne delivered a more revolutionary copyright system that gave authors the rights to their works, as well as the decision on who would print it. The term was for 14 years with an option to extend to a second term of 14 years, in order to discourage printer or bookseller monopolies. The statute also created a public domain for works that had expired their term of copyright and it granted consumers full rights of usage on the works after purchase. This event was also significant because it distinguished a work from its physical incarnation.

The battle for copyright (1774)

The booksellers opposed the limits imposed by the Statute of Anne on the term of copyrights (i.e. perpetual rights versus 14 years) and took several legal actions to try and overturn it. Their strategy centred on the position that common law viewed literary property to be same as landed property (regardless of the fact that one was intangible and the other tangible) and therefore they should have the same terms of perpetual rights. This position was finally overturned in the famous case of Donaldson versus Beckett, in which the Lords upheld that copyright was a limited right, and not absolute or perpetual, and is fully documented in the 'Proceedings in the Lords on the Question of Literary Property, February 4 through February 22, 1774' (Talmo 2006).

Dramatic Copyright Act (1833)

This was the first act to address performance rights. It protected the performing rights for a limited number of years.

Literary Copyright Act (1842)

This act introduced the system, still in use today, of granting rights to the author of a work for their lifetime plus an additional number of years (which in this case was 7 years after death).

The player piano (1863)

With the introduction of Fourneaux's player piano in the USA, it became possible to record and reproduce music. The recorder was a device that punched holes into a paper roll as the pianist played a tune. This roll could then be copied many times over and sold to people with player pianos that read and played the very same sequence of notes recorded on it. By 1902 over a million player piano rolls had been sold in the USA and this drove the market for the player pianos (an early example of content driving the uptake of the player device). However, the music composers of the day were of the opinion that this promoted the piracy of their works and led to the 1909 revision of the Copyright Act, which provided them with the right to determine whether, and on what terms, their music should be recorded. Once recorded, however, other artistes could then re-record the music without asking permission by paying a fixed compulsory licence fee of two cents per copy.

The Berne Convention (1886)

The Berne Convention was an international treaty agreed mostly by the countries in Western Europe in Berne, Switzerland. It sought to harmonise the many disparities in copyright laws of different countries and to provide some level of protection for imported works between countries. The need for this treaty was driven by the growth of international trade and communications, which quickly highlighted the situation as countries sought to make works available to their population. The Berne Convention formed the core national copyright system for its signatories, which initially comprised Western European countries (as well as Japan and Tunisia), until the mid-20th century when other countries around the world adopted it including the USA in 1988. In its revised form, it is still a key basis for modern copyright regimes in many countries today. The revisions include the 1908 extension of copyright protection for 50 years after the death of the author, the removal of the need for registration of works in signatory countries and, in 1928, the recognition of the moral rights of creators. In 1970, the Berne Convention Bureau was assimilated by WIPO, the United Nations special agency for intellectual property.

UCC – Universal Copyright Convention (1952)

The UCC treaty was created by UNESCO (United Nations Educational Scientific and Cultural Organisation) as an alternative to the 'European-biased' Berne Convention. It was supported and adopted by countries that opposed the terms of the Berne Convention, which they felt was more favourable to net exporters of copyright works such as Western Europe. Signatories included the Soviet Union, USA and many developing nations around the globe. As a consequence of this development, many countries from the Berne convention also signed up to the UCC in order to ensure their copyright was also protected in the UCC countries; however, they were restricted from leaving the Berne Convention for the UCC with the risk of penalties. With the subsequent revisions of the terms of the Berne Convention, most countries have now joined Berne, thus rendering the UCC largely irrelevant.

The Rome Convention (1961)

More properly known as 'The Rome Convention for the Protection of Performers, Producers of Phonograms and Broadcasting Organisations', this convention extended copyright protection to include the performers and their performances of the work in various formats. This was in response to technological advances such as tape recording, which were not covered by the previous 'print' focused agreements such as the Berne Convention. This protection, granted to performers, sound producers and broadcasters, enabled them to forbid the reproduction and broadcast of their work without consent.

WIPO (1967)

According to http://www.wipo.int, WIPO

> is dedicated to developing a balanced and accessible international intellectual property (IP) system, which rewards creativity, stimulates innovation and contributes to economic development while safeguarding the public interest (WIPO 2006b)

It was established by the WIPO convention of 1967, and mandated by its then 20 member states to promote the protection of intellectual property globally and in cooperation with other agencies such as the Berne Convention Bureau, which it took over in 1970. By 1974 it became a specialised agency of the United Nations responsible for administering and governing the international copyright, trade mark and patent system. Today there are some 183 member states worldwide.

FSF – Free Software Foundation (1985)

Richard Stallman founded the Free Software Foundation as a non-profit organisation dedicated to advancing the objectives of the free software movement. This 'free' ideal is often qualified with the phrase 'free as in speech, not beer' in order to clarify their alignment with the principles of freedom of information. The foundation was also established to support the GNU Project, which serves as a concrete and practical example of the free software philosophy. GNU is a recursive acronym for 'GNU's Not Unix' and it forms the basis of the GNU/Linux free operating system that has since become a viable alternative to proprietary operating systems such as Microsoft Windows and Unix. Over the years, a raft of free software for this system has been developed and distributed using the GNU General Public License (GPL), which is a legitimate intellectual property licence designed to prevent free software from being re-appropriated into the private domain. The licence works by using copyright law to ensure that every user has the right to study, use, modify and redistribute both the work and its modified version as long as the same licence terms are applied to it. This is often referred to as copyleft – as opposed to the more common and restrictive copyright.

CPDA – Copyright, Designs and Patents Act (1988)

This act of the UK Parliament restated and amended the statutory basis of UK copyright law (including performing rights), which had been governed until then by the Copyright Act of 1956. Among other things it brought the UK in line with the Berne Convention signed in the 19th century; it also simplified the categories of works protected under copyright to include literary, dramatic and musical works, artistic works, sound recordings and films, broadcasts, cable programmes and published editions.

EUCD – European Union Council Directive 93/98/EEC (1993)

This directive commonly billed as 'harmonising the term of protection of copyright and certain related rights' was created to do just that for the EU member states. The Berne Convention provided copyright protection for a minimum of 50 years *post mortem auctoris* (after death of the author) on literary and artistic works, but some countries (e.g. Germany) had set theirs to 70 years; therefore in order to harmonise the terms as per the directive most of the EU member states also extended their protection to match this for printed works, but the term of protection for sound recordings was kept at 50 years post mortem.

TRIPS – Trade-Related Aspects of Intellectual Property Rights (1994)

This international treaty saw the introduction of intellectual property law into the international trading system and it is still one of the most comprehensive international agreements on intellectual property. This treaty is administered by the WTO and it deals with copyright and other related intellectual properties such as patents, designs, trade marks and most of the others we covered in the previous section. Specifically, it covers computer programs under copyright law as a literary work and mandates the protection of databases. It extended copyright to include rental rights and granted rights for performers over the recording, replication and broadcast of their live performances, as well as the rights of producers over the reproduction of their works, for a term of 50 years. The treaty also specifies that copyright be granted without formality and that exceptions to copyright be strictly constrained. The TRIPS agreement applies to all 149 members of the WTO and it has specific enforcement and dispute resolution protocols (e.g. the 2001 Doha Declaration, which was adopted to address the needs and concerns of lesser developed countries). The treaty has a lot of critics from the anti-globalisation activists and various academics as the levels of intellectual property protection required from countries at different levels of development are not optimal. Other issues include health and globalisation, the patenting of software and business processes and the restriction of compulsory licensing (e.g. whereby third-world pharmaceutical companies might pay a set licence fee to reproduce a protected life-saving drug for use in its own domestic market).

WCT – WIPO Copyright Treaty (1996)

This was an international treaty on copyright law adopted by the WIPO member states in 1996. It was created primarily to provide copyright law with the necessary tools to address the huge advances in information technology since the previous copyright treaties. For example, it ensured that computer programs were protected as literary works and that databases also had protection on the arrangement and selection of the information they contain. This treaty also provides authors with some measure of control over the rental and distribution of their works. Perhaps most famously, it also prohibits circumvention of the technological measures employed for the protection of works as stated, as well as the unauthorised modification of rights management information contained in works. The US Digital Millennium Copyright Act and several EU Directives are the first implementations of the WCT.

WPPT – WIPO Performances and Phonograms Treaty (1996)

This second WIPO treaty deals with the IPRs for performers (singers, actors, musicians etc.) and phonogram producers (i.e. sound recordings). It grants them four types of economic rights, for their respective performance and production, which are the rights of reproduction, distribution, rental and availability. These broadly provide the right to authorise the replication of their work, the sale or transfer of the original work and copies thereof, the commercial rental of the phonograms and finally the 'on-demand' availability of the works (such as via the internet). Performers are granted, for their live (or unrecorded) performance a further three types of rights, which include first broadcast rights, other communication to the public and the fixation (or recording) rights for their performance. These rights are subject to several limitations and exceptions, as with most of other copyright laws, and they are also subject to national treatment, whereby each party is treated according to the laws of the other in a reciprocal fashion. The term of protection for these rights last for 50 years and are not subject to any formality, that is, they do not have to be registered to be considered in force.

DMCA – Digital Millennium Copyright Act (1998)

The DMCA is the USA's implementation of the WCT and makes it a criminal offence to produce, use or distribute any measures that can be used to circumvent any protection technology on copyright works. It also increased the penalties for copyright infringement on the internet and made provisions for online service providers to remove copyright infringing content if requested to do so by the copyright owner.

The US Copyright Term Extension Act (1998)

Also known as the Sonny Bono Copyright Term Extension Act, this law added 20 years to the duration of copyright in the United States. Just like the similar 1993 EU directive, this act extended the copyright term from 50 to 70 years *post mortem auctoris*. In this case, however, it was also retroactive and effectively postponed the date any US works could enter into the public domain, by mandatory expiration, to the year 2019.

EUCD – European Union Copyright Directive (2001)

This is the EU equivalent of the DMCA and it is firmly based on the WIPO Internet Treaties. It addressed the two core issues of replication and dissemination of works in a digital environment and it extended the scope of copyright to include temporary reproduction (e.g. data caching). It also made strong anti-circumvention rulings, which effectively made it illegal to:

* remove or alter electronic rights management information (e.g. metadata, digital signatures, watermarks, fingerprints, encryption etc.);
* distribute, broadcast or provide to the public copies of protected matter that have been compromised as above;
* induce, enable or facilitate infringement (e.g. adverts, how-tos etc.).

EUROPEAN UNION DIRECTIVES

Several European Union Directives have been issued on the topic of intellectual property and copyright since the early 1990s. An EU Directive is a legislative act that states what needs to be achieved, without prescribing exactly how it should be implemented, by the member states. The main European Union Directives on copyright and related rights include:

* Directive 91/250/EEC – that granted copyright protection for software (1991);
* Directive 92/100/EEC – that addressed rental and lending rights (1992);
* Directive 93/83/EEC – related to satellite and cable TV retransmission (1993);
* Directive 93/98/EEC – this harmonised copyright terms across the EU (1993);
* Directive 96/9/EC – this provided for database protection (1996);
* Directive 2001/29/EC – (or EUCD) adopted the WIPO Internet Treaties (2001);
* Directive 2001/84/EC – dealt with the resale rights on original works of art (2001);
* Directive 2004/48/EC – provided for the enforcement of IPRs (2004).

The Creative Commons (2001)

According to their UK website (http://creativecommons.org.uk), the Creative Commons (CC) is a worldwide organisation that offers copyright alternatives to content developers and owners of all kinds, for use anywhere in the world. The movement was started in 2001 by a small group of US experts in intellectual property, cyberlaw, academics and web publishing, namely James Boyle, Michael Carroll, Lawrence Lessig, Hal Abelson, Eric Saltzman and Eric Eldred. This later expanded into other jurisdictions and countries and became the International Creative Commons, which works to establish national projects that can better incorporate the many nuances of copyright law applicable in different jurisdictions. By 2005, over 15 million web pages and other types of creative works had adopted these licences around the world. The aim of CC is to provide a way for content owners to declare their copyright intentions and to enable the legal use and reuse of their works by others. It achieves this using simple 'non-legal' language and terms that are comprehensible to both ordinary people and web applications alike. Content owners may employ CC to allow others to reuse, distribute and modify their creative works, for many reasons including to increase exposure and reach a wider audience, to enable the adoption of new and innovative business models and also to contribute to the public domain if desired. The CC is not against copyright and it is actually implemented using copyright law, with which it enforces the specified usage rights. The CC is similar in many ways to the GNU GPL, from which it was originally inspired, but it addresses more scenarios by offering content owners a menu of options that can be combined to provide different levels and kinds of permissions over the usage of their work. Some examples of the options available are shown in Table 3.3 (from CC's UK website).

TABLE 3.3   *Creative Commons licences (source: http://creativecommons.org.uk)*

Licence option	Description
CC_a (Attribution)	Permits others to freely copy, distribute, display and perform the work, and derivative works, as long as the content creator is given due credit as such. This is akin to exercising the moral rights in copyright.
CC_nc (Non-commercial)	Permits others to freely copy, distribute, display and perform the work, and derivative works, for non-commercial purposes.
CC_ndw (No derivative works)	Permits others to freely copy, distribute, display and perform only exact copies of the work, not derivative works based upon it.
CC_sa (Share alike)	Permits others to distribute derivative works only under a licence identical to the licence that governs the work.

The selected option, or combination thereof, is expressed in the three forms as follows:

- **common's deed** – made of specific icons and a plain language summary of the declared usage rights;
- **legal code** – consisting of the legal interpretation of the above and that is robust enough to stand up in court;
- **digital code** – this is the machine-readable code that can be accessed by web robots and other services or applications of the internet.

It is also possible for a content owner to contribute their work to the public domain by enlisting the help of the CC team to legally declare that a work has 'no rights reserved'. Finally, the options may themselves be mutually exclusive; for example, the **CC_ndw** option cannot work with **CC_sa** option, because the latter share-alike option applies to derivative works, which are explicitly prohibited by the former option.

WIPO Internet Treaties become international law (2002)

The WCT and WPPT created in 1996 became signed into law in 2002 after ratification by 30 countries.

Copyright and Related Rights Regulations (2003)

This UK implementation of the EU Copyright Directive provides, among other things, the required anti-circumvention legislation that makes it possible for rights owners to take legal action against anyone that circumvents or makes and distributes tools designed to circumvent technological protection measures such as DRM. This legislation made necessary amendments to the Copyright Designs and Patents Act of 1988, which until now was the mainstay of UK copyright law.

DADVSI – Loi sur le Droit d'Auteur et les Droits Voisins dans la Société de l'Information (2006)

This French copyright reform bill, which roughly translates into 'law on author's rights and related rights in the information society', has proven to be very controversial right up to the time it was voted through by both houses in the French parliament. This was mostly because it not only implemented many of the WIPO Internet Treaties, but went further with some amendments that could require manufacturers to share proprietary digital music formats with others. Perhaps the most interesting and controversial aspects of DADVSI are the DRM interoperability law and the establishment of a regulatory body to adjudicate requests to provide information sufficient to enable DRM interoperability (Rosenblatt 2006a). The French law on copyright, especially with regard to copyright exceptions, is different to the UK or US implementations and, in some cases, can appear to be quite liberal. For example, the

French exception for private copies allow citizens to freely make copies of works (except software) for their private use and to freely display those works within their family circle (which may also include friends) without the agreement of the copyright holder. However, and perhaps in mitigation, the French law levies a 'tax on private copy' by adding a surcharge on blank media (e.g. CDs, DVDs, HDDs etc.) that is meant to cover the losses incurred by rights holders from this practice. In essence this could be considered a form of blanket licence that 'pays' for the private copy exception. This is so entrenched in the French system that, in a case involving a DRM-protected DVD movie, *Mulholland Drive*, the Versailles court of appeal ruled that DRM techniques that prevented the making of private copies were illegal. However, this decision was later overturned by France's highest court on civil and criminal matters, the *Cour de Cassation* in March 2006.

In conclusion, the role of copyright cannot be overstated and at its most fundamental level it provides primary content creators with some exclusive rights to their works, with the aim of ensuring some economic return on their creative investment and providing incentives for more of the same. Prior to the WIPO Internet Treaties, the existing copyright laws, which were mostly designed for tangible, physical copies of a work, could not fully adapt or apply to the digital environment, hence the need for several amendments and other initiatives. Two core aspects of copyright, particularly relevant to the new digital environment, are the reproduction rights and the dissemination or distribution rights, and these have been the focus of most of the changes implemented in the new copyright regime. However in order to maintain a practical and usable copyright system that also delivers on the original copyright goal of reward and incentives for content creators, it has been necessary to make several exceptions to copyright law and this, along with other challenges faced by copyright, is the focus of the next section.

COPYRIGHT EXCEPTIONS, ISSUES AND CHALLENGES

Copyright has had many challenges in the past, starting with the booksellers' legal actions against the Statute of Anne up to the recent cases of file-sharing services on the internet. These cases are usually connected with the introduction of new technologies that affect the way we copy and distribute content. This has been brought home in an unprecedented fashion with the rising impact of the internet in our daily lives, the direct result of which has been the introduction of technological and legislative tools such as DRM and DMCA or EUCD. The rest of this chapter deals with these challenges and the way copyright has evolved to address them over the years, starting with copyright exceptions.

Copyright exceptions

As hinted earlier the full measure of copyright law could, if literally applied, prove to be rather unwieldy, impractical and extremely difficult to use and enforce. Also it could actually become a hindrance to the propagation of creative works to a wider audience for a variety of reasons. For example, it would mean that the ability to copy and distribute content would have to be strictly policed for infringement at every level and with prohibitive cost implications for composite media industries such as film and television.

According to Black (2002), it is obvious that exceptions to the above reproduction and communications are necessary to ensure a workable, practical system, and to address such areas as fair dealing (or fair use), private uses, reprography, library and academic usage as well as accessibility for less-able users. These and other exceptions are presented here at a high level for completeness, after which we shall explore the main tests used to determine how or under what circumstances a normally prohibited activity may fall under the umbrella of copyright exceptions. In the following we outline some of the various exceptions or limitations to copyright law (CARET 2005).

Non-substantial part

It is widely accepted that copyright infringement occurs if the whole or a substantial part of a protected work is used without required authorisation from the rights owner. However, because there is no strict definition of a 'substantial part' it is therefore open to argument and imagination, on a case-by-case basis, as to what can reasonably be considered substantial in a work. From past legal cases, it can be surmised that key content, no matter how small, can be just as important as the amount of work that can be considered substantial. This effectively amounts to the quality versus quantity of the portion of the work used, which could be substantial enough to qualify as infringement. A common rule of thumb is no more than 800 words in total for books (with no single instance exceeding more than 300 words) and no more than 40 lines or 25% of a poem. Also items such as graphs, figures and illustrations may be considered as separate works to the text.

Fair dealing

Fair dealing is the term used to describe permissible activities on a copyright work. It is similar to, but more narrowly defined than, the US equivalent of fair use. This exception relates to those activities that can be considered a fair use of the purchased product (e.g. a toy, a house or a book), which can be lent out, resold or discarded as desired by the purchaser without infringing copyright. Unfortunately, this is easily applicable to tangible products, but becomes less clear-cut when applied to the digital environment. In the UK, these activities include:

- private and non-commercial research study purposes;
- performance, copies or lending for educational purposes;
- criticism and review of publicly available works;
- news reporting of current events;
- copies and lending by librarians;
- acts for the purposes of royal commissions, statutory enquiries, judicial proceedings and parliamentary purposes;
- recording of broadcasts for later viewing or listening (i.e. time shifting);
- producing a backup copy of a computer program for personal use;
- playing a sound recording for a non-profit making organisation, club or society.

Note that fair dealing, as set out above, is less applicable to audiovisual items such as video and sound recordings (e.g. film, TV and music) than the literary items. Also materials for teaching (e.g. photocopies and hand-outs of protected material) are not usually covered under fair dealing and institutions normally require photocopying licences to cover these uses. Finally, exceptions do not affect the moral rights of the creator to be accredited as the author of the work, nor does it prohibit them from stopping any use that damages their reputation.

Express or implied licence

An express licence is often found in the attached copyright notices of some publicly available materials such as websites and it states categor-ically what can and cannot be done with the content as exemplified by the CC licences. Armed with this it is not necessary to ask for permission to use the material in the specified manner. On the other hand, an implied licence is more difficult to define or prove because it relies on the argument that the content owner must have intended the work to be used in a certain way based on the circumstances or method by which they have made it available. This is often the argument used for material that has been made available on the internet without an explicit state-ment of permissions as above.

Academic purposes

Specific exceptions for education purposes include the copying of any literary, dramatic, musical or artistic work by a non-reprographic method. It permits the copying of a sound recording, film (including video), broadcast or cable programme for the purposes of teaching film-making or sound-related subjects. It also allows the performance of sound record-ing, film, broadcast or cable programmes for teaching purposes – only for students and not a public lecture. Finally, it is not an infringement to use copyright work in relation to academic examinations, apart from copying music, or mock examinations.

Accessibility

This exception usually applies to the need by people with physical impairments to make a 'one-for-one' copy of a protected work that is accessible to them for their own personal use. It applies to a whole range of physical disability including arthritis (cannot hold or turn a page) to the blind or partially sighted individual (may need an audio or Braille version).

Temporary copies

This exception for temporary copies of protected materials is intended to cater for technical requirements such as web caches and similar transient information copies made and held within a system as part of its normal functioning.

Incidental inclusion (passing shot)

This exception applies to situations where a copyright work is incidentally included in an artistic work, sound recording, film, broadcast or cable programming.

It is important to note that the above exceptions to copyright do not necessarily imply permission to use a copyright work without permission; they just make it possible for certain activities not to infringe copyright. However, the exception may be overridden by a contract that limits some of the leeway offered by copyright exceptions. If in doubt check the terms and conditions, or contracts, which may reduce or cancel the option to rely on copyright exceptions. In the absence of contracts, some tests can be applied to help determine whether an activity falls within the scope of copyright exceptions, as follows.

The three step test

The three step test was originally introduced by the Berne Convention and it is still used in some jurisdictions to establish whether the use of a protected work falls under copyright exception. The sentiment of the three step test holds that limitations to the exclusive rights of the copyright holder only apply:

(i)   in special cases; where
(ii) the use does not conflict with the normal exploitation of the work; and
(iii) it does not prejudice the legitimate interest of the rights holder.

The four factor test

The USA's equivalent four factor test, set out in Section 107 of their Copyright Act – the 1992 amendment (US Copyright Office 2006), also reflects the above and is used to determine whether the usage has infringed copyright or whether it falls under the fair use exception. The four factors tested are as follows:

(i)   What is the character of the use?
(ii) What is the nature of the work to be used?
(iii) How much of the work will be or has been used?
(iv) What economic effect would this use have on the market for the original or for permissions if it became widespread?

The above tests can be interpreted in many ways, but they generally help to maintain the position that copyright limitations apply only for exceptional circumstances that do not adversely affect the spirit of copyright to entitle the rights holder to some economic benefits on their work.

Issues and challenges faced by copyright

It may be deduced from the previous sections that the main issues and challenges faced by copyright often stem from the core areas of reproduction and communication or distribution of protected works. Technological innovations in these two areas have repeatedly been the catalyst of change in user behaviour and the law as a consequence. This is exemplified, to an unprecedented degree, by the rise of digital technology and the internet, which has been referred to as 'the world's greatest copying machine'. Table 3.4 outlines the impact of some major technology innovations on these two areas since the birth of copyright law.

TABLE 3.4   *Technology challenges and the impact on copyright*

Technology	Works affected	Area of impact	Description of impact
The printing press	Literary works and images	Reproduction	The introduction of print technology revolutionised the reproduction of literary works at an industrial scale and this helped to fuel the renaissance by democratising the education of the masses
Photography	Images	Reproduction	Photography made it possible to capture and reproduce real images
Piano roll and phonograph	Sound recordings	Reproduction and distribution	These enabled users to capture and reproduce musical works and performances
Photocopier	Literary works and images	Mass and single copies	Made it even easier, faster and cheaper to duplicate documents via optical and electronic means in comparison to printing
Fax	Textual informations and images	Communication	More of a telecommunication tool than a large-scale reproduction and distribution channel

(continued)

TABLE 3.4   *(continued)*

Technology	Works affected	Area of impact	Description of impact
Radio	Audio content	Mass communication	Dissemination of audio-based content and performances to a mass audience
Television (including cable and satellite)	Audiovisual content	Mass communication	Dissemination of audio and video content and performances to a mass audience
Audio tape recording	Sound recordings	Mass and single copies	Made it possible to create good quality copies of sound recordings and music for commercial and private uses
Video tape recording	Audiovisual content	Mass and single copies	Provided an easy means of capturing and reproducing audiovisual content by both commercial and individual users
CD and DVD	Audio, video and digital data	Mass and single copies	These optical formats came with the ability to capture and reproduce high-quality digital content – perfect copies of content
Computers	Digital content (data, audio, video)	Creation and reproduction	Enables the creation of perfect copies of any type of digital content
Internet	All digital content	Mass distribution	Digital technology and the internet have made it unprecedently easier, faster and cheaper to reach a global audience with digital content of any description and format
P2P networks	All digital content	Reproduction and distribution	A particular example of the combination of internet and computing, which provides content sharing facilities to other connected or 'peer' computers across the internet

From Table 3.4 it would be fair to surmise that the greatest challenge faced by copyright to date is directly related to these latter technological developments and the resulting shift in consumer behaviour, which have also led to the need for DRM. Some of these issues are examined in the following.

The challenge of internet and digital technology

The recent explosion of digital and internet technologies have created a step change in the capability to replicate and distribute content by making it easier, faster and cheaper to do this on a large scale for anyone with a good PC and broadband internet connection. At the same time it has shifted the traditional point of contact at which content meets the consumer from a packaged physical copy (e.g. audio CD, DVD movie, or books and magazines) to an intangible digital computer file in various formats.

It appears that the technological advancements have moved consumable content closer to the point of expression (and capture) thus dispensing with the need for physical copies of the work before dissemination to a mass audience. At some level this could be considered appropriate because content (regardless of their method of expression) is derived from human creativity and imagination hence it is in essence an intangible product. However, because we have grown accustomed to handling the physical media that delivers the content we have associated the media with the content and based our original copyright laws on this premise. This is ironic given that the first great accomplishment of copyright was to separate an idea from its expression, but it seems that the time is now right to further separate the physical instance from the expression, at least in the minds of traditional copyright owners and users of protected works. This may not be such an issue for the next generation who are growing up into a future environment where this would be the norm.

Finally, it is obvious that the landscape for the production and consumption of content has changed dramatically and this shift has been enabled in no small way by the above-mentioned technological advances in digital content production, reproduction and dissemination. For example, the proliferation of digital devices and connectivity has made it a simple matter for anyone to capture, copy and share content with other people around the world in a matter of minutes for no more than the cost of a phone call, if that. This has brought a huge headache for copyright enforcement for both pre-existing works and the newer so-called user-generated content, as we describe next.

Copyright and user-generated content

The popularity of many social networking websites (e.g. MySpace.com, Bebo.com, Flickr.com and YouTube.com) can be directly attributed to the phenomenon of user-generated (and consumed) content. This is an area that currently receives much attention in the media world, and with good reason, because the level and rate of growth in traffic shown by these sites are amazing. For example YouTube.com, a video-sharing website, grew in the space of 18 months to become the tenth most popular destination on the internet according to online information and statistics provider Alexa.com. The proliferation of user-generated content has been enabled by the availability of digital technology and connectivity needed to capture and share the content produced by individual users. Also the social networking aspect of this phenomenon, which is based on our normal human behaviour as a social animal, means that the internet is just starting to achieve its potential as an interactive mass communication tool that spans and connects the globe.

However, this explosion in user content brings with it several issues in the light of current copyright law including the following:

- **Enforceability** – how to monitor and police the vast quantities of information and user-generated content available on the internet for copyright infringement, keeping in mind that many users may not pay attention to the nuances of copyright law.
- **Culpability** – who is responsible for confirmed cases of copyright infringement, is it the user that uploaded it, the webmaster of the offending website or the ISP hosting the site (or perhaps all three and more)?
- **Awareness** – how do you educate the large number of content-generating users of their rights and responsibilities in the automatic copyright system (many people are not necessarily aware that some material should not be reused just because it happens to be 'on the internet')?

Fair dealing or fair use and copyright

Depending on whom you ask fair dealing or fair use could be considered a very good thing, because it acts as the safety valve that limits the extent of copyright and thereby makes it more practical and useable for the consumer of protected content. There are two sides to the equation (between content creators or rights owners and the end-users or content consumers) and copyright has to try and satisfy both parties by protecting the rights of the former and encouraging their creativity for the benefit of the latter. However, copyright law can become a double-edged sword when applied too firmly in favour of one side, hence the need for copyright limitations and exceptions such as fair dealing to balance and ease the tension that can arise in those circumstances. As a result fair dealing (or fair use) has become the favourite whipping boy in the many legal tussles that have attempted to define this middle ground on behalf of and usually to the benefit of one camp over the other.

Goldstein (2003) put it rather elegantly by describing the two opposing points of view in this particular battlefield as 'copyright optimists' and 'copyright pessimists'. The copyright optimist, he writes, takes the position that copyright is rooted in natural justice and entitles the author to every last penny that other people will pay for copies of their work. This would include, in the case of a book, some financial consideration from the hardback and paperback versions, the film revenue, TV and radio broadcast, video and DVD sales, online downloads, translations into other languages and derivative works such as movie sequels and games etc., as well as from future formats that do not even exist yet. On the other hand, the copyright pessimist holds the opinion that creators and rights owners should have some degree of control over copies of their work but only as an incentive to produce more works and just enough to satisfy this requirement. Anything above this would be an encroachment on other people's freedoms. From these two points of view it may be concluded that the letter of copyright law may appear to lean towards the copyright optimist, but the exception of fair dealing (or fair use) balances this by pulling towards the copyright pessimist.

If copyright prohibits infringing activities, then fair dealing (or fair use) makes it possible, in some special cases, for these same activities to be carried out by the public without fear. Examples of commonplace activities that are enabled by fair dealing (or fair use) include lending your copy of a CD or book to a friend, making backup or temporary copies or even selling your copy of a DVD movie to a second-hand shop. However, as observed earlier, it is much more difficult to apply this concept of fair dealing (or fair use) in a digital environment, because there is no tangible product to lend or resell; furthermore, there is the fundamental issue that fair use and fair dealing statutes are often expressed in terms of criteria that are nigh on impossible for technology to measure or decide. Also, the fact that it is possible to create and distribute an exact digital replica of the original adds further complexity by making it infinitely harder to police. This, according to Goldstein (2003), is the crux of the copyright debate, because copyright covers one of the few areas where it is possible for one person to use or consume a product without diminishing the ability of another person to do so. The introduction of DRM is one attempt to implement a solution that is designed to enable the control of content in just this type of environment.

Copyright and international trade (moral rights versus fair use)

The history of copyright is littered with examples of the many issues that have arisen at the juncture of copyright and international relations. They also highlight the very artificial nature of copyright law in its relationship with international commerce. A good treatment of this topic can be found in Goldstein (2003). The chapter on the 'two cultures of copyright' explores the opposing approaches to copyright adopted by countries such as the USA and France. It highlights these by observing that the USA has a utilitarian approach to copyright, similar to the copyright pessimist, and will happily champion the doctrine of fair use, while France and some other continental European countries view the rights of authors as core to copyright and promote the authors' moral rights position, in much the same way as the copyright optimist would. These positions are also indicative of the common law versus civil law origins of their respective copyright regimes. Although the underlying objectives of copyright are the same for the two countries, the main differences in their approach are manifested in the application of those two doctrines. Historically, France and some other European countries were net exporters of copyright material and they championed the moral rights doctrine in order to derive as much economic benefit as they could from their works abroad. On the other hand, the USA, at the time a net importer of foreign works, chose to ignore copyright altogether in an attempt to protect their economic interests and reduce the burden of educating their public. Nowadays the reverse is the case and the USA has become a major exporter of copyright to the rest of the world, so their position has shifted accordingly. They have become the proverbial poacher turned gamekeeper in order to protect their copyright and economic interests abroad.

However, this is not peculiar to the USA and Choate (2005) provides a good account of this practice in the history of other nations. The basic notion is that many emerging nations become powerful by appropriating other nations' intellectual property and then turn around and try to protect their power through intellectual property enforcement. Examples include Germany (after WWI), Japan (after WWII) and now China. European countries too have, at some point in their history, chosen to ignore copyright on works from other countries for economic reasons (e.g. between Belgium and France in the early 19th century). This and other similar events in the past led to the introduction of various rules and principles such as the following:

- 'Reciprocity' whereby each country agreed to provide copyright protection based on the laws of the originating country.
- A later refinement of this led to the principle of 'national treatment', which attempted to address the unequal copyright control measures adopted in different countries by ensuring that foreign works are protected to the same standard as local works in the importing country.
- Finally, the more recent development of 'neighbouring rights' makes it possible for items that are not covered by copyright law in all countries to still be protected, albeit with a less onerous regime that allows even greater flexibility in treatment between countries.

None of these principles have proven to be 'cheat proof' as countries continue to try and find ways around the rules in order to maintain or protect their own particular interests at the time. Goldstein concludes that

> copyright has been a protectionist card that nations play according to their current notion of what arrangements will best promote the national interest (Goldstein 2003)

The exhaustion of rights (or 'the first sale doctrine')

This doctrine refers to the entitlement of the purchaser of a protected work to resell their copy of that work, at their sole discretion, without having to pay any further consideration from this subsequent sale to the copyright owner either directly or via a licensing or royalty collecting body. The EU Directive on the first sale doctrine is not fully consistent across member states and effectively only applies to tangible objects and not digitally distributed copies (Black 2002). This means that rights owner cannot enforce their exclusive rights on resold physical copies of their work (i.e. get paid for the same thing twice) but may be able to do so with electronic copies.

Geographical boundaries and jurisdictions of copyright

This is a thorny problem especially for industries that have long existed with (and perhaps even thrived on) the intricate relationships and interdependencies of geopolitical and territorial rights on traditional physical content and media. These include the traditional film, record and publishing industries with their well-established legal departments and business models that have long specialised in the art of international copyright negotiations, deal-making and competitive strategies. They are now faced with the double challenge of adapting to a rapidly changing business and technology environment as well as having to work with a slower responding international legal and legislative network of agencies and governments. Basically the speed of technological developments on the internet, as well as the rapid adoption and spread of its use at a global scale, often proves very disruptive to the old way of doing business as evidenced by the uptake of Napster (which peaked at about 700 million users) and Apple's iTunes (which is still top of the legal music download services at the time of this writing).

Copyright duration and longevity

The term of copyright protection granted to the author of a literary work and their inheritors is up to 70 years *post mortem auctoris* (i.e. after the author's death) after which the work goes into the public domain. This means that an average author with a lifespan of 70 years will get some 120 years protection in total on a work they published at the age of 20. While this is not really an issue in terms of copyright, it may take longer for works to enter the public domain if people continue to live longer, as is currently the case in the developed world.

In conclusion, these challenges clearly show that the copyright system is not perfect and under certain conditions it may even be detrimental to societies, economies, creativity and even technology. However, they do help create an environment that highlights and supports the changes necessary for its survival and adaptation to these and other new challenges that result from our progressive evolution.

Some relevant case laws and landmark rulings

This last section outlines some of the more interesting and significant cases that have helped to shape or influence the course of copyright law over recent years. They have been chosen to reflect the twists and turns of the legal response to technology-based copyright issues around the world.

Video home recording (Sony Betamax): Universal versus Sony (USA, 1984)

Often referred to as the 'Sony safe-harbor' principle, this US Supreme Court ruling stated that:

> ...the sale of copying equipment, like the sale of other articles of commerce, does not constitute contributory infringement if the product is widely used for legitimate, unobjectionable purposes. Indeed, it need merely be capable of substantial non-infringing uses.

The above decision essentially protected VCR manufacturers from liability for contributory infringement because the court held that technology could not be barred if it was 'capable of substantial non-infringing uses'. It also found that time shifting was covered under the fair use doctrine.

Fair use: Campbell versus Acuff-Rose Music Inc. (USA, 1994)

In 1994 the US Supreme Court ruled that a rap parody of Roy Orbison's song *Pretty Woman* was fair use even though it was for a commercial purpose. This was because the court found that the markets for the two works may be different and there was no strong evidence of economic damage to the original. This became one of the tests for impact of 'transformational use' of a work.

Streaming media: RealNetworks versus Streambox (USA, 1999)

In 1999 a Washington federal court ruled in favour of RealNetworks against a company called Streambox that distributed a streaming media recording software called the Streambox VCR, which could obtain streamed content from a RealServer and store it on the local machine in violation of the restrictions imposed by the RealServer system.

DVD copy protection: DeCSS (Norway, 1999)

DeCSS, a DVD content decryption program, was released on the internet mailing list LiViD in October 1999. One of the authors, a Norwegian programmer called Jon Lech Johansen, was put on trial in 2001 but was later acquitted of all charges in early 2003. He was retried again later that year and also acquitted.

SDMI: Felten versus RIAA (USA, 2000)

The Recording Industry Association of America (RIAA) established the Secure Digital Music Initiative (SDMI) to research copy-protecting technologies. This initiative challenged the internet community to break six different codes with a cash incentive of US$10,000 for any successful hacks that was handed over to the RIAA. This feat was achieved by Edward Felten, a computer science professor at Princeton University, along with several other colleagues. However, because they wished to present their findings at a conference the RIAA threatened to sue Felten for violation of the DMCA. The paper was subsequently withdrawn, but Felten and the Electronic Frontier Foundation (EFF) challenged the RIAA on the grounds of violation of his right to free speech and following an agreement in 2002 Felten was able to publish the paper, which is now available online (see http://www.cs.princeton.edu/sip/sdmi/).

P2P file sharing: A&M versus Napster, Inc. (USA, 2001)

This was the first major case to address the issue of copyright laws versus P2P file sharing. Napster was created by Shawn Fanning in 1999 as a file-sharing P2P network application devoted to sharing music files and this led to the music industry's accusations of massive copyright violations and subsequent lawsuits by December 1999. The resulting publicity made it grow even more rapidly in popularity so that by the time the United States Court of Appeals ruled that the defendant, Napster, could be held liable for contributory infringement of copyrights, the user numbers had grown significantly. For example, in the last month of Napster's operation the members exchanged some 2.79 billion files (Fisher 2004). The court rejected various motions filed by the defendant such as: the argument that sampling and space-shifting fell under 'fair use'; their proposal for compulsory licensing arrangements with the record companies; or that the case bore any similarity with the Sony Betamax case of 1984 (i.e. the court ruled that Napster was not an ISP and thus could not avoid liability under the 'ISP safe-harbor' provision of DMCA).

DMCA – circumvention: Dmitry Skylarov and Adobe e-books (USA and Russia, 2001)

Dmitry Sklyarov, a Russian computer programmer, was arrested in Las Vegas and charged with trafficking a software program that could circumvent technological protections on copyrighted material in violation of the US Copyright Act and the DMCA. Dmitry had created the Advanced eBook Processor (AEBR) software, which could convert Adobe's e-book files into a generic format, while researching on cryptanalyses for his PhD. Following some intervention by the EFF, Dmitry was released from US custody and allowed to return home to Russia.

Sony Music Entertainment (UK) Limited versus Easyinternetcafé Limited (UK, 2003)

In 2003 Sony successfully sued Easyinternetcafé for copyright infringement because it provided, for a fee, a CD-burning service to its customers for their MP3 files. The English high court found that ignorance of the nature of the content did not absolve Easyinternetcafé of liability and also that the commercial nature of the activity further indicted the defendant.

File sharing and copyright infringement: MGM Studios versus Grokster (USA, 2005)

In 2005 a United States Supreme Court decision unanimously held that defendant P2P file-sharing companies Grokster and Streamcast (owner of Morpheus) could be sued for inducing copyright infringement for acts taken in the course of marketing file-sharing software. Previously, in April 2003, a Los Angeles federal court had ruled in favour of Grokster and Streamcast against RIAA and MPAA. This decision was appealed in 2003, but the US Court of Appeals again found in favour of Grokster and Streamcast in 2004 with the ruling that they were not liable for contributory and vicarious copyright infringement. However, the US Supreme Court subsequently found against the defendants in 2005 with the opinion that anyone who distributes a device with the object of promoting its use to infringe copyright was liable for the resulting acts of infringement by the users of that device.

Kazaa P2P file sharing: Universal versus Sharman Networks [Kazaa] (Australia, September 2005)

Sharman Networks, the distributor of Kazaa (a very popular P2P file-swapping service), was found to be in breach of copyright by allowing its users to illegally swap digital files. The court found that it and some of the other defendants in the case must have been aware of this activity and that their efforts to prevent it were insufficient and ineffective; the court also found that they did not bother to implement any technical measures to stop this activity. In July 2006, the Kazaa service agreed to pay compensation to the record companies and to implement filtering technologies that would help prevent copyright infringement, in order to continue operating as a legal service.

SonyBMG CD copy protection (worldwide, 2005)

Sony BMG included the XCP and MediaMax CD-3 software on music CDs as a copy protection and prevention measure. However, these software packages, which automatically installed on desktop computers when customers tried to play the CDs, interfered with the OS and opened security holes that could allow viruses to break in and cause other problems. This led to many lawsuits and as a result the company had to recall the affected CDs, with much publicity.

Polydor versus Brown et al. (UK, November 2005)

A summary judgment was granted by an English High Court in favour of some record companies against a music file sharer on the basis that the defendant's use of P2P software to place music files in a shared directory accessible by the internet constituted the infringing act of communicating a copyright work to the public (Cornthwaite 2006).

Massive copyright infringement: publishers versus Google (USA, Belgium and worldwide, 2005–2006)

In New York in 2005, The Authors Guild and other plaintiffs filed a class action suit against Google over unauthorised scanning and copying of books through the Google Library program. They claimed that Google engages in massive copyright infringement at the expense of the rights of individual writers by reproducing works still under the protection of copyright.

In 2006 a Belgian court ordered Google to stop publishing content from a dozen Belgian newspapers or risk a fine of about €1 million per day if they did not comply. In response Google dropped all of this content from its website, although their spokesperson maintained that Google's search cataloguing of content only helped to drive traffic to the newspaper sites.

Internationally, several book and newspaper publishers started litigation against Google and some also announced an initiative to tackle search engine use of their content by adopting a licence 'tag' system called ACAP (Automated Content Access Protocol), which specifies any usage conditions applicable to their content. The publishing industry bodies in support of this include the European Publishers Council (EPC), the European Newspapers Association (ENA), the International Publishers Association (IPA) and World Association of Newspapers (WAN).

BPI versus AllofMP3.com (UK, July 2006)

An English High Court has granted the British Phonographic Industry (BPI) permission to start legal proceedings against AllofMP3.com, a Russian digital-music download site based in Moscow. The site claims to be legal and licensed under the Russian Multimedia and Internet Society (Roms), but this has been refuted by the International Federation of the Phonographic Industry (IFPI) as illegitimate and not legal in other countries.

Viacom versus YouTube (USA, 2007)

The 2006 acquisition of YouTube.com, a video-sharing website, by search engine giant Google led to speculation of when, not if, the big media companies would sue for breach of copyright. In March 2007, Viacom launched a billion dollar suit against YouTube for copyright infringement over its various properties that were illegally posted onto the website.

As can be seen from the above, the challenges to copyright are numerous and despite the best effort of national lawmakers and international bodies it still appears to be full of loopholes and contradictions that can be exploited by any party so inclined.

CONCLUSION

In this chapter we briefly examined the various types of intellectual property and delved more deeply into copyright and its application in the more technologically advanced and connected world of today. We have looked at the exceptions and issues that must be addressed, as well as a provided a quick overview of some significant cases.

In conclusion we accept that copyright law is an artificial mechanism designed to cater for the expression of an idea without protecting the idea itself. However, with its main objective of providing a means to reward the creator of a work it is vulnerable to abuse by commercial buyers and holders of that copyright with little returns, in many cases, to the self-same creators it purports to serve. It also opens itself up to severe criticism as an international instrument, because of its manifest weakness in addressing transgressions by many countries both now and in the past. This is due to the fact that no single country can claim, with any moral conviction or authority, that it has a pristine history when it comes to copyright and international trade and relations. It is no wonder that users of illegal file-sharing software and services may feel some justification in sticking it to the 'big, bad, greedy establishment'. However, this only perpetuates and exacerbates the situation because the main strength of copyright is in its flexibility to adapt to any new challenge given time; it would therefore seem sensible to apply that quality in determining the way forward into the digital future we have just started to glimpse. At a fundamental level, the power of copyright lies in the very fact that when ideas are allowed to grow and flourish in the right environment and time, they tend to reach a tipping point after which they may explode and grow at a phenomenal rate to sometimes become much bigger than their original conception. The internet and its impact so far is a perfect example of this.

It all goes to support the fact that the time is right for DRM, but not necessarily in its current form. It still needs to evolve into something more of a 'digital rights enabler' that can lead the way to a more coherent paradigm of information management that is better suited to our future in a connected world. However, in order to achieve this lofty goal there has to be honest and open collaboration with all of the stakeholders in this field, which is the topic of the next chapter.

4 Stakeholders and Industries

The last three chapters provided an overview of the background of DRM from the communication, legal and technology perspectives. This chapter looks at the domain interests in DRM, which have been grouped into five logical categories. The first section explores each stakeholder group in some detail and touches on some of the strategies and initiatives they have adopted to address their particular pain points. The second section provides an overview of some of the sectors and industries affected by DRM and the impact of digital technologies and content. This is a vast area and indeed many books have already been written on it; therefore the discussion is focused on the impact felt by the five representative stakeholder groups for each industry. The next section then presents the socio-political context and examines some recent government initiatives and efforts to try and understand the various issues, with a view to facilitating their resolution. Finally, this chapter concludes with a brief look at some of the major advocacy and lobby groups on DRM and consumer issues.

THE FIVE STAKEHOLDER DOMAINS

The five categories of stakeholder and domain interests cover the whole content value chain and consist of the creative, technology, commercial, governance (e.g. legal and legislative) and consumer or end-user groups of stakeholder interests (Umeh 2004). The domains have been grouped to represent the entities found in the content value chain and content lifecycle for any industry sector and organisation that uses and consumes content. They also each represent a vital segment of the content economy, without which the others would struggle. These stakeholder interests have a direct impact on the relevance and need for DRM as follows:

- **Creative stakeholders.** Without the continuous output from this group there would be no content whatsoever and consequently there would be no need for DRM.
- **Technology stakeholders.** Digital technology enables perfect replication and easy distribution of content, but without this group DRM would not exist.
- **Commercial stakeholders.** In the absence of this group, the relevance and need for DRM to enforce IPRs would be greatly reduced or totally removed in some cases.
- **Legal, legislative and governance stakeholders.** This group produces the rules by which DRM abides and is enforced. Its absence would render DRM ineffective.

- **Consumer and end-user stakeholders.** Without content consumers the other groups would have no real purpose in this context and DRM would be unnecessary.

The term 'content economy' has been adopted in this chapter to describe the end-to-end flow of content and revenue between the primary producer and end-user (as well as all of the points and links in the value chain between them). It is used here to encapsulate all of the information, knowledge and revenue related to works and intellectual property in the digital economy into a single phrase for brevity.

Figure 4.1 is a model of the five stakeholder domains in the context of their relationship to each other and to the aforementioned digital content lifecycle. This model shows how the commercial stakeholder domain plays a central role in relation to all of the other stakeholders. This is because DRM is ultimately an economic tool and one that has been designed to help implement and enforce the concept of intellectual property in the digital environment. The two stakeholder domains on either side represent the producers and consumers of the content and the two domains above and below it represent the governance and technological groups that respectively influence and enable the digital content value chain.

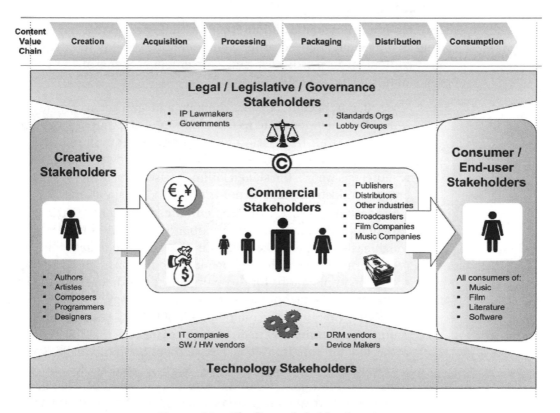

FIGURE 4.1 *The five stakeholder domains*

The creative stakeholders

The domain of the creative stakeholder interest group represents all of those entities concerned with creating content. They include all primary content producers and virtually any individual or organisation that creates or owns copyright works in any form. This group of stakeholders are well positioned at the beginning of the content value chain, because they ultimately drive the content economy in terms of the raw input of material content and products that fuel the knowledge, information and content universe. The creative stakeholders and the end-users or consumers form the two core pillars around which the whole content economy and its related services are built. The other stakeholder groups (i.e. legal and legislative, commercial and technology groups) essentially enable, support and influence the transfer of content from the former to the latter in an organised manner that is sometimes referred to as the 'knowledge economy' or 'content ecosystem'. Without the creative or end-user stakeholders, the entire model collapses, hence the emphasis placed on them as vital pillars of the content economy.

The impact of digital technology and DRM on the creative stakeholder

The main impact of digital and internet technologies on this stakeholder group is noticeably focused around the enhanced ability to create and reuse content in terms of cost and convenience. Some of the salient points in this regard are listed below:

- **Cost.** It has become easier, cheaper and quicker to create and reuse digital content due to the plethora of software applications that range from free basic tools to upmarket offerings. Also the impact of the ever-increasing availability and power of computing resources as well as the skilled labour to use them, especially in the creative industries, have all contributed to this situation.

- **Connectivity.** Apart from its enhanced content distribution capabilities, the internet and broadband connectivity have made it much easier for the stakeholders in this group to collaborate on a creative project regardless of location and this has significant cost-reduction implications for those organisations that rely on the use of cheaper skilled labour as a competitive strategy.

- **Content protection.** The main benefit of DRM for this stakeholder group is predominantly to do with the assurance that their work is protected and safe from illegal dissemination in the digital space. However, the importance of this factor is variable for different members of this group and in fact is more immediately applicable to the commercial stakeholders since they are mainly concerned with realising returns on their products. The primary content creators, especially those that are not yet established, may be happier with any form of circulation for their works in order to attract and create an audience from which they may derive economic benefits for future works.

Due to the above factors, it is no longer enough for an artiste to create content and walk away, instead it has almost become a necessity for artistes to create content that is geared for multi-purpose use right from the outset. For example, it has become commonplace for authors to publish their works online as a blog during the development phase, in order to capture feedback and comments from interested and potential readers and customers even before the book is published. After publication, some authors will maintain a website or blog as a 'live' version of the book to which revisions are applied as events unfold around the subject matter and which then becomes the basis for revised editions of the book. In conclusion it is no longer enough for a primary content creator (or artiste) to be adept at creating content in just one format, they increasingly have to embrace the idea of multi-format, multi-purpose content delivered through multiple channels and devices to consumers that have myriad choices on which content, format, channel or device to use or discard.

The technology stakeholders

The technology domain stakeholder group may be regarded by some, and with good reason, as the party responsible for majority of the issues faced by the content industry today, which has resulted in the need for solutions such as DRM. In fact it is patently clear that the more recent technological innovations have been largely responsible for the digital revolution; however, it is the use of technology and not the technology itself that is to blame for the situation we find ourselves in today. In other words the technology brings both benefits and problems depending on how it is used, and what some may consider an issue today could turn out to be a competitive advantage for others tomorrow. It is this duality of purpose that prompts the inclusion of hackers, crackers, virus writers and other denizens of the internet underworld into this group of stakeholders that otherwise lists among its members the various information technology companies, software houses, manufacturers of computer hardware, consumer devices, communication technology and broadcast equipment, the network infrastructure specialists and content protection solution providers, including DRM technology vendors. The technology domain stakeholder group also represent the interests of the entities responsible for the foundation upon which the digital content economy is built for obvious reasons. The main driving force for this stakeholder group is innovation and this is fed by the never-ending quest for competitive advantage, the result of which is also applied to the attainment of more competitive advantage. The end result is a virtuous cycle of innovation-led evolution that is both driven and exploited by members of other stakeholder groups especially those in the commercial and creative domains.

The impact of digital technology and DRM on the technology stakeholder

The effect of digital and internet technologies upon this stakeholder group is evident in the rapid acceleration of innovation that has resulted from the aforementioned virtuous cycle of technology evolution. Some of the main points of note include the following:

- **Cost.** The comparative adjectives of 'faster', 'better', 'cheaper' and sometimes 'smaller' (e.g. form factor) are now regular bywords for describing the products of technological innovation in the digital realm. The cost factor is particularly significant because successive generations of technology have displayed a tendency to be less expensive than their predecessors especially once there is a mass-market adoption and the attendant economies of scale.

- **Connectivity.** Internet, broadband and wireless technology have created the super-highway for 21st century communications and together with mass media storage and access device technologies they form the basic infrastructure for the content and knowledge economy of the future.

- **Content protection.** Piracy has always been around and given the nature of the content industry to rely on the revenue generated from the replication, distribution and consumption of intangible property assets, it will always be around. This is an inevitable fact of life that has been responsible for the development of intellectual property and copyright mechanisms in the pre-digital era. The main impact of piracy in the digital era is the ready availability of replication and distribution technologies that can be used for both legitimate and illegitimate purposes by organised criminals (i.e. the pirates) and consumers alike.

The toughest task faced by the technology stakeholder group is related to the translation of the sometimes vague, dynamic and imprecise rules that govern IPRs (in particular copyright and its exceptions) into a model that can work in both the digital and analogue worlds. It is nigh impossible to capture the real intentions of a content user whenever they copy and share a digital work and this makes it difficult to effectively apply the absolute rules that digitally implement IPRs to analogue life-forms such as human beings.

The commercial stakeholders

This stakeholder group is the lynchpin that ties the other DRM stakeholder domains together in the content economy. The activities of the commercial stakeholder involve all of the other stakeholder groups and are central to this economic milieu. They are carried out by the various members of this group who tend to be multi-purpose individuals or entities, sometimes with roles that also fall within the domain of the other stakeholder groups (e.g. a broadcaster may also create, distribute and consume content, as well as some of the technology it uses to do any of the above, such as the BBC). The commercial stakeholder group includes all individuals, groups and enterprises that acquire, process, package and distribute content as part of their business model. This includes all individuals, commercial entities and non-profit organisations that exist in the fields of media and entertainment (e.g. broadcasters, publishers, record companies, film houses, games and other content providers) and also the many corporate enterprises that rely on intellectual property for their revenue in various sectors (e.g. software, manufacturing, financial services, pharmaceuticals, fashion, construction and health), as well as institutions that both produce and consume content (e.g. universities, libraries, museums, galleries, public and private institutions, charities and foundations). The entities in this group essentially take content from the creator and deliver it to the consumer or end-user as a service or product, with or without the use of technology, and under the influence of the governance (legal and legislative) stakeholder group.

The impact of digital technology and DRM on commercial stakeholders

The main issue of concern to this stakeholder group is firmly focused on getting and maintaining a healthy return on investment (ROI) for their content business. The impact of digital and internet technologies upon the commercial stakeholder group is powerfully illustrated by the many recent sector-changing developments in the creative and content industries such as publishing (e.g. Amazon.com), music (e.g. iTunes), film, broadcast and entertainment (e.g. YouTube.com) and retail (e.g. eBay.com). These developments reflect the overall shift in emphasis from the physically bound business and information models of yesterday, to a more fluid and dynamic way of operating in the content economy and which has been enabled by the digital revolution. Some particular points of note include the following:

- **Cost.** The rapid advances in digital technology are constantly reducing the cost of doing business and this can either be perceived as harmful or beneficial to established content business models, depending on your perspective. This is exemplified by the ever-decreasing cost of content-generation technology, whereby what used to be considered 'high-end' capabilities in professional-level image and audio technology are now routinely available in consumer-level products. For example, the skilled users of consumer products and devices, such as digital camcorders and image editing software, can actually produce some relatively high-quality content, which can also be replicated and distributed easily and cheaply by using other so-called 'low-end' or free products and services (e.g. YouTube.com or CurrentTV.com). Figure 4.2 in the 'Evolving the content economy' section illustrates this point in graphic form.

- **Connectivity.** The wider availability of broadband and other high-speed connections to the internet is leading to the rapid democratisation of media sources and channels of content for the consumer. A user can easily get the same piece of news content on their TV, PC, mobile phone or newspaper, depending on their preference or particular physical context or location at the point in time. Therefore content businesses must now fight harder for a much narrower slice of the consumer's 'mindshare', 'timeshare' and 'walletshare', to use the jargon, within that consumer's greatly enlarged window of content sources.

- **Content protection.** The main effect of the technological advances on content piracy is seen in the much-reduced barrier to entry for anyone wishing to engage in digital content piracy. This includes the enhanced capability to create high-quality digital copies and the ready availability of a global distribution network courtesy of the internet. The impact of this, in conjunction with the increasing contention for consumers, has squeezed the revenue models of many established and entrenched content businesses. Unfortunately the situation is not helped by the attitude taken by some of these players to approach this evolutionary process with a tough and inflexible mindset that has resulted in the implementation of certain ill-conceived draconian technology protection measures and other legal mechanisms that invariably fail to deliver any real benefits in the long run.

The commercial stakeholder group represents a microcosm of the overall content economy and all of the changes necessary to evolve the content economy must also take place and flourish at this level first. On the surface this bodes quite well for competition and the promise that the free market dynamics will help to determine the winners and losers in this contest. However, from past experience, it is also vital to remain vigilant for any attempts by entrenched interests to grab, or try to retain, control of the content economy through unfair and anti-competitive practices or via the old-fashioned bully tactics.

The legal, legislative and governance stakeholders

This multi-partisan stakeholder domain is really focused around the rules, regulations, standards and other civil constructs or mores that govern the use of content by all of the other stakeholders. This group represents the overarching layer of governance, which although imperfect, is usable and flexible enough to serve the majority of stakeholder interests (most of the time). The group includes those individuals and organisations responsible for intellectual property laws and regulations, legal professionals, associations and enterprises right across the content value chain. It also includes the various international entities, treaties and agreements, national governments and their agencies, as well as intellectual property and DRM lobby groups that contribute to the development and evolution of the civil and legal intellectual property construct globally. Finally, this stakeholder group also counts among its members the various standards and regulatory organisations including both international formal standards and industry-led standards and their respective organisations. The influence of this stakeholder group reaches across the content value chain and other stakeholder groups including the content creator, content service provider, distributor and the consumers. It is responsible for setting the many rules by which content is created, packaged, distributed, consumed and reused in the global content economy. These rules affect many industries sectors including media and entertainment, IT, telecommunications, pharmaceuticals, manufacturing and financial services as well as all other entities that produce and trade, or otherwise rely on, intellectual property for their existence.

The impact of digital technology and DRM on legal, legislative and governance stakeholders

The main issues affecting this stakeholder group are directly related to the challenges presented by the commercial and other stakeholders attempting to apply and enforce analogue rules in a digital environment. Furthermore, despite the high-profile cases listed in the previous chapter, it appears that the level of involvement by the legal and legislative communities in the development of new digital technologies is extremely poor from the outset. It would seem that lawyers are only interested in stepping into the breach when the technology fails and the law, which is by now mostly 'out-of-step', needs applying. This attitude only serves to compound the problem and must be addressed sooner rather than later because the 'vulture culture' mentality and practice of getting involved after the technology fails is both counterproductive and rather self-serving, as it helps perpetuate the very problem it is meant to help resolve and at the expense of most other stakeholders. Some other relevant points of note include the following:

- **Cost.** The cost, in time and effort, required to produce and evolve the new and more effective rules and regulations that will govern the use of digital content, as well as the added distraction of expensive litigation and intense lobbying activities (among the other stakeholder groups) that surround this process, make it a formidable task for all of the stakeholders in this group.
- **Culture and connectivity.** A cultural shift is needed in the way that laws and rules are created and implemented, especially in the context of the evolving content economy. The days of reactive laws and legislation may well be numbered considering the rapidly increasing pace of change in the technology, business, creative and end-user domains. There is little room for the extremely slow and

reactive 'vulture culture' of the legal and legislative stakeholders, which does very little to help the dynamic and ever evolving content-based economy. The lawmakers and other governance stakeholders must be intimately connected to the evolutionary process in order to better facilitate the emergence of appropriate solutions in this context.

- **Content protection.** The role of the governance stakeholder has involved the creation of laws and treaties that uphold the existing intellectual property constructs that were mostly developed in the pre-digital world. This has included the introduction of the various legal instruments (e.g. DMCA and EUCD) discussed in the previous chapter. As might be expected there is still considerable debate and dialogue about the efficacy of these tools in combating what is seen as a problem mostly by the incumbent organisational entities that are threatened with disintermediation and obsolescence.

In conclusion this stakeholder group has a vital role to play in the future of both DRM and the content economy, and their core responsibility is to help safeguard and legitimise the push for creating holistic solutions that will be comprehensive and acceptable to all stakeholders, along with the compromises that must be made by each and every stakeholder in the content economy.

The consumer and end-user stakeholders

This last group of stakeholders represents the final culmination point in the content value chain and encompasses the point at which content is consumed, revenue derived and future markets defined. Members of this group are made up of all individuals and organisations that consume content products from members of the creative and commercial stakeholder groups, aided by the enabling products from technology stakeholders and influenced by the rules from the governance stakeholders. The fascinating thing about this stakeholder group is that although it is arguably the most powerful stakeholder group in the content economy, it is constantly overlooked or neglected by the machinations of the other stakeholder groups, except when they need to derive revenue from it. This state of affairs is made all the more intriguing when we consider that this stakeholder group consists of people that also belong to one or more of the other stakeholder categories by profession (e.g. artiste, lawyer, technologist or content salesperson). At some point or another, members of the other stakeholder groups will have consumed content (i.e. been an end-user) in many aspects of their daily lives. The true power of the new content economy will be felt only with the full realisation of the implications of this situation and this has started to happen with the rise in the so-called user-generated content and the social networking phenomena. As yet this stakeholder group is simply trying to get to grips with life on the internetworked world of today and have their hands full with the new and exciting opportunities, devices and content channels that are opening up everyday.

The impact of digital technology and DRM on consumer and end-user stakeholders

The main impact of the digital revolution on this stakeholder group is in the democratisation of information and connectivity, much like the profound effects felt by the introduction of printing press technology and the resulting increased availability of books and education for the masses, but more so in this case because it affects a global audience. Some quick points on the specific impacts of digital technology and DRM are as follows:

- **Cost.** The aforementioned 'faster', 'better', 'cheaper' and 'smaller' trends in consumer products and services have helped to create energetic markets for new content products and services that did not exist only a decade earlier (e.g. iTunes) and have also re-energised some of the more established markets with new means of reaching customers (e.g. Amazon.com books and Dell computers).

- **Connectivity.** Ubiquitous internet, broadband and wireless technology have truly made it possible for people to connect on a global scale As observed earlier, news content is readily accessible and the consumer now only has the task of deciding which channel to use in accessing it; hobbies and lifestyles are readily enjoyed and shared with people anywhere in the global village and this is only just the beginning of things to come.

- **Content protection.** User-generated content and social networking have sparked the imagination of the content industry as a possible panacea that would help cure the ills of the recent turbulent times. However, this is not without cost as the people that generated their own content also tend to reuse other people's content including copyrighted material, which harbours the potential for widespread infringement litigation. Also some of the more intrusive content protection mechanisms (both legal and technological) have not quelled the claims of economic hardship by the severely affected recording industry.

In conclusion, it would seem that the end-user or content consumer is still not fully engaged in their role as a bona-fide stakeholder in the content economy, therefore it would be in the best interest of all other stakeholder groups to help educate, communicate and cooperate with this group because, as stated in a 2005 Capgemini white paper,

> any lasting development in this context will most likely be brought about by the end-users, and it will also affect them the most (Umeh 2005)

Evolving the content economy

As already mentioned earlier in this book, although DRM technology and applications may occupy a very narrow niche in the whole content economy and ecosystem, the subject it addresses is situated right at the heart of the rapidly evolving technology, communications and media universe. DRM is predominantly an economic mechanism, which owes its very existence to the fact that content businesses rely on their ability to generate revenue from the replication and distribution of content, and that any enabler of these abilities is also a potential conduit for content leakage and a consequent loss of revenue. DRM in its current form is used to ensure that the supported content business models, as well as the protected content, are implemented and maintained according to the extant worldview (or *weltanschauung*) of entrenched and partisan content establishments. The following sections explore some major factors that need to be taken into account when looking at current evolutionary trends in the content economy.

Reducing cost

There is an increasing tendency for continuous downward pressure on the prices of products and services in the digital content economy. This may be due to the relative abundance of content, delivery channels and bandwidth, as well as competition among the many service providers and product vendors. This factor affects all stakeholder groups to various degrees, but none more so than in the commercial stakeholder domain where, as discussed earlier, the lower cost and increased capabilities associated with new consumer products and services are making it more difficult for established content businesses to compete effectively whilst maintaining their exalted positions. For example, the impact of some fairly recent innovation in digital recording technology has meant that the capabilities of the expensive and 'high-end' studio recording equipment of yore is now available, for a fraction of the cost, in the somewhat more affordable home studio recording products of today. Artistes now have the ability to produce high-quality music, including some recent commercial hits, quite literally from their bedroom studio equipment, which typically includes a PC (mid–high media specification) and a plethora of virtual studio software. Another angle to this discussion is that the trend for convergence in content products and services, adopted by some operators as a competitive strategy, also contributes to the reduction in prices. This basically means that the advancement of digital technology, which has enabled significant cost reductions and increased capabilities, also helps to accelerate these trends by enabling the support of multiple systems, applications and services on the same product or device (e.g. mobile phone, camera, radio, TV, music player, PDA etc. all on one handheld device). Figure 4.2 shows the downward pressure on prices as high-end products, services and their supported functionalities make their way into mass-market, user-centric, low-end consumer offerings. It is by no coincidence that this graph resembles the long tail economic model popularised by Anderson (2006) in his book entitled *The Long Tail: Why the Future of Business is Selling Less of More*, because they both reflect the power of the new content economy and its ability to democratise and refocus the market segmentation for content products and services to the individual (i.e. the ultimate 'market segment of one' individual).

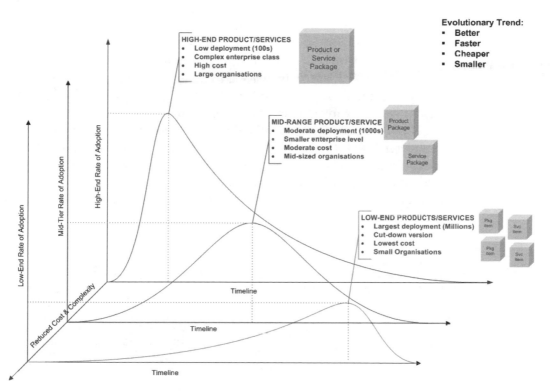

FIGURE 4.2 *Reducing cost effect of digital technology and innovation*

Blurring boundaries of the content economy

The second significant factor in the evolving content economy is the gradually dissolving traditional boundaries between the stakeholder groups. It probably began in the mid-to-late 1990s with the disintermediation of many product and service resellers (or middlemen) as a result of the direct-to-market opportunities presented by the growth of the internet and the web. Enterprises were quick to jump on this bandwagon, which effectively helped in lowering the financial cost and effort required to recruit, service and retain their customers. Members of the content industries (especially those related to music and film content) also had the opportunity to capitalise on the direct-to-consumer channels of the internet, but perhaps due to the low-bandwidth connections at the time, the lack of adequate protection for digital content and the entrenched protectionist attitudes of the industry (or a combination of these and more factors), there was a crucial lag in responding to these events. As we know this gap was rapidly exploited by some consumers to a startling degree via the rise of P2P and other file-sharing network technologies and services. This phenomenon, if left unchecked, would have effectively disintermediated the whole recording industry and even other similar content-based businesses. However it is not over yet because although file-sharing issues are slowly being addressed by the affected industries (e.g. RIAA lawsuits, iTunes, YouTube etc.), the original direct-to-consumer threat (or opportunity) still remains for the commercial stakeholders, especially those that wish to persist their with increasingly out-of-step business models. Furthermore, the increasing trend for user-generated content has also contributed to the blurring of the boundaries between content creator and consumer, as most users can now readily generate and share their own content with others aided, of course, by some of the newer commercial stakeholder business models that capitalise on the whole social networking theme. Figure 4.3 is intended to illustrate the slow dissolution of traditional boundaries between the stakeholders in the content economy, especially in the commercial domain area between content creators and consumers.

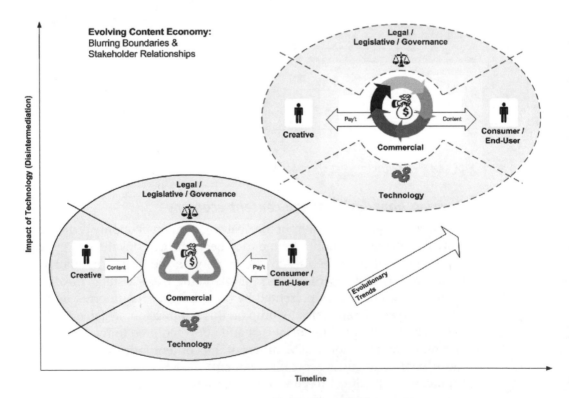

FIGURE 4.3   *Blurring boundaries*

Shifting roles and influences in the content economy

In Figure 4.3 there is a hint that the blurring of traditional boundaries has started what would seem like a slow shift in the balance of power between the various stakeholders. The traditional content businesses within the commercial stakeholder category, especially in the last century, held an iron fist over the content economy because they essentially controlled the money and as a result wielded the most power in terms of their ability to dictate terms or influence other stakeholder groups. The democratising impact of the digital and internet technologies has led to a perceivably slight loosening of this grip and as a result the members of other stakeholder groups, especially the creative and end-consumer stakeholders, appear to have found a voice that will empower the exchange of content products from one to the other in a less dictatorial fashion. However, this is only a very early stage prospect and is not guaranteed to play out as described regardless of the vociferous support by the anti-DRM lobby groups and 'content must be free' type advocates. One of the core objectives of the global IPR system and copyright is to incentivise the creation of more works by their inspired and gifted creators for the betterment of the human race. To this end it is still necessary to have a system that upholds and fulfils this goal and this has been traditionally delivered by the partnership of the commercial and governance stakeholder groups, which is not likely to disappear anytime soon. The lasting effect of any evolutionary change in the content economy will most likely result in an adjustment in the balance of power between stakeholder groups, as illustrated in the indicative example shown in Figure 4.4.

In this example, although the estimated change in level of influence wielded by each stakeholder group is offset by the overall growth in the content economy (which is represented by a multiplier factor k) it does indicate that the influencing power of the creative and consumer stakeholders will grow considerably in the new content economy. The influence of the technology stakeholders will likely experience moderate to slight growth in their role as a primary driving force in the content economy, while the commercial and governance stakeholders are likely to see a significant shrinkage in their power to influence the new content economy but only in relation to their historical levels of influence.

In conclusion the above factors, which have been derived and extrapolated from current observable events, are intended to highlight the central role played by economics in DRM. There are many examples and positions that can be taken on the subject and most likely some academic theses already exist on this topic, but there is still a need for rigorous, authoritative and industry-specific research on the actual effects of DRM economics, which ties up all of the stakeholder perspectives and defines a clear way forward in the evolution of the content economy.

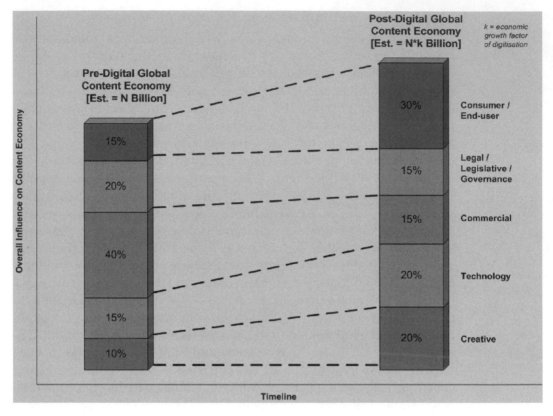

FIGURE 4.4   *The shifting balance of power*

INDUSTRIES AND THE NEW CONTENT ECONOMY

This section looks at some of the industries affected by developments in the evolving new content economy and DRM. This includes the beleaguered music industry, which has become the poster child for the impact of digital technology and the shifting sands of the evolving content economy. It is mainly aimed at providing a brief overview of the issues faced by these industries, as well as the changes that they may need to undergo in order to remain relevant and competitive in the evolving landscape. As could perhaps be expected, the majority of the most visibly affected industries belong in the media, entertainment, communication and technology sectors, but it also affects all knowledge- and content-based industries and organisations that rely on intellectual property and IT to carry out their businesses.

The music industry

As stated earlier, the music industry (especially the recording industry segment) has perhaps been the most visibly affected out of all of the industries in this context, and they have borne the brunt of the impact and challenge to long-established business models brought on by the recent innovations in digital technology and the attendant effect on music consumption. Much coverage has been given to the issues faced by the industry especially in relation to digital piracy and the numerous P2P file-sharing networks that facilitate this activity, but perhaps not enough attention has been paid to the fundamental business structure and premise of this industry, which has equally contributed to the situation. In the following we summarise the music industry stakeholder perspectives on some of the impacts of digital technology and DRM on this sector.

Creative domain stakeholders' perspective

Recording artistes can go direct to their audience thanks to the ubiquitous reach of the internet. DRM would be beneficial to the creative artiste here if it helped to develop their markets and return a larger slice of the revenue to them directly.

Technology domain stakeholders' perspective

Such is the impact of digitisation that software-based virtual studio setup consisting of standard PC-based packages (e.g. Propellerhead's Reason and Steinberg's Cubase) can be used to create decent quality productions for commercial use. Internet-based distribution coupled with relatively non-draconian DRM solutions (e.g. Apple's FairPlay) and a reasonable price point (per track) have made it a win–win situation for both artistes and consumers alike.

Commercial domain stakeholders' perspective

Music businesses stand to benefit from exploiting the opportunities presented by the increased channels to market for their products. This especially applies to music publishers and online distributors. However, existing recording industry business models may require some major adjustment to adapt to the changing environment.

Legal, legislative and governance domain stakeholders' perspective

Several organisations and societies provide the governance and management of revenue flow in the music industry and they include the likes of:

- International Federation of the Phonographic Industry (IFPI);
- British Phonographic Industry (BPI);
- Recording Industry Association of America (RIAA);
- Performing Rights Society (PRS);
- Mechanical Copyright Protection Society (MCPS);
- Phonographic Performance Ltd (PPL);

- International Confederation of Societies of Authors and Composers (CISAC).

Many of the issues that face the major labels and other record industry players in managing the challenges of the online music environment are related to the legacy structure of the music business, especially the complex rights, relationships and agreements that have evolved over the years to cater for factors such as 'territoriality', 'synchronisation' and other jargon-laced contractual clauses. An example of progress in this regard would be the UK's cross-industry agreement on the percentage royalty for online music, which is now set at 8% gross for songwriters, composers and publishers (Reimer 2006).

Consumer and end-user domain stakeholders' perspective

The music consumer has had an interesting ride since the mid-1990s, in what must be described as an industry in turmoil. They have witnessed the amazing capabilities of new digital technologies with which to discover, consume and share music; they have witnessed the reaction of the music industry with threats and litigation against their own customers; and they have had to bear the effects of technology protection measures implemented by the record industry in a bid to reduce casual 'piracy' by the end-user. Yet, and in spite of all this, the consumer cannot seem to get enough of the products of this industry. They have embraced this new paradigm for music delivery and consumption with the same enthusiasm they have for a brand new hit record and this more than anything else bodes particularly well for the music industry in the evolving content economy.

Summary and conclusions

> The recording industry as we know it may be dying, but the music business is alive and well if not booming (Fish 2006)

The global music industry is in a state of flux and uncertainty that can only be addressed and resolved with time; therefore stakeholders need to adjust their expectations accordingly.

Rights management

As stated in the previous sections, one of the major issues faced by the music industry, quite outside of the challenge posed by digital technology and online music, is mainly with regards to rights management. The various organisations tasked with managing the flow of revenue in the music industry form a small universe of entities, which are rather imaginatively captured by the 'music universe' illustration in Figure 4.5, created by UK's Performing Rights Society.

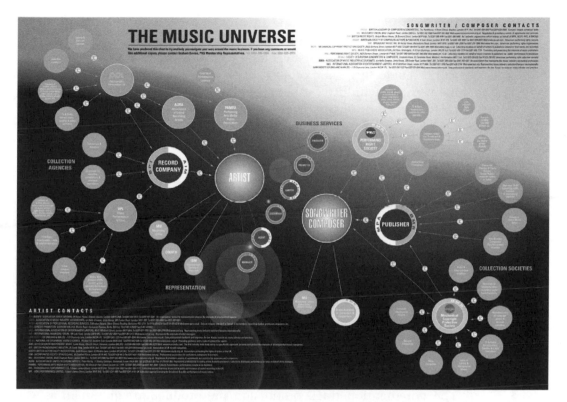

FIGURE 4.5   *The PRS music universe (source: communications@mcps-prs-alliance.co.uk)*

In this representation the music industry is focused around the two main entities of artiste and songwriter or composer (i.e. the creative stakeholder), to which are attached the main industry entities of record company and music publisher (i.e. the commercial stakeholders) respectively. The remaining entities form a constellation of supporting organisations that provide royalty collection and other business support services (including the governance stakeholders). The latter entities are mainly responsible for managing and channelling the flow of revenue between artiste and consumer via the commercial entities of music publisher and record company.

> The main functional areas in a typical royalty collection society can be summarised as: Collect Revenue; Match and Share; Make Payment; and the Support Services (Umeh 2006)

The film industry

The film industry is a different type of beast compared to the music industry, and this is mostly due to the film-making process, which can be much more complex, and involve more people, than the average music album. Furthermore, film is a composite media format that typically includes both video and audio elements together in the completed work. Due to these and other factors, such as high bandwidth requirement, the film industry is not yet as badly affected by online file sharing as the music industry. However, this situation may change as more people in the file-sharing community get faster internet (or broadband) connections. We briefly outline some of the film industry stakeholder positions in the following.

Creative domain stakeholders' perspective

Film makers are also experiencing the beneficial effects of decreasing equipment costs, and talented individuals can obtain good HD cameras on a modest budget. Also there are many cheap but good-quality post-production tools and software, such as the HD-capable Final Cut Pro, which comes with certain Apple PCs. Also there is a proliferation of filmed entertainment from other parts of the world, which are fuelled by the expanding global film industry that includes the prolific Beijing film industry, India's 'Bollywood' and Nigeria's 'Nollywood'.

Technology domain stakeholders' perspective

The aforementioned HD production/pre-production equipment as well as improved high-bandwidth and secure networks (e.g. London's Sohonet) all help to enable international collaboration on film projects. The increase in broadband and wireless broadband connectivity and consumer devices means that online film consumption is set to increase through both legitimate and non-legitimate channels and file-sharing applications such as BitTorrent and eDonkey.

Commercial domain stakeholders' perspective

Film industry productions are typically delivered by purpose-built production companies created solely for each particular project.

> This involves gathering loosely connected, ad-hoc teams of expert craftspeople, technicians, artistes and other skilled individuals that form and re-form from project to project (Van Tassel 2006)

The proliferation of film editing technology and the high-bandwidth connections required to collaborate internationally is now making the film business a truly global venture even for individual projects. Online delivery of film entertainment through operators such as CinemaNow is becoming more commonplace along with the requisite protection mechanisms such as DRM, which are necessary to secure the content and allay the fears of content owners. However, the impact of internet content delivery is also keenly felt in the multiple release window mechanism of the industry. The traditional film industry relies on commercially successful products to help subsidise the cost of the flops. However, the shifting landscape means that the big studios may not even get a chance to invest in hit projects, as more creative types resort to making their own movies independently of the studios. Even the prolific pornography industry, which may be considered a leading example of an industry embracing and benefiting from the internet, has not escaped unscathed and its members have started to complain about the influx and amount of user-generated content (i.e. amateur porn) that is increasingly diluting an already overcrowded market:

> In America alone, the porn industry is worth an estimated 12 billion dollars with some 4.2 million websites, and over 13,000 video titles released annually (Harlow 2006)

Legal, legislative and governance domain stakeholders' perspective

Some of the film industry bodies responsible for the governance and revenue flow within the sector include:

- FILM COUNCIL or The British Film Commission (BFC);
- British Film Institute (BFI);
- British Board of Film Classification (BBFC);
- British Academy of Film and Television Actors (BAFTA);
- Producers Alliance for Cinema and Television (PACT);
- Motion Picture Association of America (MPAA).

Rights management is also a thorny issue for the film industry and perhaps more so as its composite format of video, audio and literary components means that it must also face the rights requirements of other industries (e.g. music and publishing) in addition to its own.

Consumer and end-user domain stakeholders' perspective

The impact of digital technology is felt at all levels of the consumer interface including the digital cinema, HD DVDs and TVs, online delivery channels and the sophisticated home entertainment systems that help to maximise the experiential aspect of the content. This aspect stands in favour of the film industry, which bases their argument against pirated content on the unpredictable quality that seriously detracts from the whole experience.

Summary and conclusions

Despite the dire predictions and challenges faced by specific industry segments, the media and entertainment industry is still very strong overall and, in fact, according accounting firm PriceWaterHouseCoopers:

> the US media market (comprising Filmed entertainment, TV Networks and Distribution) is projected to grow from about 184 Billion in 2005, to over 230 Billion by 2009 (Gunther 2006).

Organisational structure of film projects

Figure 4.6 shows a typical film project's organisation consisting of 'the right people, for the right job, at the right time and at the right price point'. These individuals and teams of skilled people may not work together at the same time or location on the particular film project.

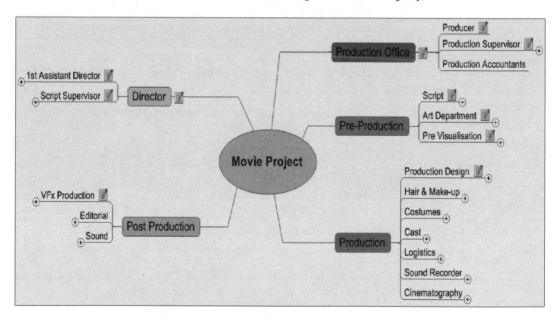

FIGURE 4.6 *Organisation map of a typical film project*

The publishing industry

The publishing industry is older than either the music or film industry and in its very beginnings was considered to be as disruptive to established business models as the internet is today. The impact of digital technology on the publishing industry is felt most keenly with the digitisation of books and other published materials, which become just as vulnerable to piracy as any other media files in a digital form.

Creative domain stakeholders' perspective

An author now has several means of promoting and disseminating their works in addition to established channels and this is great for successful works, as a multiplier effect kicks in to make them even more successful courtesy of the other channels.

Technology domain stakeholders' perspective

The prime examples of digital literature include ebooks and other digital publishing technology and formats, but it must be understood that most websites, blogs and other online dynamic content format also fall under the literary category.

Commercial domain stakeholders' perspective

The book publishing sector has always lived with 'piracy' in one form or another and, as discussed in the last chapter, it has had to fight some formidable battles with progressive technologies and usage practices that evolved and prompted some of the major changes to the ever evolving copyright laws (e.g. photocopying and exceptions to copyright). The positive impact of the internet on the book and publishing industry is handsomely exemplified by online retailers such as Amazon.com and barnesandnoble.com, which make books available to a larger market than any bookshop chain and they can sell an unlimited amount of titles with their 'long-tail' enabled business models. Publishers also rely on hit books or 'bestsellers' to help mitigate the losses from the flops.

Legal, legislative and governance domain stakeholders' perspective

Organisations that help to govern the book industry and manage its revenue flow include:

- Society of Authors;
- Author's Licensing and Collecting Society (ALCS);
- Writers Guild for Great Britain;
- PEN – The World Association of Writers.

The contract signed between author and publisher is the main guiding and driving force in their relationship and is legally binding to both parties:

> Publishers that deal direct with authors, usually request control of all rights throughout the world, including electronic formats, broadcast and subsidiary rights in all territories (Legat 2002)

Consumer and end-user domain stakeholders' perspective

The consumers of literary works are at an advantage over the other media formats because you do not need electricity or any specific device to read a book in its physical printed form. Also the introduction of digital ebook formats has helped to overcome any limitations of the physical media such as portability.

Summary and conclusions

The publishing industry is not likely to disappear anytime soon and it is likely that the industry will continue to develop the markets for digital formats, which are simply another channel for selling the same product.

The role of libraries

Certain public institutions such as the British Library have an opportunity to play an important and significant role in shaping the evolving content economy in their traditional role as custodians of the public knowledge. Libraries make it their business to acquire and preserve vast quantities of published works in several media formats and have been vested with certain powers such as legal deposit (which mandates that all publications in the UK must be deposited with the British Library). The benefits this could bring to an online world are numerous and not least of which is the ability to preserve electronic material that may otherwise be lost due to the relentless march of technology. The British Library has created some initiatives along these lines such as their UK Web Archiving project, which is intended to archive all UK-based websites. Also the potential of their Sound Archives project, which has already converted a huge amount of music and audio recordings in the digital repository system, was demonstrated in the 2006 exhibition that celebrated 50 years of the UK album charts (see Figure 4.7). It should not take much to work out the implication of that particular project for the music industry, if done on a global scale with appropriately non-intrusive protection mechanisms or DRM.

The software and IT industry

The software and information technology sector is the nucleus for the majority of the developments in the digital content economy, because it has provided the enablers for some of the more dramatic events that have occurred in the media and entertainment industries in recent times. In order to avoid repetition and overstating the obvious we briefly outline some of the main themes for each stakeholder group in the following.

Creative domain stakeholder' perspective

Software writers and computer system designers are responsible for the amazing leaps in hardware and software capabilities in the past few decades. The various technology protection measures (such as DRM) and potential

FIGURE 4.7   *British Library album chart exhibition*

content piracy tools (such as file-sharing networks and applications) are conceived by this group.

Technology domain stakeholders' perspective

These stakeholders take the inputs from the creative stakeholders and transform them into the building blocks and components from which various business services and products can be made.

Commercial domain stakeholders' perspective

The business approach and philosophies may differ according to which side of the fence the organisation sits on with respect to commercial and open-source offerings. Also ISPs now play the role of gatekeeper for the content industry and have become the initial point of call for addressing any suspected infringement activity that occurs from services hosted on their servers.

Legal, legislative and governance domain stakeholders' perspective

The Open Source philosophy is fundamentally geared towards using Intellectual Property licensing mechanisms to deny anybody the right to exclusively exploit a work (St Laurent 2004)

Some of the more popular open-source software has been used to operate the internet from its inception and these include components of the widely used 'LAMP' architecture, which stands for Linux, Apache, MySQL and PHP. There are several types of open-source licences including:

- Massachusetts Institute of Technology (MIT) licence – the earliest open-source licence;
- Berkeley Software Distribution (BSD) licence – a classic open-source licence;
- Apache licence – v1 and v2;
- GNU's licences – GPL and Lesser General Public License (LGPL).

Consumer and end-user domain stakeholders' perspective

Consumers of technology-based products have a lot to be thankful for, and a lot to be wary about, because they may unwittingly use them to infringe the IPRs of some individual or organisation. The early technology adopters are usually the guinea pigs and discoverers of hidden capabilities of the products, some of which were not even intended by the designers (e.g. SMS text messaging).

Summary and conclusions

It is evident that the future evolution of the content economy will continue to be heavily influenced by technological advances (at least in the near to medium term), and that the stakeholders in this industry will continue innovating and feeding off of these advances.

P2P networks

P2P networks use a simple network topology that shares resources among connected peers or servers in the network. There is a distinction between the networks and the applications, although most people refer to them interchangeably. Basically there are several networks upon which many P2P programs are based and through which files can be shared among the peers on that network. 'Some P2P programs like Shareaza and MLDonkey have been designed for use on multiple networks' (Wang 2004). The following is a list of some P2P networks, along with the P2P programs that work with them. Note that the illegitimate nature of some of the activities carried out with the client programs on these networks means that they do not usually last very long; therefore this 'snapshot in time' list is only included here to show the relationship between P2P clients and the networks:

- **BitTorrent** – clients include Azureus, BitTorrent, MLDonkey and Shareaza;
- **eDonkey2000** – clients include aMule, eDonkey2000, eMule, MLDonkey, Shareaza and iMesh;
- **FastTrack** – clients include Grokster, iMesh, Kazaa and MLDonkey;

- **Gnutella** – clients include BearShare, Grokster, iMesh, gtk-gnutella, LimeWire, MLDonkey, Morpheus and Shareaza.

Only a handful of these clients still exist or operate in their 'wild' state (i.e. unfettered by any legal bonds) as a result of lawsuits by the content industry. Some services that help to legitimise P2P file sharing include the likes of SnoCap, the brainchild of Shawn Fanning creator of Napster, which compares file-sharing requests against a database of approved materials before allowing the download to happen.

Other industries

Broadcasting industry

> It has become increasingly obvious that in future media companies will no longer be defined by media type (i.e. music, film or TV companies), but instead will be known as entertainment companies that create acquire and exploit all manner of Intellectual Property (Deloitte 2006)

Games industry

The online games industry in particular has become a multimillion pound industry thanks to the introduction of alternative reality games such as Blizzard entertainment's *World of Warcraft*, which has over 7 million subscribers worldwide.

Telecommunication industry

Mobile telephony, IPTV and VOIP services are the ones to watch. This industry is considered by many to be right up there with the internet in terms of impact on modern society.

Financial services industry

DRM technologies can be used to enhance regulatory compliance and the protection of highly sensitive information.

Healthcare and pharmaceuticals industry

These firms require robust information security solutions for protecting intellectual property in drug development collaborations, contract manufacturing, clinical trials and compliance.

Manufacturing and automotive industry

The processes in this industry sometimes require the flow and use of sensitive information, such as designs, product plans and engineering documents, especially when collaborating with partners and offshore organisations.

DRM AND THE SOCIO-POLITICAL CONTEXT (GOVERNMENT AND LOBBY GROUPS)

The government contribution

The various national governments have little direct input in the actual development of digital content technology or DRM, but they do have great influencing powers over the evolving content economy through the various regulatory and legislative mechanisms at their disposal. This section looks at two initiatives by the UK government to understand and address pressing issues in DRM and IPRs.

APIG Report

Date: June 2006
Title: Digital Rights Management: Report of an Inquiry by the All Party Internet Group
In November 2005 the All Party Parliamentary Internet Group (APIG) launched an enquiry into DRM, which solicited the opinions of various stakeholders and experts on what changes the UK government needs to make in the laws and regulations in relation to DRM. The group was chaired by Labour MP Derek Wyatt and a report of the inquiry with all of its findings was published in June 2006 (APIG 2006), which according to a subsequent *DRMWatch* article (Rosenblatt 2006b) was lauded as 'the best public policy document on DRM that we have ever read – ever'. The report made nine recommendations and was structured to provide an overview of DRM and the several issues to be addressed including copyright trade-offs, licensing practices and government intervention, as well as the specific issues with libraries, disabled users and interoperability. The report concludes with a proposal for a 'UK Stakeholders Group' to oversee future policy, followed by the usual end matter and other relevant information. The report can be found at http://www.apig.org.uk/ along with other details.

Gowers Review of Intellectual Property

Date: December 2006
Title: Gowers Review of Intellectual Property
In 2005 the Chancellor of the Exchequer commissioned the Gowers Review to determine whether the UK's intellectual property system was up to the task of governance 'in an era of globalisation, digitisation and increasing economic specialisation' (Gowers 2006). The review published a call for evidence and over 500 responses as well as a petition to extend the copyright term for sound recordings. The review made and published its findings in a report with a number of recommendations to improve the framework for innovation by implementing:

* stronger enforcement of IPRs to ensure practical protection is provided for rights owners and effective deterrents to infringement are in place;

- lower operational costs for business, simplifying processes such as licensing and litigation, and improving education and advice;
- greater balance and flexibility of IPRs to allow individuals, businesses and institutions to use information and ideas in ways consistent with the digital age.

It also recognised that some changes to the intellectual property system will be required both in the UK and globally, and recommended that the UK should take a lead on intellectual property policy development. Needless to say some strong reactions were expressed by certain industry bodies. For example, technology companies, especially ISPs, were vehemently opposed to the idea of a new tariff for the losses due to illegal download. Also the IFPI reacted against the recommendation by the review not to extend the copyright term on sound recordings from 50 to 95 years, and claimed that this was discriminatory to British artistes and producers.

Advocacy or lobby groups and organisations

Several organisations have undertaken the role of consumer advocates or voices of reason and conscience in the evolving digital landscape of today. These organisations focus on different aspects and issues including topics such as DRM, privacy and corporate responsibility. This section presents a few of these groups with a brief description and links to further information.

Electronic Frontier Foundation (EFF)

According to their website, the EFF (founded in 1990) is a donor-funded, non-profit organisation that has achieved eminence as one of the prime activist groups dedicated to confronting 'cutting-edge issues, defending free speech, privacy, innovation, and consumer rights in the world'. It has been very vocal on the issues around digital rights and frequently takes its battle to the courts where it has been known to take on large corporations and even the US government. The EFF also undertakes to educate the press and the general public on the issues at stake in the digital rights debate. Their DRM page at http://www.eff.org/IP/DRM/ is a good source of information about the activities and stance of the EFF on DRM.

Electronic Privacy Information Center (EPIC)

Established in 1994, EPIC is an independent US-based non-profit public interest research centre, which, according to its website, is mainly focused on bringing 'public attention to emerging civil liberties issues and to protect privacy, the First Amendment, and constitutional values'. It publishes the EPIC alert, which is an email and online newsletter that covers issues around civil liberties in the information age. EPIC is funded by contributions from individuals, private foundations and companies. Their website at http://www.epic.org/privacy/drm/default.html contains more information about the activities and position of EPIC on privacy and DRM.

Informed Dialogue about Consumer Acceptability of DRM Solutions in Europe (INDICARE)

INDICARE is a European research organisation dedicated to the pursuit of consumer education on the topic of DRM. In 2006 it published a consumer guide to DRM, which is aimed at informing and educating consumers on issues around DRM and its relevance to them. INDICARE is financially supported by the European Commission, but its views and opinions are independent. The website http://www.indicare.org/application.php contains more information about INDICARE.

CONCLUSION

From all of the points discussed in this chapter it is obvious that DRM is first and foremost an economic tool that appears to be directly linked to the money or lack thereof in the global IPR system. The role to be played by DRM and other mechanisms designed to protect content in the information economy is critical, but it can also be a double-edged sword that cuts both would-be enforcers and users of content and rights. As we saw from the film industry's project organisation model, it is most likely that the future of business (especially in light of today's world of outsourcing) may evolve along a service-oriented route whereby business service providers will need to become more dynamic and flexible in order to better serve their clients, irrespective of geographical, temporal or cultural points of origin. Such a future must embody the principle of 'the right people, for the right job, at the right time and price' to deliver their offerings. DRM has a major role to play in the creative and other content-based industries as a crucial enabler of this process by providing the appropriate content security framework and safeguards for the vital intellectual property component of the global content economy.

It is also becoming clearer that any effective solution to some of these seemingly intractable problems must happen in conjunction with large-scale changes in the attitudes and perspectives of the entrenched stakeholders in all of the domains above. It is not helpful to have an adversarial mentality and, in the words of Gantz and Rochester (2005), 'Both sides need to chill out'. Until each stakeholder can understand and recognise the *weltanschauung* or worldview of all of the other stakeholder domains, it will remain difficult for them to accept the need for a sea change in attitude. This may well be the most onerous require-ment to fulfil, but without which there will be no real understanding of the enormous potential lurking in the more revolutionary aspects of the digital revolution, let alone any realistic prospect of fully harnessing and realising it in the short to medium term.

5 Rights, Models and Issues

Rights confer the authority to permit or prohibit a specific activity on a piece of content. In the digital world these rights can be implemented by decomposing or translating them into Boolean (i.e. yes or no) tests that must be performed before an activity such as copy, print or play is executed on the system. In order for this to work there is usually a numeric attribute or logical condition against which the request is tested and these are provided by the rights model held within the DRM system. This chapter begins with a look at content rights in the real-world and digital environments and also provides an overview of the components that make up a rights model in a DRM system. This is followed by an exploration of some of the rights-enabled business models and the rights languages that are used to implement them in a computer system. The chapter closes with a look at the various issues that need to be addressed in order for DRM to be more acceptable and usable in the long run.

CONTENT RIGHTS

Before we can identify and specify the appropriate rights to a given piece of content, it is necessary to spell out exactly what constitutes the term content. In this context, content is the same as a work in copyright law and it refers to any real-world item of creative expression such as a book, a poem, an essay, a film, a music track or song, painting or photograph, but in a digital form. For our purposes, we focus this discussion mostly on content rights within the digital realm. However, to complicate matters further certain types of audiovisual content such as films and TV programming are made up of other components or 'atomic' sub-content types (e.g. sound track and still pictures etc.) and may be regarded as 'composite' content. It could be argued that any standalone instance of a work that goes into the creation of another essentially makes it a part of that new work, especially if it is 'recorded' into the new work, for example, a passing shot of a billboard or painting, or a radio jingle playing in the background of a film scene. Also it can be difficult in some cases to establish just what should be considered a standalone work, as in the case of music samples clips, a film score or audio brand marks such as Intel's four note signature tune often used on its TV adverts. The granularity of the various components that make up composite content such as films can be very fine indeed and this can be problematic in the digital domain where it is possible to include an exact copy of content into the new form or 'mash-up' as it is popularly known.

What are content rights?

Content rights in both the physical and digital worlds are basically a description of those permissions or entitlements usually derived from copyright that are applicable to a piece of content. For example:

- the right to copy or duplicate the content (reproduction rights);
- the right to forward (distribution rights);
- play (render);
- print (translate);
- forward (distribute);
- delete (destroy);
- modify (extend, shorten, restructure).

However, in the digital domain some additional capabilities are available that can extend or restrict the above rights including:

- the ability to revoke or permit **access** to the content depending on specific criteria (e.g. the number of times the content has been played or copied);
- the ability to constrain the **usage** of content based on certain conditions set by the content provider or owner (e.g. only permit playback of a downloaded movie for two hours on Sunday afternoons in Brazil, to take a feasible but complex and ridiculous example).

The latter areas of access and usage rights are core to DRM because they cover the two fundamental groups of activities that users undertake and over which the content owners can exert some level of control in the digital environment. Furthermore, they also hint at the possibilities of what can be achieved using these technologies, for example, as an enabler for desirable features such as dynamic content pricing or as an inhibitor to prevent unauthorised activities such as piracy. However, as with any tool its uneducated use can lead to unintended consequences such as the SonyBMG copy-protected CD scandal in 2005. It is always necessary to point out that DRM is not a technical implementation of copyright law and does not try to capture every nuance and subtlety of the copyright system. In fact DRM has an opposite approach to rights management when compared to copyright, and Karen Coyle summed this up beautifully:

> Where copyright law is an expression of 'everything that is not forbidden is permitted', DRM takes the approach of 'everything that is not permitted is forbidden' (Coyle 2003)

The implication of this statement is that while man-made copyright systems focus on prohibited activities, computer-based DRM systems are designed to anticipate and incorporate every single usage scenario in their model. This often means that new or modified usage scenarios may not be so easy to implement on the system once it goes live. This can be a problem for many types of content, which may become inaccessible once the rendering technology and protection system become obsolete. This and other issues with current DRM systems will be discussed later in this chapter.

Rights model components

According to Rosenblatt et al.:

> a rights model is a specification of the types of rights that the system can keep track of, and what the system can do to or with those rights (Rosenblatt et al. 2002)

This means that a DRM system may not necessarily model all of the rights applicable to a piece of content, only those deemed necessary to provide the required functionality of content protection or other types of control. Essentially a system refers to a collection of components that interact to deliver a result or achieve a goal; therefore it may also include elements from society and culture, as well as commercial, technological and legal systems. These factors all interact together and, as we shall see later on, can sometimes make it very difficult to represent the rights accurately within the digital domain. Perhaps unsurprisingly this also applies to the reverse situation of translating DRM techniques that work well in the digital environment into the analogue world that the users inhabit.

Having established just what constitutes content and rights in the previous section, this section looks to define and briefly explain the different components that make up a rights model. In this context a rights model refers to the representation of real-world rights, permissions and conditions within a DRM system. We shall look at the different types of rights and their attributes as well as the real-world rights they try to reflect in the digital domain.

Types of rights

For any given piece of digital content there exists several types of rights associated with it and that go hand in hand with the content itself whether explicitly stated or not. These rights can be grouped under three main categories as follows:

(i)   Render

- **Print** – grant or revoke permission to print the content.
- **View** – grant or revoke permission to view the content.

- **Play** – grant or revoke permission to play the content, interestingly this may be totally separate from the right to view or listen to the content.
- **Others** – may include several activities that can be performed on the content during rendition, for example, time shifting, pause, rewind, fast forward, etc.

(ii)   Transport

- **Copy** – grant or revoke permission to copy or record the content (this right may also be used to make backup or system transient copies, which raises some issues around how to identify the 'purpose of use', as we shall see later).
- **Move** – grant or revoke permission to transfer the content from one machine to another (in computing a move is usually accomplished via a copy and delete sequence of actions).
- **Lend** – grant or revoke permission to transfer the content and associated rights for a period of time (i.e. involves temporarily passing the content to another party and losing the rights to access or use it for the duration).
- **Delete** – grant or revoke permission to remove the content from the system.

(iii)   Transform (derivative work)

- **Extract** – grant or revoke permission to extract a portion of content as a new standalone work.
- **Edit** – grant or revoke permission to manipulate content by modifying or changing it (e.g. add, remove or restructure the content); this is particularly relevant to user-generated content and Web 2.0 applications such as wikis, which may or may not use some rights specification tool such as the CC licence.
- **Embed** – grant or revoke permission to manipulate content by embedding all or a piece of it into a new work (this may involve copying and inserting, e.g. audio sampling).
- **Translate** – grant or revoke permission to manipulate content by translating into another form, language or display medium (this may include content encryption and integrity checking).

These categories, derived from Mark Stefik's groupings as described by Rosenblatt et al. (2002), pretty much cover most of the rights that can be modelled within a DRM system as illustrated by the sample activities under each category.

Rights attributes

Each of the rights categories and activities discussed above come with certain characteristics, which are referred to as attributes. These attributes help to specify, among other things, the extent to which a permitted activity may be performed with or on the content. Three of the more important attributes are as follows:

- **Consideration.** This is how much or what is exchanged for the rights. Could be money, personal or contact information via forms and registration, or having to look at some adverts. Essentially nothing is truly free even when it appears so.
- **Extent.** This is a specific direction on exactly the amount of activity the permission grants (e.g. number of days, number of plays, devices that can be used etc.).
- **User types.** This defines the type of user to whom the above attributes will apply and the value of the attributes may be different for each type of user (e.g. a registered user gets to play the content five times, while a casual surfer may get to play only a short sample unless they register).

As can be discerned from the above list, these attributes are used to implement the business rules and policies used by the system to represent and execute the intentions of the business owners with regards to the access and use of their content. In other words the attributes along with the rights they specify help to make up the business model that is implemented in the system. This is further illustrated in the next section on rights-enabled business models, which includes both traditional and modern or analogue and digital formats.

RIGHTS-ENABLED BUSINESS MODELS

As stated earlier, the traditional rights-enabled business models that worked mostly for physical analogue products have been joined by the new forms designed to work with intangible and digital products to form a still-evolving mix of models and strategies, which are presented in the following.

Subscriptions

This model provides regular and scheduled income to the content provider. It is a mature and reliable model typically adopted by most media companies. Refinements to this model include stepped offerings with a higher price for more content. DRM is highly applicable to this model.

It is perhaps the most familiar model based on historical ties with other media formats such as television, cable or satellite, telephony (mobile or fixed line) and periodicals (e.g. newspapers and magazines). The subscriber generally pays a regular fee for content. This may also include 'free' subscriptions that require no cash payment, but may have other types of exchange. Various spin-offs and extensions of the subscription model include the '*a la carte*', 'all you can eat', tiered subscriptions, premium and on-demand services.

Free downloads

These are useful as a means to reach a widespread audience (e.g. loss leader) and as a means to obtain some valuable user information.

It applies to content that is freely available for download on the internet. This may be because it is in the public domain, or may be supported by adverts or by harvesting user information. This model also applies to illegal or pirated content available via file sharing but without any guarantee on the quality of content.

Paid downloads

This is the online implementation of the traditional and proven vendor–buyer model. The user pays for what they get.

The user pays a fee and downloads the content in the form of a file that can then be played or stored depending on the rights and permissions given. The attributes may be for life or a limited period of access to the content.

Pay-per-view

This is a great model for the one-off or live event that is briefly in high demand, but which rapidly drops in interest and value afterwards.

The user pays for each rendition of the content and this may be found in the 'live' or analogue performance arena (e.g. concerts, film shows) or digital types such as VOD.

Pay as you go

This has many similarities to the previous method, but includes other activities not just viewing.

The user pays for each activity in the content, for example, to play, copy or forward. The remuneration may be in form of micropayments (i.e. very small amounts per activity).

Pre- or post-paid content

This is similar to the pay as you go model except for the time of payment. This is the model used by mobile phone and some utility service providers.

The user may use pre-paid vouchers (e.g. iTunes) or be billed separately (perhaps included in another service such as mobile phone bills with some 3G content).

Usage monitoring and data mining

The strategy is to make use of valuable user data as a source of revenue and a useful market-targeting tool.

The user gains access to content by agreeing to have their usage data or other information gathered and repurposed by the content providers who then use it to position more relevant offers to the consumers based on their inferred preferences. This can be very powerful in the hands of seasoned marketers.

Superdistribution or viral marketing and distribution

This is a twofold strategy that is designed to market and distribute content via existing users for free or via incentives of cash or more 'free' content. The content so distributed may also have DRM protection.

Users pass on the content including rights and attributes to other users who are then bound by the same or slightly modified conditions. Examples include P2P distribution using DRM-protected content that allow a preview or limited play functionality before mandatory purchase.

Rights assignment

This is the basis of licensing, which is a well-established mainstay in the traditional world of the publishing and music industries. DRM systems could be used to enforce the assigned rights in a digital environment.

Licensing occurs where one party (usually the content creator) assigns all or some rights to a specific content to another party (i.e. the publisher) for a specified period of time.

All you can eat

This is virtually unlimited content for a specified period of time on a premium price point or tariff. Can be used to complement subscription or other paid access models.

The all you can eat proposition for the user in this model is usually granted in exchange for a higher flat fee.

Bundling

This is the use of multi-content and multi-service packages to attract more than the usual demographic.

Users may get various types of content (e.g. music tracks and videos, ringtones, games etc.) in each attractive bundle for a special price.

Syndication

The reuse of content in different media or formats exposes it to a larger audience. The scope exists for including automated contract management and royalty collection mechanisms into this model.

The traditional syndication model used in periodicals and TV is now available online via technologies such as RSS feeds, which employ a content-pull mechanism to update their content on the subscriber's client or agent software. This is useful for audience-specific content portals and user communities.

User-generated content

This is the social network and community-based strategy for content–audience interaction on a massive scale. The revenue model here may include advert support.

There is an unprecedented opportunity for users to create and share content online on any topic and in any format of their choice with a like-minded audience. Examples include the Web 2.0 darlings such as MySpace (music), Flickr (photographs) and YouTube (video), as well as blog sites and wikis (e.g. Wikipedia).

Content portals

In this strategy aggregated content is made available to a wide or narrow segment of consumers and usually positioned as a start-off point to deeper content in other locations.

Branded portals from ISPs, media content owners and search engines are normal. Niche or subject-based portals (e.g. women's health or games sites) also exist, as do industry- or sector-specific offerings.

Affiliation and affinity models

This strategy includes affiliate programs as used by content vendors (e.g. Amazon.com) and affinity-based webrings, which are both based on traffic or customer building strategies that help bring similar minded people to related content.

These models work by using peer recommendation to drive consumers towards content of interest to them. The web with its network of linked resources excels at this and online operators such as Amazon.com are great exponents of this model.

Release windows

This strategy maximises the content revenue by targeting various audiences and formats at specific points in a release cycle. There is opportunity for DRM technology as an enabler for this particular model by using the rights attributes to model the time constraints.

This strategy is used mostly by the movie industry, which can obtain multiple revenues from the same customers and from the same content. An example sequence would see a film released in separate windows as follows:

Theatrical release → Pay-per-view → DVD → Cable and satellite TV → Major network TV → Syndication to smaller TV outfits and endless reruns

The revenue decreases with each step but is still made nonetheless. However, piracy and new release formats have meant that the windows are shortening in length but increasing in number.

Walled garden

This strategy restricts users to selected content within a closed network. This is fast becoming an obsolete strategy but DRM could be used to implement it even in an 'open' network based on user profiles and rights.

The early ISPs tried to use this model to protect users and promote their own content but did not succeed. The users wanted to be able to access content outside the wall.

Cross-media or cross-platform

This is an obvious strategy for today's media companies, but one that is still difficult to implement in a streamlined fashion. This also represents one of DRM's biggest hurdles to date.

The ability to purchase and use content anywhere, anytime and on any device is highly desirable for users and most content owners. Some organisations already offer multi-purpose content with all of the necessary translational processing required for their provision on different media and platforms, but this currently involves heavy investment in several industry-specific solutions to manage the same elements of content rights, creation and distribution.

Long tail

This strategy applies the phenomenon documented by Anderson (2006) about the viability and proliferation of niche content on the internet. Basically any content will have some value to someone, somewhere and the internet does a great job of enabling this discovery and subsequent purchase.

This strategy works by using the vast resources of the internet with its huge bandwidth to provide unlimited shelf space for all types of content on the internet. This is the ultimate release window model with a virtually infinite tail window.

Big bite

This is a strategy used to obtain maximum revenue from the first release of content on the internet. It is applicable to providers of volatile content such as games.

This is the opposite of the long tail strategy from a vendor point of view. Premium prices are charged on the first release of the content and thereafter it drops quite rapidly. Users interested in 'fresh and hot' content are the most likely targets.

Advert-supported models

This strategy is another favourite of old media such as broadcast and publishing. Some issues exist regarding the measurement methods used in the online environment (i.e. viewer impression 'eyeballs' versus actual interaction and purchase or 'click-thru' and 'sell-thru').

This model is used by some 'free' content sites and portals as well as other services such as search engines (e.g. Google), but the user is subjected to varying degrees of advert placement in their experience (e.g. the more-intrusive pop-up adverts are widely disliked). This model can be quite lucrative for the site owner or content provider depending on their site traffic.

Recommendation engine

This is related to the affiliation and superdistribution models and may in fact be the enabler behind both. Some vendors have taken it a step further and automated the process with intelligent programs and algorithms to make the recommendations. DRM technology could be a great enabler for this model as it has all of the elements needed to interact with and guide agent-based technologies.

This model provides recommendations to the user by using their historical (data mining) or actual current activities and usage information to infer their preference for a particular piece of content. The user is presented with a selection of potential content and their reactions (e.g. reject or select) are used to further refine the next proposition. This model is useful in industries such as telecoms and music or film retailers as a customer retention tool.

Dynamic user profiling

This involves evolving the services to match the changing needs of a user. It is an effective and market-segment-oriented approach that can address the fabled and ultimate 'market segment of one'. DRM can be very useful in this context.

Each user or group is unique and dynamic so this approach will change to accommodate them as they grow and develop, anticipating and servicing their needs over time. The user sees a provider that uniquely caters to them and all of their content needs. Used in conjunction with the recommendation model, this can be quite powerful.

Multiple play

This strategy is mostly seen in the convergence-led business acquisitions where companies in the telecoms, ISP, broadcasting and general content and media space combine or 'mash-up' to offer these services in *N*-numbered plays (e.g. triple play or quad play).

The users are able to get several services from one single provider such as telephony, cable, broadband and others. This model is beneficial to the customer due to competitive pricing but the services may not always meet the hype.

Cybermediary

This is another name for middlemen or intermediaries in an online context. These providers may also include value added services that add to the appeal of the product to the consumer. DRM can be applied to the content services.

eBay.com is a prime example of this type of business, as are price comparison services such as kelkoo.com, shopper.com and dealtime.com. Others include sites such as lastminute.com and even Amazon's stores.

Mash-ups

'Mash-up' is a Web 2.0 term that describes the combination of different models, processes or business types to create a new one

The mash-up of search and video in Google's acquisition of YouTube.com is a prime example of this hybrid model.

The above models were derived from many sources, including the excellent works by Rosenblatt et al. (2002) and Van Tassel (2006). The list is by no means exhaustive since new models and variants of old ones are springing up all the time. For example, according to an ex-Silicon Valley venture capitalist there are even more exotic variations of mash-ups arising in places such as India, where the online matrimonial websites or traditional marriage bureau have been combined with web and social networking services (e.g. shaadi.com) to add an edge to the tradition. Many of these models could be better enabled by DRM or other technologies, such as user authentication or content management (see Chapter 6).

RIGHTS MODELLING AND LANGUAGES

This section looks at the various ways that rights can be expressed in the digital environment. This is usually accomplished by the use of rights expression languages (RELs), which have been designed to do exactly that. These languages can be used to model some of the rights-enabled business strategies within a computer system and as such they are a fundamental aspect of DRM technology. The next three sections cover the sort of information required by the rights languages (i.e. metadata), the various types of RELs in existence and, finally, a high-level example of their use in the superdistribution model.

Metadata

The term metadata simply translates to 'data about data'. It refers to the overarching information about a piece of content that is used to describe that content. The importance of metadata cannot be overstressed, because it is vital for rapid search and identification of a piece of content in the vast repositories of content that may be found in media companies. The two activities of search and identification reflect some of the more generic uses of metadata that are not specific to DRM, but metadata can also be used to specify rights information for content and this is known as rights metadata.

Metadata can come in various styles and levels of granularity; from the comprehensive and complex to the high-level and simplistic types as shown below:

- author – <Author's name>;
- title – <Document title>;
- date created – <Date of creation>;
- date modified – <Date of last modification>.

The above rudimentary metadata are often used with computer files and Figure 5.1 shows a simple example of this in the Microsoft Word document properties box.

1. General Properties **2. Security Properties**

FIGURE 5.1 *File properties in Microsoft Windows*

The left-hand side of Figure 5.1 shows some descriptive metadata in the general properties tab such as document title, type, location, size, dates created, modified and last accessed, as well as attributes such as 'Read-only' or 'Hidden', whereas the right-hand side displays the security properties along with rights and permissions granted to the administrator user and group on this file, which specifies the allowable actions of read, write, execute and modify via the tick boxes next to these items.

Metadata can be applied to all types of digital content and they help to enable the three valuable capabilities of content identification, content search and content rights, each of which we now describe.

Content identification

This can be achieved with a unique identifier in the metadata. It is a fundamental requirement for any DRM system and without which it will not function properly. Examples include the following:

- **International Standard Book Number (ISBN).** This is usually located near the barcode in most books.
- **Globally Unique Identifier (GUID).** This is used to identify software components.

Content search

The various descriptive items and keywords included in metadata fields help search engines to match the content to a query, easily and quickly, without having to open the content itself. Examples include the following:

- **Dublin Core.** This is bibliographic data and a description of different media types including online content. This standard format includes descriptive information such as title, author name, date, publisher etc.

Content rights

These are usually found in the header or property fields of digital files that will be manipulated by certain DRM systems and they help to specify the rights associated with the content. Examples include the following:

- **XrML and Open Digital Rights Language (ODRL).** These are examples of rights languages that are used to model the rights and permissions on digital content similar to the security properties shown in Figure 5.1.

In a later chapter on standards (i.e. Chapter 7) we look more closely at some of the metadata standards that cover the areas of activity outlined above.

RELs

RELs have evolved as an important means of specifying the rights that are applicable to a given piece of content. These rights may be bound to the content by specifying them within the metadata and that way they can persist in and travel with the content from producer to user via any number of intermediaries. Certain types of RELs have inbuilt capability to enforce the applicable content rights on a user's device or system. Also RELs are used provide the structure or syntax for expressing the rights, but the semantics or vocabulary may be organised and held separately in a rights data dictionary (RDD) with which it must work to provide the required rights management functionality. There are several RELs in existence today and they are easily identified by their rather arcane acronyms that usually include letters that represent 'markup language' or 'rights language'. Some of the major ones, mostly based on the eXtensible Markup Language (XML), are described briefly in the following sections. These have been sourced mainly from XML Cover Pages website (XML Cover Pages 2006) and updated as appropriate from other sources.

DPRL – Digital Property Rights Language

Probably one of the earliest DRM related rights languages, this was the rights specification language developed by Dr Mark Stefik at Xerox PARC in the 1990s. DPRL was based on the concept of 'trusted systems' and aimed to provide a way for these systems to implement the rights, access and usage permissions on digital content. It also relied on the idea of a digital repository that would store the protected content and the rights specification for its use. Overall, DPRL was designed with the following aims:

- To describe the rights, fees and conditions applicable to digital content.
- To provide standard terms for usage rights.
- To provide operational standards for use in checking compliance of trusted systems.
- To be flexible and extensible with inbuilt capability to incorporate new features in a controlled and non-disruptive fashion.
- To support multiple pricing models, for example, subscription-based, outright purchase, purchase of individual rights (view, print, copy, edit etc.), metered usage, time-based usage and membership pricing.

DPRL was based on XML syntax and used its element and attribute model to represent the usage rights specification on a piece of content. Today DPRL is not used much as a REL but has instead been supplanted by an offspring called XrML, which is described next. DPRL was, however, implemented by ContentGuard (a Xerox spin-off company) in a product suite, which included:

- **ContentGuard Publisher** – used to encrypt and change ordinary documents into Self-Protecting Documents (SPDs);
- **ContentGuard Marketplace** – an online storefront that integrated with ecommerce servers;
- **ContentGuard Rights Server** – for tracking and enforcing the rights on the SPDs;
- **ContentGuard software development kit (SDK)** – for developing applications that use or interact with DPRL and the SPDs.

XrML – eXtensible rights Markup Language (www.xrml.org)

A direct descendant of DPRL, XrML was developed in 2000 by the Xerox spin-off company ContentGuard and it has grown to become one of the most important competing 'standards' in this area. XrML is XML based and is a large and complex rights specification language that is used in many products and systems to specify the form and structure of the rights model without the implementation details. This is because different OSs or digital environments employ different methods to carry out the same action (e.g. 'play', 'copy', 'print' etc.), therefore XrML has to provide the command in a language that the system will understand and this is achieved by use of software called an 'interpreter', which does just that, that is, interpret XrML-based commands into a native form that can be implemented by the underlying system. This is very similar to the Java programming language from Sun Microsystems and works on different computing platforms. In addition XrML also includes the definition of security protocols and other information needed to make DRM work between trusted systems.

An XrML specification is usually located in the content's metadata and it includes a 'WORK' component that contains the rights information as sub-components such as OBJECT, CREATOR, CONTENTS, COPIES, SKU and RIGHTSGROUPS. The latter RIGHTSGROUPS, of which there may be several, specify the rights to be granted to each type or group of users ('Standard', 'Professional', 'Education' or 'Enterprise' etc.). Each RIGHTS-GROUP contains a RIGHTSLIST that holds the supported rights as shown in the example list of Table 5.1.

TABLE 5.1 *XrML rights elements*

Rights category	Rights	Description
Render rights	PLAY	One-off transient rendering of the content
	PRINT	Permanent rendition of the content
	EXPORT	Send out unprotected copy of the content
	VIEW	Similar to PLAY but better suited for visual content such as images
Transport rights*	COPY	Create another copy of the document
	TRANSFER	Move the document from one repository to another
	LOAN	Copy the document to another repository and disable the original until the copy has 'expired' on the other system
Derivative works rights*	EXTRACT	Create a new work from a portion of the original with its own separate XrML document for inclusion into another work
	EDIT	Permits the modification of the extracted content
	EMBED	Explicitly permits the embedding of the extracted content into a new composite work
File management rights	BACKUP	Permits the creation of a backup copy of the content
	RESTORE	Permits the restoration of the backup copies of content

(continued)

TABLE 5.1 *(continued)*

Rights category	Rights	Description
	VERIFY	Allows verification of the content by another program
	FOLDER	Allows the specification of permissions or rights over a repository structure that maps onto the target system's file structure; this right can override individual file settings
	DIRECTORY	Permits the listing of the repository content
	DELETE	Allows the deletion of the protected file
Configuration rights	INSTALL	Install software on secure systems or repositories
	UNINSTALL	Uninstall software from secure systems or repositories

*The 'Transport' and 'Derivative works' rights have an optional **clause** called NEXTRIGHTS that is used to specify the rights (added, reduced or modified from the original set) to be passed on when a copy of the content is forwarded to another entity's 'File management', as in superdistribution.

Each right in the RIGHTSLIST has a set of attributes, or terms and conditions, associated with it that defines the extent (including constraints) to which the rights may be exercised. They cover the following areas:

- access – specifies who can exercise the right and how they can be identified;
- time and duration – specifies the applicable period of time for that right;
- location – specifies geo-spatial or 'cyber-spatial' territorial constraints;
- consideration – specifies the transaction required for exercising the right.

XrML also supports watermarking and content or usage tracking by means of a property called WATERMARKING through which it can supply necessary information to a watermarking program if required. The TRACK property enables the monitoring of any content, rights or their usage through an appropriate logging mechanism on the system. All of these capabilities make XrML a heavyweight REL that has a significant footprint on the host system, in comparison to its main competitor Open Digital Rights Language (ODRL), which is discussed separately below.

The above description is a very high-level overview of XrML and further information including the full specification of the language may be found at: http://www.xrml.org or http://www.contentguard.com (the latter organisation owns and controls Xerox's patents on DPRL and XrML).

XrML is a fully featured REL and has been widely adopted by industry heavyweights such as Microsoft, which owns some equity stake in ContentGuard, and the Moving Picture Experts Group (MPEG) who have adopted it for the MPEG REL (which is described next). As of the time of writing XrML is very much alive and competing to be the single universal REL standard. However, the fact that it is controlled by ContentGuard and is not a truly open standard may give some individuals, groups and organisations pause for thought in deciding whether to adopt it. According to http://www.xrml.org the specification is now frozen at version 2.0 in order to maintain a stable base from which organisations can develop future implementations and standards.

MPEG REL – Moving Picture Experts Group (http://www.chiariglione.org/mpeg/)

MPEG is a working group of the International Organization for Standardization (ISO) in charge of the development of international standards for multimedia content formats. According to its chairman's website (http://www.chiariglione.org/mpeg/) the group was established in 1988 and it consists of a large international committee of experts, researchers and engineers in various and related fields of video, audio and technology. This group was responsible for developing various standards including the award-winning MPEG-1 and MPEG-2 standards that are used in CD-ROM, DVD and digital television today. Their list of standards includes the following:

- **MPEG-1.** Officially designated as ISO/IEC 11172, in five parts, this is a standard for the storage and retrieval of moving pictures and audio on storage media. It is widely used for storing video and audio on the internet and in millions of video CDs (VCDs).
- **MPEG-2.** Also officially designated as ISO/IEC 13818, in nine parts, this is the standard for digital television and was very useful in helping to transition the satellite broadcasting and cable television industries from analogue to digital. Hundreds of millions of STBs incorporate MPEG-2 decoders.
- **MPEG-4.** Officially designated as ISO/IEC 14496 this standard built on the work done in the areas of: digital television, interactive graphic applications (e.g. animation) and online multimedia. It also provided the technology elements that enable the integration of production, distribution and content access in those areas.
- **MPEG-7.** This is a content representation standard for information search and its first version was completed in 2001.
- **MPEG-21.** This is a multimedia framework standard that is still currently under development with different parts being completed in phases. According to ISO (2006a) the vision of this to-be standard is to 'enable transparent and augmented use of multimedia

resources across a wide range of networks and devices used by different communities'.

The latter MPEG-21 standard is of particular interest because among its various parts it has some significant work on DRM related aspects such as the REL and RDD (i.e. in parts 5 and 6 respectively). As part of its process the MPEG selected XrML among a field of other prospective RELs as the basis for their MPEG REL standard.

The basic MPEG-21 architecture revolves around the concept of a 'digital item'. This item represents a structured digital object with standard representation, identification and metadata, and it forms the basic unit of transaction in the MPEG-21 framework. Essentially the digital item is a combination of digital content, its metadata and structure (including relationships with other objects). Part 5 of the MPEG-21 standard defines the ISO MPEG REL as

> an XML-based language for expressing rights related to the use and distribution of digital content as well as access to services (Chiariglione 2006)

and part 6 describes the RDD as

> a Rights Data Dictionary which comprises a set of clear, consistent, structured, integrated and uniquely identified terms to support the MPEG-21 Rights Expression Language (REL), IEC 21000-5 (Chiariglione 2006)

The key elements of the REL are as follows:

- **Principal.** The entity to which the right is granted. This principal must be identifiable via some authentication mechanism.
- **Resource.** The object to which a principal can be granted a right. This includes digital works (e.g. audio, video, ebook or image), a service or information (e.g. an email address).
- **Rights.** This is granted to the principal to be exercised against some resource, under some condition. It specifies the action that may be performed on / using the resource.
- **Condition.** Specifies the terms, conditions and obligations under which rights can be exercised.

ODRL – Open Digital Rights Language (http://www.odrl.net)

ODRL is an XML-based rights expression language that provides a lightweight formal mechanism for specifying rights independently of the content type and transport mechanism. As the name implies, ODRL is free of licensing restrictions unlike its major competitor XrML. ODRL was created by Renato Ianella and a team of engineers at IPR Systems Ltd, an Australian technology company, during 2000 and formally released as ODRL v1.0 specification in November 2001. The following year ODRL v1.1 was endorsed by the Open Mobile Alliance (OMA) as their preferred rights language and this put it into the mainstream right alongside XrML as a prime REL. In 2003 ODRL v1.1 was also chosen by the OMA and several telecom products and services companies such as Nokia, Samsung, Sony-Ericsson and Vodafone to protect copyright-protected content over the 3G networks. The education community also joined the bandwagon in 2003 by developing rights solutions based on ODRL and CC licensing. This Joint Information Systems Committee (JISC) funded project called RoMEO (Rights Metadata for Open Archiving) was aimed at protecting the integrity of academic and research papers in an open environment. This was accomplished by an interoperable set of metadata elements and methods of incorporating the rights elements into document metadata processed by the Open Archives Initiative Protocol for Metadata Harvesting (OAI-PMH).

Compared with XrML, ODRL is lighter and more immediately applicable to media transactions. It has a concise and compact rights modelling schema that affords it a much smaller footprint on enabled devices, which is an important consideration for mobile technology. The language constructs used are similar and reflect the rights components described in earlier sections of this chapter, some examples of which are listed below:

- permissions – corresponds to the Render, Transport and Derivative works rights categories of Table 5.1;
- constraints – reflects the rights attributes that describe the extent to which the right and permissions can be used;
- requirements – translates to the consideration including fees and other exchanges that are needed for the right to be exercised.

ODRL has positioned itself very well as an open standards-based REL that can be used to model rights in any domain by developing a standard profile for that domain. According to the ODRL web page at http://xml.coverpages.org/odrl.html:

> ODRL Profiles were first announced at the ODRL International Workshop in April in Vienna (2004), as a formal means of showing how to use ODRL in specific technical environments. Profile Working Groups have now been formed to create ODRL Profiles for Geospatial Data, for Dublin Core Metadata Initiative (DCMI) encoding, and for Creative Commons (CC) licenses (XML Cover Pages 2006)

This latter profile is designed to describe the semantics of the CC licences and define how they can be represented by extending ODRL via an XML schema. For example, the CC Reproduction Licence, which includes the right to copy and convert the work into another format, can be directly mapped to ODRL's Play, Display, Execute and Print Permissions. However, the CC 'Distribution' licence, which includes rights to distribute, display or perform a work publicly (including digital formats such as webcasting), are new semantics that have been captured in the ODRL/CC Profile. These and other developments just go to show the viability of ODRL as a bona-fide candidate standard in the race for a single standard REL for interoperable DRM.

OMA DRM REL (http://www.openmobilealliance.org)

The OMA is a consortium of the mobile and wireless industry, which is focused on standards and collaborative interworking. The OMA is responsible for successfully creating the comprehensive OMA DRM framework, which boasts by far the most comprehensive multi-vendor DRM community among its ranks. OMA DRM is based on ODRL and just like CC, the OMA DRM REL v2.0 is also defined as a mobile profile of the ODRL. This could be attributed to the concise and compact feature of the language, which is very appealing to the mobile products and services industry.

The OMA DRM 1.0 Enabler Release was developed and published in 2002, and rapidly implemented by mobile product vendors, in order to address the requirements of this market. The release included three levels of functionality as follows:

(i)   **forward lock** – prevents the forwarding of content from the device;

(ii)   **combined delivery** – adds rights definition;

(iii)   **separate delivery** – provides content encryption and supports superdistribution.

The third functionality was designed to protect higher-value content and to enable superdistribution, whereby the device can be used to forward content but not the usage rights, which are sent via a separate channel. The subsequent OMA DRM 2.0 Enabler Release in 2004 was designed to use additional features and functionality of modern mobile devices and supports streaming content, multi-device access to protected content, as well as improved audio and video rendering.

XACML – eXtensible Access Control Markup Language (http://www.oasis-open.org)

This REL is more applicable to enterprise content protection and its related field of E-DRM (which is described in Chapter 9). The eXtensible Access Control Markup Language (XACML) was released and approved to become an OASIS (Organization for the Advancement of Structured Information Standards) standard in February 2003. It started life as part of the search for security standards for web services (WS) and is functionally related to various authorisation and policy-based access control mechanisms such as the Security Assertion Markup Language (SAML). XACML primarily tries to address the need for a standard framework that can be used to establish trust relationships between unknown parties via trust negotiations. It is based on XML and has extensible rights and access management functionality designed to provide flexible control of the various types of access rights to digital objects. XACML is perceived as a significant step towards standardising a language for security policies and access decisions.

PRL – PRISM Rights Language (http://www.prismstandard.org/)

PRISM (Publishing Requirements for Industry Standard Metadata) is an extensible XML metadata standard for syndicating, aggregating, post-processing and multi-purposing content from magazines, news, catalogues, books and mainstream journals. The PRISM Rights Language (PRL) provides elements and controlled vocabularies for describing the rights and permissions granted to the receiver of content. It is intended to facilitate reuse and clearance processes for parties with established business relationships by explicitly specifying the rights and restrictions connected with a resource. PRISM PRL works by evaluating a collection of PRL statements known collectively as a PRL expression in order to determine whether a party has the necessary permissions to make use of a resource in a particular way. It is important to note the following limitations on PRISM and PRL:

- PRISM is **not** concerned with digital rights enforcement;
- PRISM does not specify policy or provide instructions to trusted viewers and repositories on how they should behave;
- PRISM also does not specify fee or payment details.

PRL was basically created by the working group as an interim measure that would provide the rights and permission vocabulary for the publishing industry until a common interoperable DRM REL standard is agreed (e.g. XrML or ODRL). According to the XML Cover Pages, the design goals of these rights and permissions are as follows:

- to be able to describe reuse rights in a precise and consistent manner;
- to make simple cases such as no rights or unrestricted use simple to specify;
- to provide the capability to indicate common types of uses or restriction;
- to allow for graceful evolution to future accepted standards for specifying rights.

XMCL – eXtensible Media Commerce Language (http://www.xmcl.org/)

This REL (included here only for completeness) was created by RealNetworks as an alternative to XrML and although it was submitted to the World Wide Web Consortium (W3C) as a prospective standard, it failed to gain much traction thereafter.

Superdistribution

As an example of the use of a REL to represent and specify the underlying content business model within a DRM system, the superdistribution model is perfectly suited to highlight the important requirements from the perspective of the business, technology, security and usability aspects that need to be addressed in a DRM system. The excerpt below is a portion of the requirements for the MPEG-21 REL and RDD taken from the Internet Engineering Task Force (IETF) website (IETF 2006):

> 2.6.15 Superdistribution
>
> Requirement: The RDD-REL shall support superdistribution of Digital Items in terms of associating the same or different sets of rights, conditions, and obligations for the superdistributed Digital Items.
>
> Note: Original users retain rights granted to them, and new users are required to acquire rights granted to them.
>
> Example: Information on where rights are offered can be used to refer new users of a Digital Item to acquire rights for themselves. In order to issue different sets of rights, use different usage/business models for new users.

This encapsulates the capabilities that must be enabled by the MPEG-21 RDD and REL in implementing the DRM system. The subtleties and complexities of achieving these requirements are many and some of them (e.g. enabling different business models for different users) are discussed in the next section, which talks about various DRM issues.

DRM ISSUES AND LIMITATIONS

There are several issues that still need to be addressed by DRM solutions and these have not been made any easier by the fact that they exist in the consumer space and cut across several domains, industries and stakeholder interests. Some of the major issues are outlined below.

User experience

This is perhaps the biggest hurdle that most DRM systems need to overcome because unless consumers are willing to adopt and use DRM-protected content in their daily content consumption it will remain the unenviable responsibility of content providers and owners, legal and legislative mechanisms and technology and trade associations or standards bodies to try and force the issue. Some of the main areas to be addressed before users can be expected to endorse and willingly adopt this technology are described in the following.

Usability

Most DRM implementations currently intrude into the whole consumer experience of purchasing and using content and this can be quite off-putting to customers. As far as many consumers are concerned 'good DRM is invisible DRM', therefore those business models that rely on features such as superdistribution need to be implemented in such a way that the prompt (or 'nag') to purchase forwarded content is kept in line with (if not actually enhancing) the user experience.

Interoperability

Users want to be able to play their content anywhere, any time and on any device. In many cases DRM-protected content cannot be used on all of the consumer's devices and this becomes an incentive for hackers to try and crack the protection. For example, in 2006 the 'unlocking' of Apple's iPod to enable it play music from other download stores by DeCSS hacker Jon Lech Johansen may be considered a step in the right direction by both Apple's competitors and online music consumers.

Privacy concerns

Users think DRM is an invasion of their privacy (to do whatever they want, in the privacy of their homes, with their bought and paid-for content). However, this privacy concern may be more applicable to physical media bound content than untethered digital content because an internet connection effectively means that the cyberworld is open for business even inside the user's home.

Perception

DRM is often perceived by some end-users to be more of an anti-piracy tool than an enabler of both old and new content business models. This perception is enhanced by the established content industry's wholesale backing of 'protective measures' for their precious content at the expense of usability and the opportunity for technology-enhanced business processes and services.

143

Social issues

This Includes addressing DRM's limitations in the various social and contextual usage situations that users may encounter such as divorce, marriage, inheritance, transfer, first sale etc. The consumer is not a static entity with a profile that can be sold the same thing over and over again. They tend to change in preferences and circumstances, therefore a successful DRM-enabled model must be flexible and adaptable to the user's changing needs.

Business models

As hinted in the 'Social issues' point above, digital technology operates in a precise manner that makes it extremely difficult to capture and represent the many complexities and subtleties of real-world business models such as those described in the earlier section on rights-enabled business models. The major limitations that, if addressed properly, could prove to the biggest selling point for DRM systems include the following.

Dynamic model support

This has been touched on in some of the previous sections. Basically if the protected content can be presented under different business models to different users, it would be more applicable to real-world dynamic business and social environments than the restricted synthetic digital models foisted on end consumers. This is unsatisfactory mostly because both businesses and consumers are forced to adapt to a technology-influenced reality.

Flexible pricing

This is an adjunct to the above dynamic model support limitation. It covers an area that is well established in certain industries such as air travel and hospitality, where depending on the time or purchase; type and profile of customer (e.g. regulars); and the prevailing business circumstances, the prices for the same service can vary tremendously. DRM has an innate ability to support this especially when linked with usage and rights tracking, which is discussed next.

Usage and tracking

It is extremely difficult to capture and model all of the actual uses of content, as well as the various intentions of the user. For example, certain business models allow for different rights or prices for the content depending on context of use (such as different rights or prices for commercial and non-commercial use of the content). Also fair use and other copyright exceptions make it necessary to understand the intention of the user before an unauthorised activity can be recognised and prohibited by the system. Other related issues include user and device identification, as well as privacy concerns raised by tracking the user's activities on the system. Undoubtedly DRM and digital technology are extremely well suited to providing usage and tracking features, but extremely poor (in so far as the abilities of the modeller) in making qualitative judgements as to the intentions or implications of the user's activities. The positive aspect to this is that both the usage and tracking features can become the enablers of many desirable features such as flexible pricing and business model support to the mutual benefit of the consumer and the business.

The analogue hole

This refers to the gap that exists between the digital content in its DRM-protected state and its rendition in the analogue format necessary for human consumption. As analogue creatures, humans require a translation of the digital 1s and 0s in a content file (e.g. music, video, speech etc.) into a form that is perceptible to us. This is usually output in 'clear' analogue format and nothing prevents anyone from capturing the admittedly lower-quality or degraded output and re-encoding this into an unprotected digital form – which can then be copied and distributed. The reality of this particular issue is demonstrated by the screenshot in Figure 5.2.

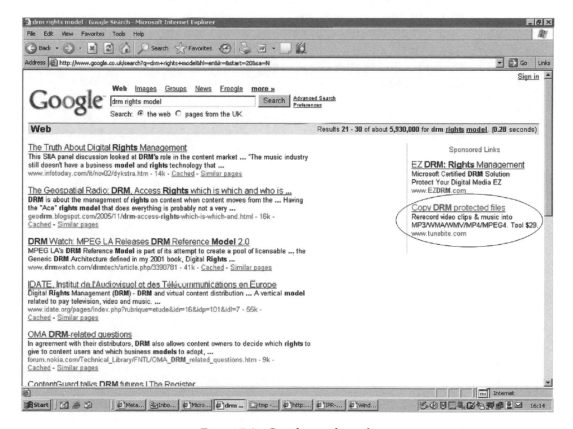

FIGURE 5.2 *Google search result*

The circled sponsored link on the right leads to a website that has the following statement:

> Tunebite Platinum legally converts DRM copy-protected music, audio books and video clips in formats like WMA, M4P, AAC, M4B, WMV and M4V into unprotected MP3, OGG, WMA, WMV and MPEG4 files by recording them while they are being played (Tunebite 2006)

In other words this outfit sells software that can copy DRM-protected files by capturing the content when it falls into the analogue hole (i.e. during playing).

CONCLUSION

In this chapter we have looked at the concept of rights and examined the components and examples of rights models and various rights-enabled business models. We have also explored the representation of the models using the REL and presented an example requirement for superdistribution. Finally, there was a brief look at some of the major limitations and issues to be addressed by DRM systems. In the next chapter we discuss the technologies that come together to form the DRM systems we have discussed here.

6 DRM Technologies

DRM is the term used to describe the collection of technologies and standards that combine to provide some control over the access to and usage of content both within and outside a digital environment. As discussed earlier, DRM's main objective, at least in the world of media and entertainment, is to protect the content and to enable the monetisation of that content. This chapter explores those technologies that combine to make up the various DRM solutions in existence today. It begins by exploring the various component technologies that deliver the ability to protect the content and control various activities that can be performed on it including access. The next section then looks at the core reference architecture of DRM systems and examines common components and services that provide the required functionality for a complete end-to-end DRM system. Finally, we conclude with an overview of the whole DRM ecosystem, which provides a context for DRM and how it fits into the various systems commonly found in the content provider, enterprise and consumer environments. This 'bottom-up' approach (i.e. moving from components to architecture to context) is a deliberate departure from the traditional 'top-down' model found in many architectural methods and is used to highlight the fact that DRM is not a single and comprehensive technology, but an arrangement of discrete (or standalone) capabilities that can be combined to provide the desired functionality. Also, because the previous chapters have set the wider context of DRM, this chapter focuses on the technologies that make up DRM and its ecosystem as well as the issues they bring.

One major thing to always bear in mind is that DRM also covers content usage and access permissions outside the digital domain, and this presents a particular challenge to the digital technologies used, because the analogue world is filled with relativity and approximations that are opposite to the precise nature of DRM's digital 1s and 0s. Other challenges include accurate user identification, encryption and content protection solution issues (such as 'break once, break everywhere'), as well as the need for a dynamic and predictive permissions modelling capability to cater for the ever-changing relationships of the content provider and consumer. The following sections delve into these issues as they are encountered under the appropriate headings.

CONTENT AND COPY PROTECTION AND ACCESS CONTROL

The majority of people tend to associate DRM with protection and access restrictions on content and this is mainly due to the use of encryption to protect and secure the digital content. This section provides an overview of cryptography, encryption and their application in the field of DRM, as well as a brief look into the related area of CA.

Cryptography: overview

This section provides an overview of modern cryptography, a subject with a long military history but which is also firmly grounded in the mathematics that provides the necessary difficult problems (e.g. factoring large numbers) upon which many cryptographic applications and techniques depend. Cryptography consists of many components and may be defined as follows.

Definition

> Cryptography is primarily concerned with keeping information private. This is normally achieved via several mechanisms such as: the encryption engine, the keying information and operational procedures, that all work together in what is known as a cryptographic system or cryptosystem (Cobb 2004)

Cryptanalysis is concerned with the ways to break cryptographic systems and together with cryptography makes up the field of study called cryptology. Encryption is the process of transforming a piece of information, which is known as the 'plaintext', into a form that is unintelligible without the use of a special key. The encrypted message is usually referred to as the 'ciphertext' even though the protected message may not be text-only information (e.g. audio, video etc. files are also referred to as plaintext and ciphertext in cryptology). Decryption is the opposite process of transforming encrypted information back into its original form. The encryption key is usually made up of a complex sequence of characters that is used to convert the plaintext to ciphertext (or the reverse in the case of decryption). Obviously the longer the length of the key, the more difficult it would be to 'guess' the value as is done in so-called 'brute force' attacks. The key is a vital part of a cryptographic system and the secure exchange of keys between the message sender and receiver can present quite a challenge even for the most secure cryptosystems. The main issue is that the key has to be shared at some point with the recipient and could fall into the wrong hands during this process. So a whole field of sometimes quite elaborate key exchange strategies and protocols have developed over the years to address this issue.

Encryption algorithms

'An algorithm is a well-defined computational procedure that takes a variable input and generates a corresponding output' (Oppliger 2005). To put it simply, 'a cryptographic algorithm is the instruction set that is used to scramble and unscramble data in a cryptosystem' (Cobb 2004).

It sets out the logical steps to be used in encrypting the content, including key generation, which is then implemented as a program in the cryptosystem. The main differentiator for algorithms, which also determines how they are used, is based on whether a key is present and whether that key can be used to both encrypt and decrypt the same message (this latter aspect is referred to as key symmetry). These characteristics are briefly described as follows.

No-key algorithms

This class of algorithms does not use any key to encrypt data and its output is not normally decipherable. Examples of this include one-way functions, random bit generators and hashing functions (a hash function is a transformation that takes a variable size input or content and returns a fixed-size string, which is called the 'hash value' of the content). These algorithms use their characteristic one-way encryption to provide a 'fingerprint', signature or digest of the plaintext information. Figure 6.1 shows how this algorithm works (note that the plaintext message is not converted by this process).

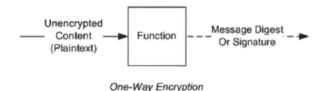

One-Way Encryption

FIGURE 6.1   *No-key algorithm (source: adapted from Oppliger (2005))*

Symmetric-key algorithms

Modern encryption methods use symmetric-key algorithms to implement the so-called 'secret-key' cryptography whereby both the sender and receiver of the encrypted message must have a copy of the same key that is used to encrypt and decrypt the data. This obviously means that the information will remain secure as long as the key remains a secret. Figure 6.2 shows how this algorithm works in a graphic format.

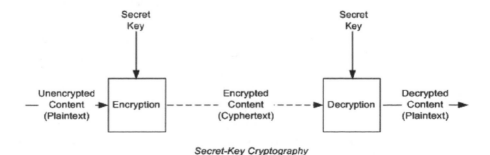

Secret-Key Cryptography

FIGURE 6.2   *Symmetric-key algorithm (source: adapted from Oppliger (2005))*

Asymmetric-key algorithms

The asymmetric-key algorithm, which is used to implement 'public-key' cryptography, is relatively more complex as it provides two separate keys, one of which is used by the sender to encrypt the data (the public key) and the other (the private key) is used by the receiver to decrypt the message. The private key must correspond mathematically to the public key used for encryption otherwise the output will be unintelligible, therefore both public and private keys are usually generated by the same encryption function for the same party who can then publish their public key whilst keeping their private key secret. The publicly available key can then be used by anyone to encrypt and send a message to the owner, secure in the knowledge that only the holder of the corresponding private key can decipher and access the content.

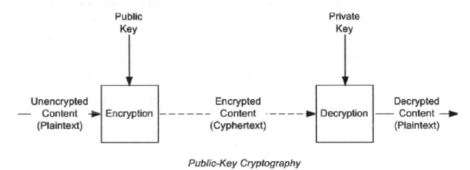

Public-Key Cryptography

Figure 6.3   *Asymmetric-key algorithm (source: adapted from Oppliger (2005))*

Another differentiating characteristic of the various algorithms is related to their mode of encryption as follows:

- **Stream ciphers.** This includes algorithms that encrypt data one bit at a time. They are usually quicker to process.
- **Block ciphers.** These encrypt only a specific block of data (e.g. 64 bits) at a time.

We outline and briefly describe some of the major cryptographic algorithms as well as their category based on the above factors as follows.

DES (Digital Encryption Standard) and 3DES (Triple DES)

This symmetric algorithm uses block encryption. Created in 1975, DES was one of the more popular encryption algorithms and became a standard in 1981. It uses a 56-bit encryption key and works by combining the key with the plaintext and reshuffling it around 16 times. Despite this, in 1999 DES was broken by brute force using a special computer. 3DES works by sequentially applying three different keys to encrypt data. The keys used can be longer than the 56-bit key of DES for even stronger protection. However, it can be slower than some other algorithms.

RC4 (Rivest Cipher 4)

This symmetric algorithm uses stream encryption. Developed by Ron Rivest for RSA in 1987, RC4 is a variable key-size stream algorithm based on random permutations and is used in the secure socket layer implementation in browsers.

RC5 (Rivest Cipher 5)

This symmetric algorithm uses block encryption. RC5 is a fast block algorithm created in 1994 by Rivest for RSA and it is designed to offer great flexibility with variable block size, key size and number of rounds.

MD2, MD4 and MD5 (Message Digest 2, 4 and 5)

These one-way algorithms were developed by Ron Rivest in 1989, 1990 and 1991 respectively. They are used for digital signature applications to compress a message of variable length into a 128-bit message digest or signature.

IDEA (International Data Encryption Algorithm)

This symmetric algorithm uses block encryption and has been implemented in the Pretty Good Privacy (PGP) program, which is an email encryption program that also uses other algorithm options. The IDEA uses a 128-bit key that is broken up into 56 sub-keys by a process of permutation and combination of the original 128-bit key in a very efficient process that means it can run faster than DES.

AES (Advanced Encryption Standard)

This is a symmetric algorithm using block encryption. It was selected from an entry to the NIST's (National Institute For Standards and Technology) AES competition, which ran from 1997 to 2000 when the winner (the Rijndael Algorithm) was chosen.

SHA-1 (Secure Hash Algorithm)

This one-way algorithm is used to create a message digest or fingerprint of data. It works by padding out the message with extra data and encrypting the result from which it takes a portion of the cipher as the signature of that message. This is very reliable for integrity checking because it can pick up even the smallest changes to the original data (which show up as a different hash value).

Blowfish and Twofish

These two symmetric algorithms use block encryption. Blowfish is a 64-bit block cipher developed by Bruce Schneier in the early-to-mid 1990s and it works by means of a series of key- or data-based permutations and substitutions on the data. Twofish, which was one of the AES contestants, is based on Blowfish.

RSA (Rivest, Shamir and Adelman)

This asymmetric algorithm is one of the most popular public-key cryptosystems and was invented in 1978 by Ron Rivest, Adi Shamir and Leonard Adleman. It works by using large prime numbers to create the public and private keys that can then be used to encrypt the message. The RSA FAQ (RSA Lab 2000) contains some good information on this and the website http://world.std.com/~franl/crypto/rsa-example.html gives an example.

DSA and DSS (Digital Signature Algorithm and Digital Signature Standard)

These are both asymmetric algorithms. DSS was selected in 1994 by NIST as the US government's digital signature authentication standard. DSA is only used to provide digital signatures and is based on the discrete logarithm problem that is described in the RSA FAQ as one of the types of hard problems used by public-key cryptography (RSA Lab 2000).

ECC (Elliptical Curve Cryptography)

This asymmetric algorithm was introduced in the mid-1980s and it is used to encrypt large amounts of data, usually for secure data storage. It is based on plotting the intersection points between several lines and an elliptical curve and may be referred to as the elliptic curve discrete logarithm problem.

Diffie–Hellman key-agreement protocol

This asymmetric key-exchange algorithm is a protocol invented in 1976 by Whitfield Diffie and Martin Hellman (also independently derived by Ralph Merkle), which is squarely aimed at addressing the issue of exchanging encryption keys in a non-secure environment. It works by allowing the correspondents (who may be unknown to each other) to generate a session key with which the sender can encrypt and send the message along with a temporary public key that the recipient uses to derive the session key and decrypt the message.

In the following we list some of the advantages and disadvantages of public-key versus secret-key cryptography.

- **Security.** Public-key cryptosystems are inherently more secure because there is no need to transmit the private key.
- **Non-repudiation.** Public-key cryptosystems can be used to provide an undeniable digital signature from the sender by encrypting it with their private key.
- **Speed.** Public-key cryptosystems are not renowned for their speed and the secret-key algorithms have a definite advantage in this category. Both systems are often combined to provide the best of

both worlds (i.e. security and speed) in what is known as the 'digital envelope' protocol.

- **Single-user environment.** Public-key cryptosystems may be overkill in this scenario and secret keys are more suited as there is no need to transmit keys.
- **Horses for courses.** Public-key cryptography was introduced to help secure the transmission of secret keys and it is still used primarily for this activity. It will not replace the secret-key system as they perfectly complement each other in the speed versus security trade-off; therefore it is usually a matter of using whichever type of algorithm is most suitable for the task at hand.

Modern cryptography has many uses and applications beyond the encryption and decryption of data. Some of these uses include authentication via digital signatures, access control to data, content and information, security for ecommerce transactions etc. As a subject cryptography is quite extensive and fascinating, and a variety of books have been published about it including Schneier's (1996) 'bible' of *Applied Cryptography*, which is widely referenced by experts and novices alike.

DRM applications of cryptography

This section outlines some of the ways in which cryptography can be employed to help protect content in DRM systems. It is only a high-level generic overview of the relevant encryption applications and does not cover the various implementations, which may differ significantly in the various DRM systems in existence.

To ensure content integrity

This is accomplished by use of one-way encryption functions, as described above, to create a unique fixed length digest of the content, which can then be used by the player device to verify that the content has not been tampered before it will render it.

To verify identity

Digital certificates can be used to establish the identity of the actors in a DRM system. According to the RSA FAQ:

> certification is a scheme by which trusted agents such as certifying authorities vouch for unknown agents, such as users. The trusted agents issue vouchers called certificates which each have some inherent meaning. Certification technology was developed to make identification and authentication possible on a large scale. (RSA Lab 2000)

This aim is accomplished by use of encryption techniques, and it obviously applies to DRM, which is used to provide protection to content that may be distributed globally.

To verify content and identity

Digital signatures are used to bind encrypted content to the owner of the signature. This is useful for establishing ownership of content and it also protects the content from tampering as this would invalidate the signature. Signatures are usually created from the content owner's private key thereby ensuring that their public key establishes their identity.

Public Key Infrastructure (PKI)

This has been included here to emphasise the complex nature of the cryptography element in DRM. Basically PKI is made up of several components, standards, services and protocols that work together to support the various applications of public-key cryptography (such as implementing the trust models of DRM systems and services). It includes components such as the public-key cryptosystem, the certification authority or trusted third party (TTP) and the authorisation and authentication services, which we discuss later in this chapter. The main job of the certification authority is to provide certificates that effectively authenticate a user and, in some cases, also specify the rights and authorisation they have over the content. Typically the certificate is sent to a licence server that then proceeds to create and send the licence key to unlock the authorised functionality over the content. The latter process is covered in more detail under the 'DRM reference architecture' section.

The rest of this section is devoted to some of the other content protection and access control technologies or mechanisms that may or may not include a cryptography component, but nonetheless provide some level of protection and control over the content or the access to it.

Fingerprinting

This technology is used to identify a digital file by a digital fingerprint, which is created from inherent characteristics such as the length, time, size and other specific qualities of the content. This technology does not really qualify as DRM, but it is most applicable in situations where it may be necessary to identify digital content in the wild such as with music discovery services. In fact several providers of audio fingerprint services and products already exist, notably Shazzam, Gracenote, Snocap, MusicIP and Audible Magic. Some of the music identification and recognition services offered can be used to enable various types of business models ranging from online music catalogues to music recognition and recommendation engines for mobile phone services.

Some major features of fingerprinting that differentiate it from other mechanisms such as encryption or watermarking include:

- the fingerprint is created by the extraction of information from the material;
- fingerprints need to be created for each piece of material;
- fingerprinting can only identify the material and cannot differentiate between individual copies;
- fingerprinting can be applied to pre-existing content;
- fingerprinting does not encrypt content or embed any information into it;
- fingerprinting does not need to be updated.

Watermarking

Watermarking is the term used to describe the practice of embedding certain information into the media content. The data thus embedded may be used for identification of the content and could be perceptible or imperceptible to the casual observer, but in all cases it is more or less inextricably linked to the content in which it is embedded. This means that watermarking can be used on a wide range of products with features that range from the highly visible brand identification markers, to completely hidden and sometimes encrypted information in a manner similar to steganography.

Steganography

Steganography, or stego, is the art of concealing private or sensitive information within a carrier that for all intents and purposes appears innocuous. It originates from the Greek words for 'covered writing' and relies on the fact that human perception is not particularly efficient at detecting hidden patterns in the seemingly innocuous bits of noise in a given media. Although steganography may sometimes be confused with cryptography since they are both used to protect information, they are not the same thing because:

> steganography is concerned with concealing information thereby making it unseen while cryptography is concerned with encrypting information thereby making it unreadable (McGill 2005)

Some characteristics that both describe and differentiate watermarking from other protection mechanisms such as encryption and fingerprinting include:

- watermarks embed information into the material prior to distribution (usually during the creation of the content or its copies);
- watermarks can be used to identify every single instance or copy of the content and they can be read (or edited) using special devices or software;
- good watermarking does not detract from the experience of the media;
- watermarks are robust enough to survive translation into other media formats and are normally resistant to alteration or removal;
- the watermarks may be used to contain identifying or rights management information and in these cases may also be encrypted for added security;
- watermarks are increasingly being used in association with DRM applications to convey encrypted rights metadata or authorisation for the content and under these conditions they need to be easy to read or edit by the rendering device in order to be considered usable.

Applications of watermarking in DRM include visible identifiers (e.g. brand logos in stock photos or broadcast footage) and invisible watermark 'tags' for auditing and monitoring of content usage and which can be extended to include metadata information. The Europe4DRM website at http://www.europe4drm.com/demos/hp_demo/0.htm has a good demonstration of watermarking on an image file. Also the combination of watermark and encryption helps provide DRM systems with several levels of protection for the content and these are usually implemented in one of three ways:

- **Plain file, encrypted watermark.** This scheme provides the verification for ownership of the content and may include timestamps and other metadata that can be used by rendering devices to enforce the rights.
- **Encrypted file, plain watermark.** This scheme provides the dual advantage of content protection and content identification and usage monitoring.
- **Encrypted file, encrypted watermark.** This scheme combines the above schemes to provide possibly the most secure form of content protection and can be implemented to interact with the rendering device to enforce the rights associated with the content, monitor content and provide usage tracking data to the provider.

Other copy-protection technologies

Various other technological schemes, protocols and techniques exist for implementing copy protection across various media and formats, and some of the more relevant methods are briefly outlined in the following sections. These copy-protection methods and several others are described to various extents in Van Tassel's (2006) excellent book on DRM content protection and monetisation.

CSS

This system used a weak 40-bit encryption algorithm to encrypt DVD content and it uses several encryption keys to implement a series of authentication steps on the DVD player before it will play the disc. The DVDCCAA is the non-profit organisation responsible for licensing CSS to DVD disc and device manufacturers. This system was famously cracked by Jon Lech Johansen's DeCSS program around the year 1999.

AACS (Advanced Access Content System)

This scheme uses 128-bit AES encryption to protect the content along with advanced functionality such as a key management system that can provide services such as key renewal and revocation. It offers these services through a licensing authority called the AACS-LA and its website at http://www.aacsla.com provides further details. However, in January 2006 Jon Lech Johansen posted a provocative statement on his blog at http://www.nanocrew.net about how initiatives such as CSS and AACS are primarily aimed at controlling the market for players and suggested that AACS will also be broken by spring 2007 (Johansen 2006).

CGMS (Copy Generation Management Systems)

This allows the content provider to assert different levels of copy limitation to their product by inserting two bits that specify whether the copy is unlimited copies, unlimited single generation copy only (no copy of copies), single copy per original file only or totally restricted (i.e. no copies whatsoever). CGMS comes in two forms that address analogue (CGMS-A) and digital (CGMS-D) copies.

ExCCI (Extended Copy Control Instruction)

This is often regarded as the film studios DRM. This scheme uses a more complex copy control instruction set than CGMS to specify the permissible activities (and the extent to which they apply) on audiovisual content.

SCMS (Serial Copy Management System)

This was an initiative by the recording industry to prevent digitally perfect copies of content from digital formats such as MiniDisc or DAT. It allows unlimited first-generation copies but degrades or prevents subsequent replication of those copies.

CPPM (Copy Control for Pre-recorded Media)

This scheme was developed and owned by a group of companies under an umbrella organisation called the License Management International Inc. (http://www.lmicp.com) and it is used to provide and enforce copy protection for pre-recorded DVD-Audio. It is similar to and can work in conjunction with CSS. However, in July 2005 it was claimed to have been circumvented, just like CSS:

> but this time by exploiting the analogue hole that allowed the rendering audio stream to be saved as an unencrypted .WAV file format on the hard drive (Fisher 2005)

CPRM (Copy Control for Recorded Media)

Developed and owned by the 4C Entity (http://www.4centity.com), this technology provides and enforces copy protection on recordable digital media via the CPRM-enabled recording devices. It works by encrypting and binding any protected content that is recorded onto a disc such that any subsequent copying onto another blank disc will not be readable because the new disc ID will not match the original.

DTCP (Digital Transmission Content Protection)

This system originated from a call by the Consumer Electronics Association (CEA) for a digital copy protection system (DCPS) that could prevent the copying of content in transit between players or source devices (e.g. DVD players, STBs and HD devices) to their destination rendering or recording devices (e.g. DVD recorders or digital TVs etc.). This effectively protects content even within the so-called home entertainment network (HEN) of connected media devices by forcing them to authenticate each other via certificates and establish secure transmission between each other. These certificates are provided by the Digital Transmission Licensing Authority (DTLA) to device manufacturers that wish to license DTCP and the scheme also provides for key renewal and revocation.

HDCP (High-Bandwidth Digital Content Protection)

Similar to DTCP but geared more towards the HD content and device market this scheme employs similar key exchange and secure content transmission protocols along with key renewal and revocation etc. It also uses a licensing authority called the Digital Content Protection LLC to provide licences to equipment manufacturers that wish to incorporate HDCP into their products. This applies to virtually all high-bandwidth player and recorder devices produced since 2003.

CPSA (Content Protection Security Architecture)

This architecture framework was developed by the 4C Entity as an overarching guide and specification for the end-to-end content and transmission protection system, between linked consumer devices in the home. It was based around policies and watermark and encryption technologies and described via 11 architectural axioms covering areas such as content and access management, as well as transmission, playback and copy controls. Figure 6.4 taken from the draft CPSA document (4C Entity 2000) shows the digital content protection chain.

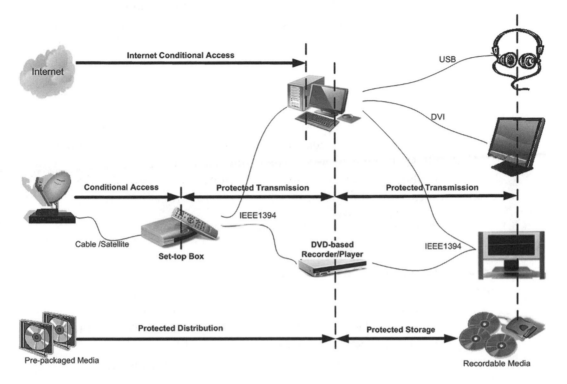

FIGURE 6.4   *Digital content protection chain*
(source: Derived from 4C Entity's Draft CPSA)

Conditional access (CA)

CA technologies are primarily used to restrict access to content unless a predefined condition has been met such as a fully paid-up subscription or membership that entitles the subscriber to view the content. It is traditionally linked to the paid broadcast services such as cable, satellite and digital TV and almost all other content provision services that require the use of a STB or other similar device. It supports various business models such as pay-per view, subscription, VOD and streaming media-based services. A generic CA system works by sending a scrambled signal along with encrypted authorisation information from the head-end (transmitter) to the client's STB, which has a signal descrambler and security module that unscrambles the signal and enables access only to the content and channels with the appropriate authorisation. Authorisation is based on the provided services or bundles that have been selected by an authenticated subscriber. The process of authentication and subscription management is normally handled outside the provision and content delivery channel and it usually involves a smartcard- or software-based client that holds the user identity as well as the decryption keys that are used to read the authorisation data and to unscramble the content signal. This arrangement requires a reliable connection to the network not only to receive the content signal and authorisation, but also to provide regular system updates and key refreshes necessary to maintain the security and integrity of the system. Digital satellite and cable operators such as BSkyB or VirginMedia also require a constant connection to facilitate the interactive services they offer.

The main difference between CA and DRM is in the scope of content and access protection offered by the respective systems. Basically CA technology only restricts access to content before it reaches the subscriber or external environment (i.e. in the pre-content acquisition phase), while DRM systems offer persistent protection of content even in the hostile environments that may exist outside of the provider–subscriber systems (i.e. the post-content acquisition phase). Table 6.1 outlines some of the differences between CA and DRM.

TABLE 6.1 *Conditional access versus digital rights management*

Features	CA	DRM
Protection phase	Pre-content acquisition	Post-content acquisition
Type of content	Protects pay TV, primarily live content (also applicable to streamed content). Used to secure a high percentage of pay-TV revenues	Protects audio, video, image, text and multi-format documents (primarily downloadable content)
Target media devices	Primarily television	PCs and mobile phones
Supported business models	Subscription-based and on-demand services	Includes paid downloads and pay-per-view or pay-per-listen models with flexible price, e.g.: • £ for 1 time; • ££ for N times; • £££ for copying; • ££££ for CD or DVD burning. All with or without time and other restrictions
Anti-piracy measures	Mainly hardware-based security	Mostly software-based security
Solution security design	Traditionally linked to MPEG2-TS transport layer	Linked to content type and encoding format
Client	Embedded software library and dedicated component (in decoder or smartcard)	Application, plug-in or OS level and integrated into a player
Standards	Coexistence of minimal standardisation with proprietary elements	Fully proprietary (e.g. Windows DRM) on PCs or fully standardised systems (e.g. OMA DRM) on mobile phones

It may appear from the above that CA and DRM systems represent competing content-protection schemes and in fact several debates have been held on this very topic at international conferences, some of which were moderated by this author, but the truth is that they can and do actually coexist in a unified end-to-end protection scenario. This has become increasingly evident with the trend towards convergence in consumer devices (e.g. personal video recorder (PVR) or PC), content services (IPTV and mobile TV) and with newer usage configurations such as the HEN in Figure 6.5, as well as a move towards user-bound rights and authentication, as opposed to device-based rights and authentication mechanisms.

Figure 6.5 *Devices for the home entertainment network*

Other access protection technologies include the following:

- **Regional Protection Control (RPC).** This is used mostly to support the traditional film entertainment business models, which rely on various release windows and schedules around the world. In this way a DVD bought in one region is encoded with a regional mark that prevents it from being played on devices bought from another region. This has resulted in the creation of region-free players and other hacks that can be used by the consumer to get around these restrictions.
- **Restricted DVDs.** These included DivX-encoded discs that allowed only a specific number of plays before they stopped working (required a player that could read and enforce this restriction). Another example was the EZ-D self-destructing DVDs that decayed over a couple of days once opened. Needless to say these technologies have not found much traction with consumers.

Analogue protection technology

The main problem with digital content protection is that it does not work so well in the analogue world, as discussed in the previous chapter. This is primarily due to the 'analogue hole' that is present whenever decrypted digital content is converted and rendered in the analogue form necessary for human consumption and through which it may be easily copied and redigitised in the clear (or non-protected form). However, certain technologies and vendors have evolved to address this issue and examples of successful operators in this space include Macrovision with their Analog Copy Protection (ACP) technology. This technology works in DVDs by incorporating certain protection activation information during the DVD authoring process that can trigger the ACP circuitry that is embedded in most DVD players and video cards. The effect of this is to disable, or heavily distort, the recordable signal of the player device thereby making any copies unusable. This solution requires the continued support of device manufacturers to include the required ACP circuit as well as the insertion of the triggering information by DVD content authors in order to work effectively. However, because this initiative was championed by the content owners themselves and held up as a requirement before they would release their content to DVD, there is no immediate danger that this type of protection will cease anytime soon.

DRM REFERENCE ARCHITECTURE (HIGH-LEVEL EXAMPLE)

DRM technology is based around a simple set of core service components that form a reference architecture upon which the various solutions can be built and this is best illustrated in the high-level logical reference architecture diagram in Figure 6.6 and which has been adapted from the work by Rosenblatt et al. (2002). It is important to note that this is a high-level architectural example and actual implemented systems may differ greatly in both the component groups and details used. This is because many technology solutions that fall under the umbrella term of DRM actually tend to focus on those particular aspects that meet their business and technology strategies. Therefore this example will not be looking at any particular implementation but will instead demonstrate the typical logical components and how they interact with each other to provide DRM functionality. Furthermore the grouping of these generic components into three logical services is intended to demonstrate their logical independence from each other, as well as their compliance with the logical boundaries in a service-orientated architecture. This is not coincidental because these services could easily be implemented in a distributed manner across various geographical, physical, systems and network domains.

Note that the numbers included in the Figure 6.6 represent the high-level interaction sequence (described later) of the steps involved in accessing and rendering DRM-protected content as an illustration only.

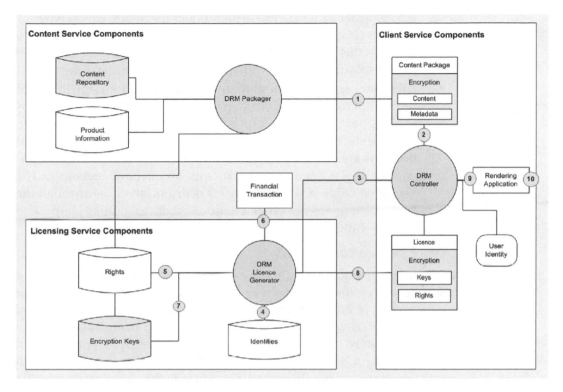

FIGURE 6.6 *DRM logical reference architecture and interaction sequence (source: adapted from Rosenblatt et al. (2002))*

DRM core service components

Content service components

This group of components typically sits within the domain of the content provider and are mainly concerned with preparing the content for protection and distribution to the outside world. The group is made up of three major components, which are briefly described as follows:

- **Content repository.** This holds the content that is to be protected along with its metadata and may actually be part of or integrated with the content provider's content management system (CMS) or linked to their media or digital asset management systems (MAMs or DAMs). The repository may be a database or file server and it may also be used to store the content before or after it has been protected by the DRM packager ready for distribution. Obviously this component has to be kept secure, especially if it stores unprotected content.

- **Product information catalogue.** This component is used for packaging the content in a sellable form, which may be standalone products (e.g. books, movies, music tracks, albums, videos etc.) or in the form of bundled products (e.g. a bundle of a music track, ring tone and the artiste poster or image file). The product metadata, which typically includes such items as price information or special offers, will also be stored in this catalogue. The product information may be integrated with or fully incorporated into the providers' ecommerce system.

- **DRM packager.** This component is responsible for applying DRM protection to the actual content and this may be accomplished by encryption, watermarking or simply adding the rights information metadata. If encrypted content protection is used then the encryption keys are normally stored in a separate secure repository that is part of the licence services in this architecture example. The packaged content is now ready for distribution either through the DRM system or via other channels such as online shops and superdistribution.

Licence service components

The DRM licensing service typically handles the rights management and IDM aspects of the system as well as the generation and storage of encryption keys and licences used for granting the appropriate level of access and usage rights to the client and end-user. This group of components may also sit within the content provider's domain (and implemented on a single server) or be distributed or interfaced with external systems across other domains such as the certificate authority for a DRM system that uses PKI for authentication. The components are briefly outlined below:

- **Rights repository.** This component stores the various rights, attributes and combinations applicable to the DRM packaged content. It supplies this information to the licence generator for use in creating the licence key, which enables the user to access the protected content.

- **Encryption key repository.** This stores the various encryption keys generated by the DRM packager for use in authentication and decryption of the content. This must be implemented as a secure repository within the system.

- **DRM licence generator.** This component generates the licence that is required by the DRM client when accessing and using the content. The licence specifies the rights and permissions applicable to that particular content–user combination and it is composed of the rights, the decryption key, authenticated user information and a confirmed financial transaction as appropriate.

- **Identities repository.** This stores all of the identities of the consumers that have been authenticated by the system; it supplies this information to the licence generator in order to bind the licence to the authenticated user or their system as the case may be. Accurate identification and authentication are vital aspects of any DRM system and can be tricky to implement without a clear strategy from the start.

Client service components

The client service is composed of the DRM controller, client application and end-user as well as their interaction with the content and licence provided by the other services. The components in this group are usually located in the consumer's client device, which will have several interfaces and connectivity to the other external systems it must interact with including the users themselves. The two components in this group are described briefly as follows:

- **DRM controller.** The component provides the DRM functionality for the consumer end of the equation. It is a multifaceted component whose functions include content decryption, licence request, user identification, information transmission and rights enforcement. The DRM controller may also be used to package content for superdistribution, along with some default rights (such as play three times then request purchase) depending on the model or if offline. DRM controllers may be implemented into the client or rendering application, integrated into the OS or be a standalone control function that interacts with the client device.

- **Client or rendering application.** The client application may be an ebook reader, a media player for music or video or other media applications that reside on the user's device (e.g. mobile phone, PC or media and consumer devices such as MP3 players and home entertainment products). DRM-enabled functionality on these devices can be implemented as standalone player applications (designed specifically for DRM systems), plug-ins to existing players (modifies the behaviour of existing applications), virtual machines (operates like a mini-DRM environment) or integrated into the client OS (e.g. secure computing platforms). The main goal is to ensure that the rendering application does not allow any restricted activities to be performed on protected content as this could compromise the whole DRM protection.

The interaction sequence

The following example sequence of steps included in Figure 6.6 serves as an illustration of how the various components interact with each other to render a DRM-protected content package. The steps presented below are meant to represent a typical straightforward download, purchase and play scenario that occurs with many DRM-enabled content distribution systems:

1. The user downloads a DRM-protected content package (e.g. a music file, film or research report document) and tries to open or play it on their system using an appropriate player application (e.g. media player or word processor).

2. This triggers the DRM controller, which immediately gathers the relevant details needed to create a licence request for the specific usage requested (i.e. to view the content). This information may be pre-existing (e.g. the user may have viewed similar protected content before) or may need to be generated by filling out a form etc. and be authenticated via the user profile on the system, credit card number or a user ID and password from the download website etc.

3. This licence request along with the content identity and user's details are sent to the DRM licence generator for fulfilment.

4. The licence generator checks that this user identity is present in the identities repository before it can build a licence to fulfil the request. If this is a new user then it may insert the new identity into the repository as part of this step, but only if the requirements for inclusion have been met (e.g. confirmed payment details or user ID and password).

5. The licence generator also checks for the appropriate rights information of the content in the rights repository and matches this against the requested right (to confirm that the content should indeed be played on the user system).

6. It may then initiate a request for payment (e.g. via supplied credit card number or online via the download website) or other types of consideration as appropriate.

7. Finally, with all of the necessary information and confirmed details (including the appropriate encryption key from the key repository) the licence generator then creates a licence for that user solely for the requested activity.

8. This licence (which is typically encrypted or otherwise secured) is then sent back to the client.

9. The DRM controller uses the key to decrypt the protected content package and releases it to the player or viewing application. Note that the viewing client may need to have been authenticated to render the content for that user and it must also be restricted from performing any other non-permitted activities such as copy or print etc. without the appropriate licence.

10. The client application then proceeds to render the content to the user.

The above sequence has been greatly simplified for illustration only and will most likely be much more complex in practice, but it does trace the sort of interactions that happen in a typical usage scenario.

Various other functionalities (e.g. superdistribution and play count restrictions) are variations on a theme in terms of the interaction required.

Superdistribution interaction model

Figure 6.7 shows a dynamic interaction model for the superdistribution of protected content and includes two scenarios or business models of superdistribution with and without content preview enabled. Figure 6.7 is adapted from the OMA DRM Architecture, which is the standard for mobile devices (OMA 2006).

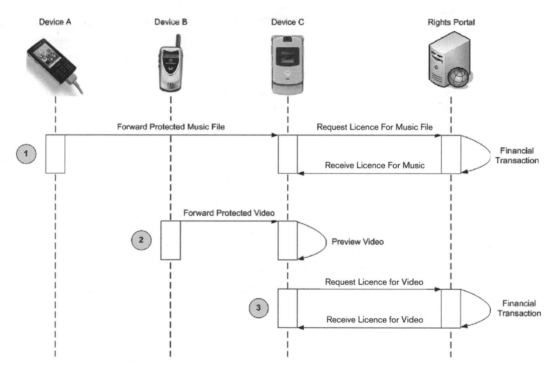

FIGURE 6.7 *Superdistribution interaction diagram (source: adapted from OMA (2006))*

The numbers shown in Figure 6.7 correspond to the following scenarios:

1. Device A forwards some previously received DRM-protected music file to device C. This may be via local connectivity or removable media. When device C tries to play the content this triggers a request for the appropriate licence or rights object to the rights issuer's URL that is embedded in the DRM header or wrapper. In OMA DRM the ensuing session is referred to as a Rights Object Acquisition Protocol (ROAP) session. On completion of this session and after a successful financial transaction to pay for the content, the licence or rights object for the music file is delivered to device C, which can then play the content for the user.

2. Device B transfers a DRM-protected video file to device C. This video file has a 'preview' function enabled in the DRM header and can provide an 'instant preview' on device C. This enables the user to 'preview' the video (typically a short clip) and decide whether to purchase it (or rather the rights to view it).

3. Once the user of device C has decided to purchase the rights for the video, it again initiates the ROAP session with the rights issuer to obtain the appropriate licence or rights object with which to view the complete video.

Note that different scenarios may be played out according to the various business models that are implemented and supported by the DRM system. For example, the preview functionality described in scenario 2 may also require a separate rights object, which has to be obtained from the rights issuer with or without a financial transaction depending on the business model. This could be a great way to track the spread of the content and perhaps also obtain information from potential new customers for later reference or targeted campaigns.

DRM ECOSYSTEM

From the above section it is obvious that DRM does not exist in isolation and needs to work within the context of both the user and content-provider systems or environment, as well as the various authentication, distribution, payment and fulfilment functions that enable the whole process of supplying protected content to the end-users. This external environment and systems, in conjunction with the core DRM services and the interactions between them, all combine to make up the DRM ecosystem. In any ecosystem, to borrow a biological analogy, there has to be a balance between the various component parts in order to maintain equilibrium and deliver optimal service and this may be chieved in this case by having seamless integration between DRM technology and the external components in the ecosystem.

Overview of the ecosystem

Figure 6.8 shows the core DRM architecture, described in the previous section, in the context of the larger ecosystem within which it must operate.

The DRM ecosystem comprises the following external components that surround and encompass the DRM system as shown above:

- **The rights management environment.** This is made up of the various sociological, civil, economic and governance structures that influence the whole content lifecycle, as well as the value

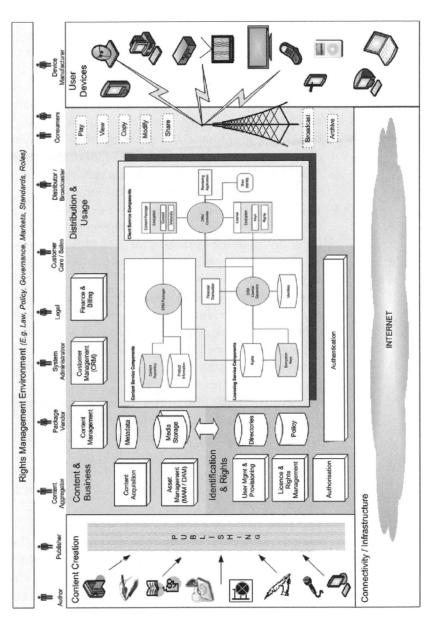

FIGURE **6.8** *High-level DRM ecosystem*

chain processes of content production, management, distribution and consumption. It also forms the overarching context in which the human actors operate in the DRM ecosystem.

- **The content creation environment.** This covers the vital activity of creating the content, which drives all of the other subsequent steps and processes in the value chain. It also includes publishing the content and making it available to the content provider environment.

- **The content and business environment.** This area includes the various systems and processes that are used to manage the content and prepare it for provision to the end-user. It also covers the customer care and financial aspects of the DRM environment, which directly affect the commercial viability of the whole enterprise, as it is here that the results of the success or failure of the business model and implementation are first felt.

- **The identification and rights environment.** The management of the rights, identities, policies and licences necessary for the overall functioning of the system is located in this area and it covers the systems and processes that provide both user and consumer authentication and authorisation.

- **The distribution and usage environment.** This area is concerned with the actual delivery and usage of the content (protected or otherwise). It covers all of the interfaces with the consumer on the supply side and includes the systems, processes and delivery channels for distributing the content and controlling and monitoring the use of it by the consumer.

- **The connectivity and infrastructure environment.** The whole digital content lifecycle mainly takes place in an electronic environment apart from some analogue processes involved in the original creation and final consumption of the content by humans. This environment is made up of an extensive infrastructure of resources and connectivity needed to support the whole value chain.

- **The user devices environment.** The end-user devices that are used to render and manipulate the content are the main components in this environment. They form the final link in the chain from the original creator of the content to the consumer and in many cases may also be the conduit for usage tracking and monitoring information, feedback and remuneration for the usage rights etc.

The above ecosystem environments and systems are encountered at various stages during the content lifecycle as they traverse the content value chain, as illustrated in the Figure 6.9.

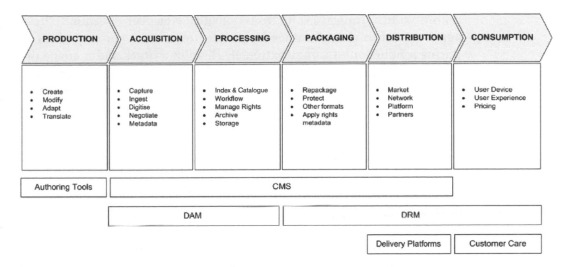

FIGURE 6.9 *Content lifecycle and value chain*

From Figure 6.9 it can be seen that the DRM system will need to be integrated with some of the neighbouring systems in order to access the metadata and rights information provided by these systems. This can usually be accomplished by using a common rights language or metadata standard to act as the glue that helps to bind the separate systems together.

The rest of this section will focus on some of the more relevant components found within the various environments of the DRM ecosystem. These represent the principal touch points and systems that typically work and interface with the DRM system. By necessity most of the descriptions have been kept as brief and high level as possible and very much focused on their intersections with DRM, our main topic of interest. The expansive nature and subject matter of these components guarantees that a plethora of material, research and treatments already exist for those who may wish to explore them further. Every attempt has been made to include links and references to further sources of information.

Rights management

This is a core component in the DRM ecosystem and could rightly be considered at the very heart of the rights-enabled content enterprise. In the media and entertainment world the rights that apply to content are usually defined and written out in a contract between the various parties that supply, aggregate, repackage (e.g. bundle) and distribute the content. These contracts normally address such things as 'licensing, clearance, audit, geographical and temporal exclusivity, finance and royalties' among other things (Van Tassel 2006). However, because these agreements can change rather frequently (even on a per-deal basis or during production) it can be extremely difficult to track and manage the complex interrelationships that exist between content partners and contributors, as well as the various degrees of exclusivity that may apply to their contribution. Furthermore these same contractual specifications effectively determine the rights that can be applied and enforced on a given content by the DRM system.

Even though it is possible to manage and administer these contracts manually, as is still done by some smaller operations, it can very quickly become extremely complex and difficult for the larger operations such as film studios, book, magazine and music publishers as well as large broadcasters. As a result there exists a healthy market for the makers and vendors of various rights management products and these run the gamut of scale from small standalone modules to large global enterprise-level systems. The rights management products usually comprise various modules or sub-components that address specific aspects of the rights management landscape such as the following:

- **Contracts management.** This provides the ability to create, modify, store and distribute the contracts from a single source or location. The two main types of contracts cover the two areas of content acquisition and development, and sales and licensing, and these may apply (either one type or the other) to most of the actors in the value chain (i.e. contributor, rights holder, distributor, manufacturer, delivery channel operator and the consumer).

- **Rights distribution and repository.** This specifies and manages the different rights contained in the contracts from a centralised location and covers particular attributes and requirements such as rights level, clearance, restrictions and protection. These may be applicable to different extents for each combination of factors such as territory, channel, exclusivity and content usage.

- **Financial settlement and royalty management.** This addresses the financial and transactional aspects of the rights in relation to the commercial use of the content. This particular component is very useful for accounting, royalty calculation and distribution as well as regulatory compliance requirements. It handles the flow of transactional information within the value chain, i.e. from the consumer to the channel operator, to the distributor, to the rights holder, and through to the contributors in the form of royalty payments. This component also implies the need for an effective usage tracking facility.

- **Integration and collaboration support.** This is necessary at two levels, for working with the other enterprise systems (e.g. finance, billing, customer relationship management (CRM) etc.) and for enabling the interaction of various actors in the value chain and within the content enterprise. The need for integration with DRM and content management rights repositories may also be a vital prerequisite.

Major vendors of rights management systems include Jaguar, SAP, Ness, iRights and Sophoi. The main principle behind the existence of these systems could best be summed up in a Jaguar System 7 product update, which states that:

> The drive to organise wholesale, retail and consumer use of these products in relation to an incorporated intellectual property profile remains valid in perpetuity (Jaguar 2004)

This requires the ability to provide consistent rights-related reporting and payment processing information for the contributor, licensor, service provider and all other stakeholders and participants in the content value chain. In essence this effectively supports and enables the whole sentiment behind intellectual property.

Content management

Content management is a key component or enabler of the digital content value chain and the digital content lifecycle. It can be described as the integrated business and technology strategy that delivers the ability for an organisation to create, manage and distribute content. It can be a very complex and painstaking endeavour, not least because it involves the management of the different processes of content ingestion, storage and distribution, but also because it has to handle the metadata necessary to leverage the content and realise the enormous potential of the digital technology infrastructure to provide added value to the content enterprise. The systems tasked with delivering content management functionality are known by various generic acronyms such as 'CMS', 'WCM' or 'ECM', as well as more specific types such as 'MAM', 'DAM' and 'DMM'. This is mostly attributable to the complexity of the topic, as well as the diverse nature of the content management industry and the products they offer in this space. We outline and describe these acronyms as follows:

- **Content management system (CMS).** CMS is the generic umbrella term that describes the overall concept of content management technology. It is widely used and accepted in that role, but certain distinctions are made depending on the primary use of the systems as described in the next items.

- **Web content management (WCM).** 'Web Content Management refers to the discipline and technologies around managing content for publication via the web' (Boye 2006). It provides templates, editorial workflow and publishing environments for web and other internet-based content delivery platforms.
- **Enterprise content management (ECM).** ECM is described in the CMS Watch website as

> a discipline, rather than a particular technology solution, that is concerned with the management of all kinds of content found within the enterprise (Boye 2006)

It facilitates the use of this content both internally and externally with the company's partners, customers and suppliers as well as the public.

- **Media asset management (MAM).** This is a term mostly used in the traditional context of the movie, music and broadcast industries to describe the management of the various elements of media content. It also encompasses analogue media assets such as film reels, tapes and scripts etc.
- **Digital asset management (DAM).** DAM is the term most often used in and associated with the web development and management arena. It is mainly used to describe systems that manage rich media assets such as digital audio, video and images, text including code and other types of digital assets.
- **Digital media management (DMM).** This usage of this term is similar to DAM, but may be more specialised and restricted to systems that only manage digital media items.

For our purposes, the generic term CMS will be used to refer to all of the content management technologies and disciplines described above, except where a particular functionality or domain is referenced such as the enterprise content space. Furthermore, the latter three terms (i.e. MAM, DAM and DMM) are most commonly used to describe systems that manage the elements that are brought together to create a composite content product such as a movie DVD or magazine publication, whereas the remit of the others (i.e. CMS, WCM and ECM) also includes distribution and delivery of the finished content to the content provider or customer. Regardless of these nuances the core requirement of any CMS is to provide the enterprise with ways to organise the content and metadata, automate the workflow around the content and provide some measure of security and an audit trail for the content.

In the context of the business and content environment as described in the DRM ecosystem, the CMS will need to work or be integrated with various other systems in a software landscape that typically includes some of the following:

- **information and content** – information lifecycle management, document and records management, DAM, imaging, WCM;
- **business and enterprise** – business process management, knowledge management, business intelligence, collaboration and workflow management, enterprise search, product data management and catalogues;
- **infrastructure** – storage, software and configuration management;
- **delivery** – portals and WS.

> There are typically two major phases in Content Management which may sometimes overlap, but which broadly address the twin aspects of content production and delivery (Byrne 2006)

For example, a WCM system will typically address several activities and processes under each phase as shown below:

- **production phase** – role management, authoring and transformation, aggregation, tagging (metadata), workflow, library service, localisation and promotion path;
- **delivery phase** – page generation, index and searching, personalisation, privilege management, caching and replication, other format support, syndication and vending.

One feature that cuts across both phases is the requirement and use of content information or metadata. This is a crucial enabler of the CM functionality and integration capability with other systems in the content enterprise. This includes the information that surrounds and supports the business and customer needs such as: the product documentation (manuals and guides), the help files and customer feedback information, which need to be captured and managed in a consistent manner using appropriate standards such as the Darwin Information Typing Architectures (DITA).

A generic WCM architecture

The CMS architecture illustrated in Figure 6.10 is adapted from a tutorial presentation given by CMS Watch's Tony Byrne at the Gilbane San Francisco Conference in April 2006. It shows a typical WCM architecture with the common components that can also be found in many other types of CMS.

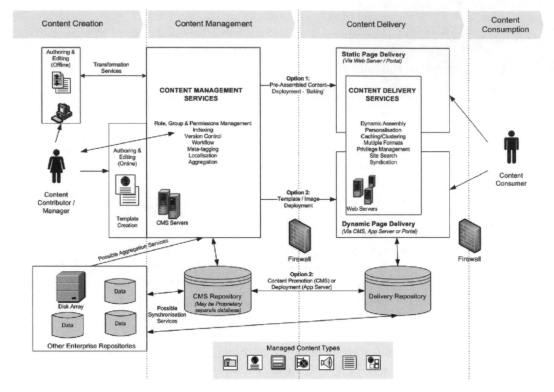

FIGURE 6.10 *Typical web content management architecture (source: adapted from Byrne (2006))*

The main CM architecture components comprise the following:

- **the repositories** – including the CMS repository (for holding or staging content and metadata), the delivery repository and other enterprise information sources;
- **the content services** – made up of the various services for content management and content delivery, as well as other services that support content creation;
- **the infrastructure** – including end-to-end connectivity and other support functions such as software management, version control, security and portal services.

Some integration touch points for DRM and content management

The following outlines the major areas of commonality that can be leveraged to enable the integration of DRM and CMSs:

- **Metadata.** 'The metadata creation process is the most crucial point of integration between rights management systems and CMSs' (Rosenblatt and Dykstra 2003). In the production phase, one of the key processes that enable the integration of content management with DRM is the creation and application of content metadata. As stated earlier, this is the common vocabulary that helps to bind the systems and allows the seamless exchange of rights information between them. In this situation the use of a standard REL ensures that the rights and other metadata are used in a consistent manner between the various systems in the environment. The production phase is probably the optimal stage in which to create and apply the metadata to the content, this is because the content is usually assembled at this point in readiness for distribution and it makes sense to apply the metadata about it at the same time. Doing this beforehand may not be practical especially where the content is composed of various digital media elements (that may already have metadata attached) and adding the metadata after the production phase brings in the risk of omitting or forgetting some of the metadata information.

- **Content repository.** Another key feature of a CMS is the ability to provide storage for the content and all of its sub-elements including metadata. This feature is also very relevant for integration with DRM because as described in the DRM reference architecture a CMS may be used to provide content to the DRM packager for protection before it is delivered to the consumer or stored in the DRM content repository (which may also be the CMS).

- **Content generation.** The CMS will usually be designed to handle content generation for delivery in one of two ways: pre-assembled content or by 'on-the-fly' assembly of the 'page' content in a WCM system and this is sometimes called 'baking' or 'frying' the assembled content. The pre-assembled or 'baked' content is ready to serve instantly and this makes for faster performance, but has low dynamism or customisability, whilst the 'fried' content can be dynamic and customisable because it is assembled only after the user requests it, but this can be very resource intensive and hence may carry a performance hit on the system. The latter generation method coupled with 'on-the-fly' DRM packaging can be used to implement a flexible and adaptive content solution, but one that will probably need all of the bandwidth and connectivity available to make it work smoothly.

- **Other content and information.** Other types of information that are produced around the CMS-DRM system such as product specification information, manuals and guides, help systems and user-generated content also need to be managed and handled in a coherent and consistent manner across the two systems. This is the area where rapidly spreading standards such as OASIS DITA may be invaluable because according to a Gilbane Report 2006 white paper:

> the benefits of this standard will not only be felt in single source publishing of technical documentations, but also in areas like web-publishing, e-learning, and user generated content applications like online real-time customer support, support blogs and message boards (Trippe 2006)

For the DRM-enabled content business this can be a useful way to interact with and support the customer outside of the main content transaction.

- **Persistent protection.** There are many benefits to be derived from integrating CMS and DRM, and one of the most important is that this combination can cover a larger span of content protection within the content lifecycle. This is important because a lot of the piracy that occurs during the content production phase may be addressed by using DRM protection even during this period as it will protect the content within the CMS automated workflow. Other benefits include the ability to work with partners, suppliers and outsourcing organisations on the same content in a safer and more secure manner with DRM protection. Also the ability to modify the rights over time means that the same protective DRM mechanism can be used right through the content lifecycle, from creation to distribution, consumption and superdistribution. Finally, in the business or enterprise environment DRM and ECM systems may combine to provide a higher level of security, compliance, audit, governance and usage policy control on enterprise content than can be obtained from either system operating alone.

Identity management (IDM)

According to Datamonitor:

> the term Identity Management is now increasingly used by the industry to describe the collection of solutions designed to help create, manage, enforce, and utilise user profiles and other identities (Datamonitor 2004)

Prior to this the most common description was the 3As of authentication, authorisation and administration. IDM as a functional capability is mainly associated with the enterprise context because it is vital for the normal functioning of the corporate environment with all of its enabling systems and information and workflows. In this environment, the main drivers for adoption include security, cost reduction for administration, regulatory compliance, policy enforcement, improvements in productivity and the ability to take on new services.

The main components that combine to deliver IDM are illustrated in Figure 6.11, which was adapted from Datamonitor's (2004) report, and described as follows:

- **Identification and authentication.** Examples include hardware and software tokens, digital certificates, smartcards, USB tokens and biometric solutions.

- **Access control and authorisation.** Examples include web-based access control, enterprise access control including single sign on (SSO), CA systems and the product activation process used by certain software and games product vendors.

- **Provisioning and user management.** User-lifecycle management (e.g. create, modify and delete user identities and profiles) provides the information associated with the user ID and is used by the authorisation system to grant or prohibit access to content. Provisioning also covers other identities such as server certificates and can be used to provision the various goods and services to users (e.g. enterprise assets such as laptops, mobiles and even software).

- **ID management infrastructure.** This includes directory structures (Lightweight Directory Access Protocol (LDAP) and Sun one), audit tools and logs, as well as specific infrastructure (e.g. smartcard readers and management tools).

- **ID management services.** Examples are PKI services (certificate generation, verification and revocation), TTPs and other services (consulting, integration, maintenance and managed services including outsourcing, education and training).

Note that the above component categories are not mutually exclusive as different product vendors may implement one or more of the above components to various degrees in their products.

Major IDM considerations in DRM include such questions as what to identify and which recipient entity to grant the rights for the protected content. This debate is usually split along the lines of the user versus the device and both have their pros and cons, for example, a user may wish to be able to use their content on multiple devices but that raises the question of how to address multi-user devices. Some features of user and device identification schemes include the following:

- **User identification.** It is widely thought that a user can be securely identified through three pieces of information that cover the three areas of something they know (e.g. password or PIN), something they are (e.g. biometric data such as a fingerprint or iris scan) and something they own (such as a digital certificate or signature).

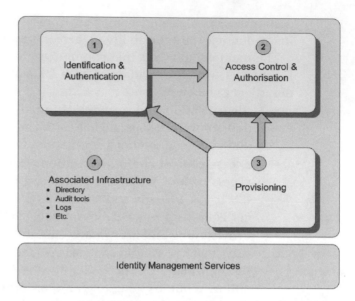

FIGURE 6.11 *Identity management components (source: adapted from Datamonitor (2004))*

- **Device identification.** This is usually approached by using authentication methods that can read a unique reference such as a hardware serial number or networked device IDs such as media access control (MAC) addresses.

In both cases there are limitations to systems and they are not completely foolproof, but the consensus seems to be leaning more towards the user-based identification and authentication systems in conjunction with device identification as a secondary or alternative route. In any case the providers of solutions in this space tend to focus on particular types of identification mechanisms that could be grouped in to the following categories:

- **directory solutions** – Siemens, Novell and Critical Path;
- **system management** – IBM (Tivoli), Computer Associates, BMC and Net IQ;
- **OSs** – Microsoft, Sun Microsystems and HP;
- **authentication** – RSA, Entrust, Ultimaco, Verisign and ActivCard;
- **others (specialist)** – Netegrity, Oblix and Thor;
- **others (generalist)** – Oracle, Evidian and Citrix.

Customer relationship management (CRM)

At the business end of the content value chain is the interface between the consumer and the content provider. This is the channel through which the customer may interact with the business on matters relating to the product, their user information and profile and the issues that they may encounter in the use and exercise of the purchased rights. The systems that enable these and other activities are often referred to as CRM systems. The CRM product is now a mature technology-based solution that may be implemented by the content enterprise as a stand-alone package, an integrated collection of functional components, an outsourced service from an application service provider (ASP) or even as a proprietary system developed in-house within the enterprise itself. The fundamental principle and key requirement of CRM is to enable organisations to become much more customer-centric in order to drive new growth by better exploiting the customer lifecycle (i.e. acquire, retain, cross-sell).

CRM provides the means by which a content enterprise can manage their customer information and relationships and in some cases this has been extended to include the management of information on and relationships with their suppliers (SRM), employees (ERM) and partners (PRM). Radcliffe et al. (2001) of Gartner Research defined eight building blocks of CRM that can be used to create the customer-centric business approach that organisations need to embrace in order to derive the benefits of CRM, as shown in Figure 6.12.

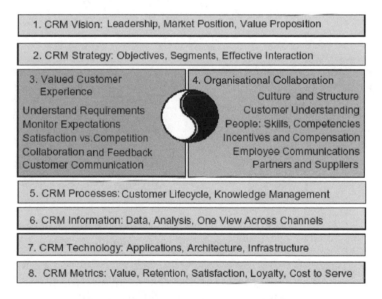

FIGURE 6.12   *The eight building blocks of customer relationship management*
(source: derived from Radcliffe et al. (2001))

These eight building blocks still remain valid today and according to a headline on the 2007 Gartner conference schedule at http://www.gartner.com, 'CRM is back on the agenda in a big way'. It can be surmised therefore that organisations are even more likely to need the benefits that CRM can bring in the new collaborative, socially networked and connected enterprise environment of today. This is directly applicable and related to DRM technology, especially with the last three blocks of information, technology and metrics.

CRM architecture and touch points to DRM

The high-level CRM architecture diagram in Figure 6.13 is adapted from a HP technical white paper (Janjicek 2001) and shows the main components of a CRM system as well as how they interact to deliver the required customer-centric capability.

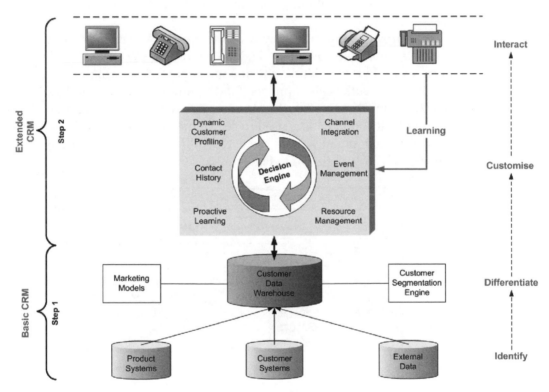

FIGURE 6.13   *Customer relationship management architecture (source: adapted from Janjicek (2001))*

The main themes of the system involve the phases of customer identification, differentiation, customisation and interaction, which fall into two segments of:

- **basic CRM** – that is, identification and differentiation;
- **extended CRM functionality** – that is, customisation and interaction.

The basic CRM section consists of a central customer data repository that serves up a single, unified view of the customer (or master data) and which is fed into by the product repository, customer systems (including contact management) and external data sources. The warehouse is the source of data upon which various operations such as market modelling and segmentation can be performed. The extended functionality section contains the more dynamic elements such as the analytics and decision engines, which support operations such as dynamic customer profiling, proactive learning, campaign and resource management, as well as integration (via various translation services) with the customer-facing front-end interfaces such as call centres, web-based ecommerce and telephony access.

The main touch points and relationship between CRM and DRM is embodied in the saying that CRM comes before DRM in the hierarchy of systems relationships. This highlights the fact that DRM is dependent on systems that help in managing customer relationships, hence it can be enhanced by integration with them in the following areas:

- **Customer information.** The high quality of customer data required for good and efficient CRM and contact management can be leveraged by DRM systems in the identities repository and for user authentication and authorisation. Furthermore the single unified master data model means that a view of this data can be taken from a trustworthy source that spans the enterprise.

- **Dynamic customer profiling.** CRM analytics are used to enable customer segmentation for campaign management and other activities and when coupled with the extended CRM system's ability to dynamically update and modify customer profiles this could be quite beneficial to DRM systems in many ways. For example, it could be tied into services such as recommendation and offer management, similar to Amazon.com's recommendation of products related to those in the user's shopping cart.

- **Feedback and learning.** Conversely, the usage tracking information that can be obtained from some DRM systems could be fed into the inference and learning modules of the CRM analytics engine. This could further enhance the dynamic customer modelling capability of the CRM system, and help to realise the ultimate goal of many marketers to model a highly individualised customer profile or 'segment of one'. Further refinements, perhaps with artificial intelligence engines, may provide the ability to predict customer behaviour and likelihood to accept an offer based on their current observable activities and past preferences. This would also capture the customer's changing tastes and circumstances and respond accordingly, thus better enabling the dynamic nature of the customer-to-business relationship.

- **Innovation and customer segmentation.** This is related to the above point and specifically addresses the idea of creating innovative products and services that are influenced by the customer's activity and feedback. This idea is encapsulated in several white papers by

Strategyn's Anthony Ulwick on the 'Outcome-Driven Innovation™' methodology, which is based on the observation that

> many businesses use demographics and market segmentation classifications which are mostly internally defined (ignoring the customer's desired outcome), and which effectively aim their products and services at phantom targets (Ulwick 2002)

In the content industry, DRM can help improve this process by providing accurate and definitive information on the usage of content based on the customer's activities.

These are just some of the synergies that could be leveraged in deploying CRM and DRM systems in a well-integrated manner. As stated earlier CRM as well as the other external components of the DRM ecosystem make up a vast and interesting subject with many resources available online or offline for anyone interested in further research.

Other systems

Some of the other systems and services that also need to work with DRM and which are quite relevant to this discussion include the following.

Financial systems, billing and payment services

Generally speaking a DRM system many not need to be too tightly integrated with the billing and payment processing systems or services because it mostly only requires an acknowledgement or confirmation that appropriate payment has been received in order to carry out the generation of the licence or rights object that is sent to the consumer's device. However, the rapid rise in the number of digital content service providers in the online and mobile environments are driving the development of a robust payments infrastructure that can handle different payment options and models especially for the so-called micropayments that involve 'low-value and high-volume' transactions such as the purchase of ring tones. As a matter of practicality, the payment methods used for these types of transactions do not usually include credit cards as they are just not cost-effective for very small amounts, therefore some of the alternative methods that are slowly being introduced include:

- the charging for purchases via the customer's mobile phone bill;
- the use of services provided by smaller operators such as SimPay;
- online accounts for micropayments such as BitPass, which does not require the storage of credit card data.

Content or service provisioning and fulfilment

This is applicable to situations where the DRM system or CMS is not used for delivery of the content. This may occur in the case of specialist or high-bandwidth requirements for certain types of content (e.g. feature-length movies) that require dedicated delivery facilities, which may be outsourced to other providers such as Akamai with their Edge Computing infrastructure. Other services such as live-event streaming may choose to deploy a CA model alongside DRM protection for both the streamed and downloaded content (e.g. archive). In this scenario, the protected content is only delivered via web-streaming or downloads after payment has been made.

CONCLUSION

In this chapter we have covered the major areas of DRM technology at a high-level and provided an insight into the various services and technologies that combine to provide the overall DRM functionality. We have touched on several copy-protection and access-control technologies, which included a fundamental overview of cryptography and its applications in content protection, as well as the use of encryption and watermarking techniques to implement various protection schemes. We also examined the features of CA and analogue protection technologies in relation to DRM and then went on to look at a DRM reference architecture, with interaction maps for download and superdistribution scenarios. Finally, we looked at the various environments and systems that interact with DRM technology in the context of a DRM ecosystem. In all of the above discussion, where possible, an attempt has been made to maintain a generic picture of DRM systems and technology in order to create a high-level picture that can provide a context for the more specific treatment of some real DRM products, vendors, standards and organisations in the subsequent chapters.

7 DRM Standards and Organisations

There are several competing standards in the different areas touched upon by DRM. As stated in the earlier chapters, DRM occupies a rather significant intersection in the content economy and ecosystem. The main objective of this chapter is to examine the various standards that exist in these areas and also to highlight some of the organisations and bodies that help to develop and control them. In order to keep this chapter free from too much noise, every effort is made to ensure that the discussions on standards and organisations are kept as brief and focused as possible and to provide links to other sources of information for those interested in digging deeper.

OVERVIEW

According to the ISO:

> Standards are documented agreements containing technical specifications or other precise criteria to be used consistently as rules, guidelines, or definitions of characteristics, to ensure that materials, products, processes and services are fit for their purpose (CEN/ISSS 2003)

There are several types of standards, which may be described as follows:

- **Formal standards.** These are produced by officially recognised organisations at a national, regional or global level.
- **Industry standards.** A consortium of industry organisations may be formed for the express purpose of creating a standard, based on the consensus by its members within that industry, but which may not have formal standards status.
- **Open standards.** These are publicly available standards that are open to any individual or entity willing to participate in their definition and maintenance.
- ***De facto* standards.** These are widely accepted, non-formal standards that have achieved widespread acceptance in the market over other competing specifications.
- **Proprietary standards.** These are established and maintained through a closed process under the control of an entity or consortium and which may be based on their proprietary intellectual property. These may also be adopted as an industry or *de facto* standard.

One of the main benefits of standards is that they offer an organised, consistent and coherent method for carrying out an activity in a particular area. Without standards there would be utter chaos in the component products and services used and produced by the stakeholders because they would not be able to fit and perform well together even if only affected by a modicum of imprecision. Standards therefore make it easier for stakeholders to get on with the business of providing and consuming content services without worrying too much about the detail in areas outside their control.

The hierarchy of DRM standards

DRM is made up of a suite of technologies, protocols and services that work together to provide some control over the usage rights to a piece of content and, owing to this very fact, it is virtually impossible to have a single standard for DRM systems that will cut across all of the layers through which it provides this service. Table 7.1 describes a hierarchy of standards that map to the different layers and stakeholders in DRM systems as described by Rosenblatt (Rosenblatt et al. 2002; Rosenblatt 2004a).

TABLE 7.1   *DRM standards hierarchy*

Hierarchy layers	Category	Description and examples
Publisher	Content management	This relates to the many different CMSs and methods in use by the various content service providers. It is not a likely candidate for standardisation in DRM systems and is not discussed in any detail here.
	Rights and holder management	Some standards exist in this category such as the <indecs2> RDD, which is briefly discussed later in this chapter.
	Business models	These are not likely to be standardised as they form the area in which many content businesses try to differentiate themselves. Some established and innovative business models were presented in Chapter 5.
Content and metadata	Content identification	Several unique intellectual property identification standards already exist and include DOI, ISAN, ISWC and UMID. These are described further in this chapter in the 'Identification standards' section.
	Content and product metadata	Many industry-specific standards exist in this category including ONIX, PRISM and NewsML, and these are also explored briefly in the 'Metadata standards' section.

(continued)

TABLE 7.1   *(continued)*

Hierarchy layers	Category	Description and examples
	Content rights	Rights metadata standards include the XrML-based MPEG REL and ODRL, which we discussed in Chapter 5. They are mentioned briefly in this chapter in the 'Rights standards' section.
	Content formats	This relates to the various formats that are used to distribute and consume the content (e.g. MP3, Windows Media, AAC (Advanced Audio Coding) or RealMedia). These standards are not under the purview of DRM systems and hence are not covered in any detail in this chapter.
Transactional and ecommerce	Payment scheme	This covers the various transactional methods used to purchase content. The standards for payment systems and technologies are not necessarily unique to DRM or influenced by it, so they are not discussed here.
	Authentication	Authentication standards and protocols already exist as part of corporate and ecommerce systems. Examples include the .Net passport authentication technologies used by Microsoft.
	Encryption	Various encryption technologies including some standards were discussed in Chapter 6 and are not presented again here. They include some standard strong encryption algorithms such as AES, Blowfish and RSA.
Connectivity	Internet	The internet standards are the foundation for digital content transmission and distribution in DRM, and they include HTTP (HyperText Transfer Protocol), HTML (HyperText Markup Language) and XML.

The remainder of this chapter is devoted to describing some of the various standards in the different layers above and also the organisations that are responsible for maintaining them. However, before we proceed to that point it is important to take a quick look at the overall benefits and characteristics that standardisation brings to DRM and related areas.

Characteristics and benefits of standards in DRM

There are several factors that influence the push for standards in DRM and its related technologies, processes and business practices and these are also the hallmarks that characterise the benefits of standards to DRM as described in the following sections. The following headings describe some of the main aspects of standards in general and DRM in particular.

Compliance

One major aspect of standards are that they set a certain level of expectation by consumers on any adopting system, therefore those organisations that create and maintain standards must encourage compliance from their adopters. In the same vein any entity, product or service that claims to conform to a particular standard must be able to proclaim and prove compliance with the standard to the prospective buyers or users. This is usually accomplished by some form of accreditation or certification service provided by that standard's organisation or proprietor. After successfully undertaking and passing these compliance checks or tests, the product, service or entity is normally entitled to proclaim itself as compliant to the standard.

Compatibility

A desirable benefit that can be brought by standardisation is the compatibility of products and services from different vendors and service providers. The decision to make a new product or service compatible with existing standards can be relatively easy because of the obvious benefits this can bring for the provider by opening up an existing market of compatible products and services already in use by consumers. Adopting a strategy to ensure that new products are compatible with existing standards (*de facto* or otherwise) can often help in the path to succession of new product standards. This was exemplified by the success of Creative's 1989 SoundBlaster soundcard, which maintained compatibility with the then widely supported AD-LIB soundcard of 1987. Many vendors try, although it is not always possible, to maintain backward compatibility with their own past products for the same reasons. However, product or service compatibility is not the same thing as interoperability, which is a major issue for DRM at the moment and which is also discussed below.

Encourage competition and market growth

One of the loftier ideas of standardisation is to level the playing field for all entrants and operators in a domain and thereby help ignite the market for the resulting standards-based services and products. There is ample historical evidence of this outcome but it is usually found in the more mature fields of enterprise such as in manufacturing, engineering and construction. In the newer (i.e. emerging and converging) fields such as IT, electronics and communications there is a more dynamic flavour to the standards that develop to maturity and this is mostly because the standards themselves often face stiff competition right from the outset unless they are mandated and protected by government agencies, international or commercial bodies. This type of competition by standards may appear at first to be ultimately advantageous for the quality of products and services developed under them; however, the results may be unpredictable unless they are developed with a fair and open system that enables quality to rise to the top. This is particularly true of those standards developed by commercial entities that may become *de facto* standards due to their greater market share and consumer mindshare, at the expense of arguably better-quality rivals (e.g. Betamax versus VHS). These are not negative issues in themselves because ultimately the market determines who wins or loses in these contests; however, the competition for market share by entrenched commercial interests can often stifle some of the major benefits of standardisation (e.g. interoperability).

Interoperability

This is perhaps the most important benefit of standardisation with respect to DRM systems and it has the most to deliver in terms of real benefits to all of the stakeholders in the content value chain. However, and again because of the complexity of the technological, legal, commercial, content and usage intersection occupied by DRM, it is one of the most difficult to achieve across the board. The main issues around DRM standards and interoperability were elegantly portrayed in a presentation by Rajan Samtani in the DRMStrategies 2005 Conference and summarised as follows (Samtani 2005):

- **The Problem**
    - Content – the DRM-protected content of one system cannot be used, distributed and protected by another
    - Rights – the rights, privileges and conditions imposed or granted by one DRM system are not recognised/ enforced across the board by other systems
    - Protection – the protection techniques used by one DRM system may not be recognised and processed by another
    - Trust – the trust models that are used and established by one system may not be usable and/or maintainable by all DRM systems
    - Business models – the models established by or for each DRM system may not be adopted and executed by others
- **The Stakeholder Expectations**
    - Consumers expect that any DRM-protected content should be consumable at any time, any place and on any DRM device or system. Therefore the DRM proposition must offer real choice, flexibility and convenience
    - Rights holders expect that content and rights can be prepared once, distributed by most profitable channels and consumed

(continued)

(continued)

by any DRM system. The DRM proposition must offer choice, flexibility and be cost-effective

- Vendor – system components can replace similar components from other vendors. The proposition must provide for market share and cost-effectiveness

- **Obstacles to DRM Interoperability**
  - Consumers need to own/access various items like: the devices (e.g. hardware devices, consumer electronics and gadgets); the data (including content, rights, metadata, identification, keys and certificates); and the applications (e.g. software players, decoders and other services)
  - DRM systems need to address numerous items like: metadata (for identification and declaration of content, users and devices); rights (e.g. rights expression, rights data and usage data); protection (e.g. encryption, signatures and watermarks); key management (key hierarchy for encryption and signing); as well as trust management (e.g. trust hierarchy and enterprise policy)

- **Factors that Contribute to Non-Interoperability of DRM Systems**
  - There is a lack (and low adoption) of open common standards for things like: content packaging and protection, rights specification and interpretation, trust establishment and maintenance, business model description and execution
  - There is a hefty cost implication to implementing an interoperable system
  - Some vendors have a high motivation to stay non-interoperable for business reasons. Interoperability requires at least two systems to work together but the owners of these systems may also be competitors for market share (e.g. Apple FairPlay and Microsoft WMDRM or Real Helix systems)

- **Suggested Approaches to Interoperability**
  - Adopting a common open standard (industry-led or *de facto*) for data/content formats, interfaces and protocols
  - Integration with non-interoperable legacy entities by using a shared standard exchangeable data/content format, adaptive interfaces and intermediate protocols
  - Exploiting commercial and other methods to drive some non-interoperable entities out of market, and to reduce alternative, non-compatible standards either by legislation or competition

Figure 7.1 illustrates the important role of interoperability in DRM with a simple electric plug and socket analogy that depicts: the ideal situation of unified, open and interoperable standard; the reality of multiple, fragmented and competing standards; and the compromise solution of adaptation and translation technologies and standards that may be both ugly and inelegant, but which make it all work together anyway.

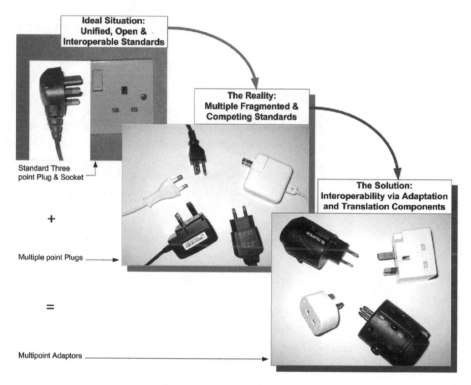

FIGURE 7.1   *Interoperability*

Rights locker

Another approach to DRM interoperability is the use of a rights locker to provide interoperability for content consumers. Basically a rights locker is a central repository for the digital rights of the individual or groups of content users. It works by providing users with a single place to store, maintain and retrieve their usage rights for their content on any connected device (e.g. PCs, mobiles, PDAs, etc.) at anytime and from any place. This is the holy grail of device interoperability and it is very much in line with the trend for service-oriented architectures, which advocate the creation and provision of discrete services by dedicated components that can function independently of the clients or users of that service. The rights locker provides services to the consumer that enables them to download encryption keys and usage rights from a central location irrespective of the device they use to access the content. This may be implemented using established standards for WS standards such as the Simple Object Access Protocol (SOAP):

> The rights locker may also apply internal rules and policies governing how the user accesses the rights and keys from multiple devices; and it could also be used to limit the number of devices allowed etc. (Garnett and Sander 2002)

The above observations adequately sum up the interoperability issue in DRM and point out some of the paths to reaching an interoperable future for DRM systems. In the next section we look at the various standards that exist in the world of DRM and related technologies.

DRM STANDARDS

The following headings are used to group the various standards in the content value chain and DRM landscape into sensible categories of descriptive functionality. This is solely intended to make it easier to present and is neither an exhaustive list nor an authoritative grouping of the standards, but it should provide a fair representation of the types of standards that currently exist in this field.

Identification standards

Content identification schemes started out in the analogue world of books and other physical products to help with the management of stock and other related activities such as cataloguing, shipping and reconciliation. Several content identifications schemes have since evolved or been adapted to cater for online content and they are used to identify different aspects of content including the atomic IP item (e.g. music track), the composite product (e.g. music album or film), the manifest product (CD or DVD versions), as well as the specific product instance (physical media item, e.g. disc ID). Some general guiding principles have been developed and observed in the online content identifier standards and these are outlined below as follows:

- **unique** – online identifiers are designed to be globally unique from the start;
- **dynamic** – independent of physical location;
- **generic** – not dependent on content type;
- **backward compatibility** – can be used with legacy schemes without need to reassign existing identifiers;
- **registry enabled** – global registry functionality to ensure uniqueness, provide lookup service and ownership tracking.

In the following we describe some of the identification standards (including formal international and industry standards) adopted by the different content related verticals. Their home page addresses have been included as a primary source of more information.

International Standard Book Number (ISBN)

This publishing industry standard was originally intended to help with stock handling in the supply chain, but it is now also widely used to aid the identification of books for purchase even in ecommerce systems.

http://www.isbn.org/

International Standard Serial Number (ISSN)

According to the ISSN website, 'the ISSN is an eight-digit number which identifies all periodical publications as such, including electronic serials'. It uses a global database as the register for each serial publication and its assigned ISSN, and the web portal at http://portal.issn.org can be used to access the publication online.

http://www.issn.org/

International Standard Audiovisual Number (ISAN)

This international standard is used in it the film industry for audiovisual content. It uses a 16-digit number to identify a work, that is, the intellectual property item not the physical instance or medium it is manifested in. The ISAN concept includes both an ISO standard international numbering system for audiovisual works and a works database (CEN/ISSS 2003).

http://www.isan.org/

International Standard Work Code (ISWC)

Similar to the ISAN, the ISWC is an international standard used in the music industry to identify intellectual property. It is described on the ISWC website as 'a unique, permanent and internationally recognised reference number for the identification of musical works'. It is composed of a letter 'T' followed by nine digits and an additional check digit at the end (e.g. T-123456789-1), which is allocated by an authorised regional ISWC agency.

http://www.iswc.org/

International Standard Recording Code (ISRC)

According to the International Federation of the Phonographic Industry (IFPI) website, ISRC

> is the international identification system for sound recordings and music video recordings. Each ISRC is a unique and permanent identifier for a specific recording which can be permanently encoded into a product as its digital fingerprint. Encoded ISRC provide the means to automatically identify recordings for royalty payments (IFPI 2006)

http://www.ifpi.org/content/section_resources/isrc.html

Global Release Identifier (GRid)

The GRid system is used to identify sound recording releases for electronic distribution. Like the ISRC above, it is an international standard that is governed by the IFPI on behalf of the international music industry. They have appointed IFPI as the registration authority for the system. The GRid has been designed to allow integration with other identification systems in use by the various music industry entities. The GRid system consists of a release ID, a metadata schema, and data and element definitions for messaging and interfacing with systems (also mentioned in Table 7.2).

http://www.ifpi.org/content/section_resources/grid.html

Unique Material Identifier (UMID)

The UMID is an international industry standard created by the Society for Motion Picture and Television Engineers (SMPTE) for use in creating a unique identifier or reference for any type of audiovisual content. The UMID acts as the link between the content (usually referred to as 'the essence' in this context) and its metadata, and it can be used for identification at a very granular level (e.g. individual still shots or frames in a film). It is a system-generated identifier that uses the automatically generated SMPTE time code in creating the identifiers. The UMID can exist in either a basic or extended form map to 32 or 64 bits respectively:

> The Basic UMID is composed of: A 12-byte label, 1 byte length value, 3 byte Instance number and a 16 byte unique material number. The Extended UMID is comprised of the basic UMID plus another optional 32 bytes of metadata source information which specifies the creation time and date, recording location and name of the organisation and/or content maker (SMPTE 2003)

http://www.smpte.org

cIDf Content Identifier (cID)

The Content ID Forum (cIDf) created this ID system as a robust unique content identifier designed to be used for identifying content instances over a distributed network such as the internet. This level of copy-specific identification is obviously suited to DRM and that is its primary use, along with content instance tracking (each individual copy of a file), copyright clearance, usage monitoring, royalty allocation and anti-piracy surveillance. The cID works by binding the content ID to the content via watermarking, XML signatures and content hash for robustness, and it uses a two-tier issuing authority model to specify the two-part content ID, which is composed of a prefix issued by a central registration authority and a suffix issued by one of many ID management centres:

> The Content ID is applied at the distribution end of the content value chain, hence its ability to track individual instances or copies of files, and it can work in conjunction with other content identification systems either by reference, or by embedding into the content via watermarking (SMPTE 2003)

http://www.cidf.org

Content Reference Identifier (CRID)

The CRID system is designed to facilitate the acquisition of specific audio-visual content instances and it is returned as the location-independent result of a search for content. The CRID may be made up of other CRIDs and used to identify a related group of content (e.g. serial programming):

> The CRID syntax takes the form CRID://<authority>/<data>, and the data portion is similar to, and compliant with, the Universal Resource Identifier (URI) in form and function; it also has to be meaningful to the defining authority (SMPTE 2003)

http://www.tv-anytime.org

Globally Unique Identifier (GUID)

A GUID is a unique 128-bit number that is created and used by applications to identify various item instances (e.g. component, file, application, database record or user). Although typically associated with the Microsoft Windows OSs and applications, which make great use of it, GUIDs are part of the Universally Unique Identifier (UUID) family of identifiers, which are also implemented in other systems and services both online and offline. The sheer number of possible UUIDs means that it is virtually impossible to have a collision (i.e. two components with the same GUID) and they are very useful for identifying even transient content such as online ecommerce transactions or user activity. The IETF has published a proposed standard RFC1422 (http://tools.ietf.org/html/rfc4122) for UUID, which is based on the original specification from the Open Group's Distributed Computing Environment (DCE).

http://msdn2.microsoft.com/en-us/library/aa373931.aspx

Digital Object Identifier (DOI)

The DOI system is an ISO identification standard that is designed for use in the publishing industry to identify any content object in the digital environment. The DOI names, which can be assigned to any object in a digital network, are used to provide information (e.g. location) about that object and although this information may change over time the DOI name remains the same. This persistent identification feature helps to facilitate areas such as content and metadata management, media asset management, ecommerce and interoperable exchange of intellectual property on digital networks. The DOI system is an implementation of the 'handle system' (http://www.handle.net), which is a general-purpose distributed information system with a suite of protocols and features that enable the provision of a secure identification and resolution service over a distributed network. The International DOI Foundation, a non-profit organisation, manages the development, policy and licensing of the DOI system to registration agencies around the world.

The DOI is composed of two parts, the prefix and the suffix, which can be represented as *NN.<PREFIX>/<SUFFIX>* (e.g. 10.9999/ISBN.0-7645-4889-1), where NN is the DOI handle, <PREFIX> is the registrant number and <SUFFIX> is the suffix that may incorporate other identifiers such as ISBN in the above example. There is no limitation on the length of a DOI. The two components of the DOI are described briefly as follows:

- **Prefix.** This is assigned to any organisation that needs to register DOIs and there may be multiple prefixes assigned to an organisation. The prefix is separated from the suffix by a forward slash.
- **Suffix.** This identifies the entity and must be unique for each prefix. The suffix may be obtained from an existing identifier (e.g. ISBN) in which case it should be used to refer to the same original entity in both the DOI and ISBN systems.

The DOI system uses the CNRI Handle's Resolution System to ensure persistence of the current associated value (e.g. URL) to the DOI regardless of any changes to the URL over time. The DOI system also uses a metadata system based on the interoperability of data in ecommerce systems (INDECS) activity, consistent with metadata systems such as Online Information eXchange (ONIX) and MPEG-21 RDD. The DOI metadata enables mappings between application areas to be made consistently. DOI supports added value features such as multiple resolutions to associate a DOI with several data items or related intellectual property items (e.g. versions, derivatives etc.).

http://www.doi.org/

Universal Resource Identifier (URI), Uniform Resource Locator (URL) and Uniform Resource Name (URN)

URIs are short strings that identify resources on the web such as documents, images, downloadable files, services, electronic mailboxes and other resources. According to Sir Tim Berners-Lee a URI can be further classified as a locator or name as follows.

> The term 'Uniform Resource Locator' (URL) refers to the subset of URIs that, in addition to identifying a resource, provides a means of locating the resource by describing its primary access mechanism (e.g., its network 'location') (Berners-Lee 2005)

> The term 'Uniform Resource Name' (URN) has been used historically to refer to both URIs under the 'urn' scheme [RFC2141], which are required to remain globally unique and persistent even when the resource ceases to exist or becomes unavailable, and to any other URI with the properties of a name (Berners-Lee 2005)

A URI syntax generally takes the form of a hierarchical sequence of components, which include the scheme (e.g. protocol such as FTP, HTTP, mailto etc.), the authority (e.g. http://www.bcs.org), the path (starts with the first '/' after the authority), the query (the optional query string starting with '?') and the fragment. Examples of URIs include:

- ftp://ftp.is.co.za/rfc/rfc1808.txt – FTP address;
- http://www.ietf.org/rfc/rfc2396.txt – HTTP address;
- mailto:John.Doe@example.com – Simple Mail Transfer Protocol (SMTP) address;
- news:comp.infosystems.www.servers.unix – Network News Transfer Protocol (NNTP) address.

http://www.w3.org/addressing
http://www.ietf.org/rfc/rfc2396.txt

These standards are used to identify content in a standard and meaningful fashion, but the identity information, while useful in its own right, can be further enhanced with additional information about the content (i.e. the metadata) and there are several standards in this area as we show in the next section.

Metadata standards

As stated above identification systems must be intimately linked to description schemes in order to help deliver DRM functionality. The data/information description schemes are usually referred to as metadata schemes, and they are used in conjunction with the identification schemes to uniquely and unambiguously identify and describe the protected content in the DRM systems. They are also essential for monitoring content usage and the reconciliation of payments to the content owners and other stakeholders in the value chain. This section lists some of the various metadata schemes and standards in use today as follows. Websites have again been included as a source of further information.

Online Information eXchange (ONIX)

This metadata standard has been adopted by book publishers and resellers (including online giants such as Amazon, and Barnes and Noble) where it is used both for physical goods (books) and digital goods (ebooks). It is perhaps the best developed and most adopted metadata scheme in the content industries.

http://www.editeur.org/onix.html

Dublin Core

This standard is mostly used for bibliographic metadata and it is quite general; therefore adopters usually need to customise or extend it to suit their particular needs. The Dublin Core metadata scheme originated at the Online Computer Library Center (OCLC), also formerly known as Ohio College Library Center.

http://dublincore.org

Publishing Requirements for Industry Standard Metadata (PRISM)

This metadata standard is based on the Dublin Core metadata scheme and is mainly used by the magazine industry. PRISM also has an XML-based rights language associated with it and this was discussed earlier in Chapter 5.

http://www.prismstandard.org

CrossRef

This standard is mainly used by the scientific journal community for reference linking via a specified set of bibliographic metadata, which may include DOIs.

http://www.crossref.org

Learning Objects Metadata (LOM)

This scheme covers educational materials (e.g. anything from lecture notes to complete courses work). It is also based on the Dublin Core scheme and is overseen by IEEE's (Institute of Electrical and Electronic Engineers) Learning Technology Standards Committee.

http://ltsc.ieee.org/wg12/index.html

News Markup Language (NewsML)

This metadata standard caters for all types of news content (including text, images, audio and video clips). It was developed by the International Press and Telecommunications Council (IPTC).

http://www.newsml.org/

MPEG-4

MPEG-4 is a standard for multimedia content and is designed to include a large amount of metadata on the multimedia content object. MPEG also has standards for video and audio compression (i.e. MPEG-2 and MP3 respectively). The MPEG-4 standard has some built in support for IPRs via the Intellectual Property Management Protocol (IPMP) interface.

http://www.chiariglione.org/mpeg/standards/mpeg-4/mpeg-4.htm

INDECS

This is an international initiative for rights owners to create standard metadata for use in ecommerce systems; therefore it has been designed from the ground up to cater for all content types. The <indecs> project delivered a framework and approach for interoperable metadata that addressed five distinct areas of interoperability: across media (e.g. books, periodicals, audio, audiovisual, software, abstract and visual works); across functions (e.g. cataloguing, discovery, workflow and rights management); across levels of metadata (from simple to complex); across semantic barriers; and across linguistic barriers. The resulting framework has been adopted by some metadata-focused organisations such as DOI, EDItEUR and Muze Limited.

http://www.indecs.org/
http://www.dlib.org/dlib/january99/bearman/01bearman.html
http://imageweb.zoo.ox.ac.uk/wiki/index.php/DefiningImageAccess/
Standard/INDECS

Rights standards

DRM rights standards are used to implement rights models and they are composed of the following items: the rights (e.g. play, view, copy, lend, extract, edit etc.), the measure or extents (e.g. length of time, number of times etc.) and the payment or consideration (e.g. money, user data, membership or promotion or loyalty scheme details etc.). The standards are also used to describe rights relationships between the various entities (e.g. devices, users, institutions) and content items. This section is intended to present some of the main rights description standards and languages used by DRM systems, however, these have been previously covered in Chapter 5 (see the 'Rights modeling and languages' section) so we focus mainly on the two main contenders of competing rights description or language standards in the DRM space as follows.

MPEG REL

The MPEG REL is wholly derived from XrML, which was created by ContentGuard around 2000. XrML was in turn derived from DPRL, which was created by Mark Stefik and others at Xerox PARC circa 1994.

This REL can be used for rights in all types of media and enterprise applications. This standard (as well as XrML) is used by many software and DRM vendors including Microsoft. It is also supported by many standards organisations including ISO, MPEG, Open eBook Forum, CRF and the TV Anytime Forum.

ODRL

Dr Renato Iannella created ODRL while working for IPR Systems Ltd in Australia around 2000. As the name suggests it uses an open specification and uses freeware licence terms.

This rights language is more specific to media applications than XrML and it is extensible via the use of profiles, which are domain specific implementations of its subset. It has been adopted heavily in the mobile telephony space via the OMA DRM profile. It is also positioned for adoption in the open-source community with its CC profile. Standards bodies supporting this language include the OMA.

Other DRM-related standards and initiatives

The following standards are also related to DRM systems and have been included here for completeness. Some of them have been grouped into specific categories, derived from a tutorial by Bill Rosenblatt in 2004, and they range from home network standards to interoperability-focused initiatives, as well as obsolete standards, in order to cover the quagmire of different standards that exist in this field.

MPEG-21

MPEG-21 is a framework for standards in networked multimedia and it encapsulates most of the current existing standards as well as those under development. It is applicable to all content types, formats and networks.

DRM support is focused on the IPMP module, an enhancement to the original MPEG-4 IPMP specification, which had little support for interoperability. MPEG-21 also supports XrML and <indecs2>RDD for its REL and RDD respectively. MPEG-21 became an ISO Standard in 2003.

Home networking standards

DTCP

Already covered in Chapter 6, the DTCP standard is intended to protect digitally transmitted content within the HEN. It was created by the 5C Entity of Hitachi, Intel, Matsushita, Toshiba and Sony, and is discussed later in this chapter.

CPRM and CPPM

Also covered in Chapter 6, the CPRM and CPPM standards provide copy protection for digital content on physical media. They were created by the 4C Entity, which is made up of Intel, IBM, Matsushita and Toshiba.

Secure Video Processor (SVP)

The SVP standard is a hardware DRM specification for use in STBs and other video-enabled content devices. It works by adding security enhancements to a standard video processor in order to make it a secure video processor that can be used to implement the business rules and rights associated to content within the SVP-enabled device and beyond. SVP licensing is handled by its own licensing authority (SVPLA), which issues and manages all of the licences for all of the intellectual property required to implement SVP by any organisation. SVP is supported by some of the major industry players such as NDS, Thomson and STMicroelectronics. The SVP Alliance website at http://www.svpalliance.org/svp.html contains further information.

Meta-DRM standards

Digital Media Project

This meta standard initiative was started in 2003 by Dr Leonardo Chiariglione (who also founded the MPEG organisation) and its aim is to help codify and automate traditional rights usages (TRUs).

Coral Consortium

This was the first major alliance formed specifically to address DRM interoperability issues and it comprised major technology vendors and content providers along with InterTrust. The Coral Consortium proposed to create DRM interoperability through services that would be based on InterTrust's Networked Environment For Media Orchestration (NEMO) technology. The NEMO technology provides an interoperability layer that enables communication between DRM systems via a translation language or service. The proposal relied on the use of a standard specification for interfaces and services that would provide a uniform DRM experience for consumers of any compliant DRM-protected content. The consortium website news pages at http://www.coral-interop.org/main/news/pr20060222.html state that although much has been made about its demise, the consortium is very much alive and increasing its membership, and updated its interoperability specifications in February 2006.

Marlin JDA

The Marlin Joint Development Association (JDA) was created by the members of the Coral Consortium (including Sony, Philips, Samsung, Panasonic–Matsushita and Intertrust) as an alternative approach to interoperability, which is based on the idea of common building blocks for DRM systems in order to enable compliant devices to interact with DRM-protected content using a single toolkit. Marlin is XML-based and built around the technologies of its member community including Intertrust's NEMO and Octopus technologies. The latter technology is a toolkit for creating DRM engines based on selected components from a menu of DRM building blocks that include several rights languages, encryption methods and supported business models. Marlin requires the formation of a licensing authority that will enforce standards compliance and administer patent licensing. Marlin provides user-based authentication (not device dependent) with a 'federated identity' approach from the Liberty Alliance, which is also discussed later in this chapter. Marlin supports a sophisticated domain model that can be enforced locally or by a server and allows temporary sharing such that user of a content service can play their content on other 'guest' devices.

Industry- and application-specific standards

Content Reference Forum (CRF)

This interoperability standards initiative is aimed at providing automated multi-tier distribution for content. CRF uses a content reference concept, which is similar to DOIs and other content identification standards. Its Contract Expression Language (CEL) is complementary to the more common RELs and is based on the MPEG REL. The forum members include industry players such as ContentGuard, Macrovision, Microsoft, Nippon Telegraph and Telephone, Universal Music Group and VeriSign. The CRF's website at http://www.crforum.org/ contains more information.

ISMAcrypt

Internet Streaming Media Alliance (ISMA) created this AES-based encryption standard for streaming media. The Alliance's website at http://www.isma.tv/ has further information.

Obsolete and inactive standards

SDMI

SDMI was originated by RIAA as a DRM mechanism for music players, which was based around encryption and watermarking protection.

OASIS Rights Language

This was originated by ContentGuard as an OASIS-backed standard but was officially discontinued in favour of XrML.

eXtensible Media Commerce Language (XMCL)

XMCL, created by RealNetworks, did not gain much traction and was overshadowed by developments in MPEG-21 around 2001.

The above discussion gives a fair overview of the state of affairs in the world of DRM-related standards and, as can be discerned, it is not an ideal state in which to develop and maintain steady momentum in the quest for a solution that will satisfy all of the stakeholders. There is no doubt that these standards and initiatives are currently rather fragmented and perhaps too numerous to be immediately beneficial to all stakeholders; however, this will likely change in the long run.

DRM STANDARDS ORGANISATIONS AND INITIATIVES

This section looks at some organisations that are involved in creating and maintaining standards for DRM and related technologies. It is purely intended as a quick overview of typical entities that exist in this space.

DRM standards organisations

OMA

The mobile telephony-focused OMA was formed in June 2002 by the consolidation of the WAP Forum and the Open Mobile Architecture Initiative and with the support of many of the leading mobile operators, device and network suppliers, IT companies, as well as content and service providers. Its main purpose is to enable the development of mobile services specifications that support interoperable end-to-end mobile services. A major focus of OMA activities is DRM and their OMA DRM 1.0 standard was designed specifically for simple, low-cost devices with little memory and provided three DRM methods of forward-lock (used for subscription content, no forwarding), combined delivery (caters for rights-enabled content) and separate delivery (supports superdistributed content). OMA DRM 2.0 extended the capability of the OMA system to cater for richer content on more powerful devices and support for more diverse and sophisticated business models, improved security with PKI support and content integrity checking. As stated earlier the OMA DRM standard is based on a profile of the ODRL standard and its specifications are made by the Content Management License Administrator (CMLA) with members that include content providers (e.g. Warner Bros.), mobile operators (e.g. Vodafone, Orange, O2 and T-Mobile etc.), mobile device makers (e.g. Nokia, Matsushita, Samsung), chipmakers (e.g. Intel) and software and DRM vendors (e.g. RealNetworks, CoreMedia and BeepScience). The OMA website at http://www.openmobilealliance.org provides further OMA-related information and documentation.

MPEG

MPEG was established in 1988 and was formally known as 'Working Group 11 of Sub-committee 29 of the Joint Technical Committee 1 of ISO/IEC'. It is responsible for developing standards for encoded digital audio and video such as MPEG-1 (VCD and MP3), MPEG-2 (DTV and DVD), MPEG-4 (multimedia for web and mobile), MPEG-7 (video and audio description and search) and the latest MPEG-21 framework, which is a standard in 14 parts that includes major DRM components such as MPEG-REL (Part 5) and MPEG-RDD (Part 6). Licensing of the patents in MPEG standards is provided by the MPEG Licensing Authority (MPEG LA). More information can be found on the MPEG homepage at http://www.chiariglione.org/mpeg/, which is maintained by the group's founder Leonardo Chiariglione.

International Digital Publishing Forum (IDPF)

Formerly known as the Open eBook Forum (OeBF), IDPF is the trade and standards association for the digital publishing industry, with membership that includes the academic, trade and professional publishers, various hardware and software companies, as well as digital content retailers, libraries, educational institutions and other related organisations. IDPF has done a lot of work on DRM-related specifications for the publishing industry especially in areas such as rights language (e.g. OeBF REL) and container technologies. According to their website:

> the Open eBook Rights Expression Language is the result of many months effort to create an OeBF Rights Grammar Requirement for digital books based on XML and an industry specific extension of the MPEG REL (OeBF 2003)

Also IDPF is currently working on its Open eBooks Container Format (OCF) specification to be used in creating secure containers for digital content. Generally speaking, the publishing industry has been very active in generating standards for identifiers and metadata (e.g. DOI and ONIX) and the IDPF is geared to pushing this innovation forward through its many working groups. The IDPF website at http://www.idpf.org contains more information.

Coral Consortium and Marlin

As already mentioned, the Coral Consortium and Marlin JDA were formed for the express purpose of promoting interoperability in DRM systems. Their website at http://www.coral-interop.org/ contains further information.

Digital Living Network Alliance (DLNA)

The DLNA is an organisation composed of some major players in computer hardware and software, consumer electronics and content provision. Its main objective is to promote a seamless end-to-end HEN that supports interoperability. To this end the DLNA provides guidelines on interoperability among other things and has adopted the Internet Protocol as the networking standard for connectivity in the home. The DLNA website at http://www.dlna.org/en/industry/about has further information.

4C Entity and 5C Entity copy protection standards

These two entities have technologies that combine to protect content and distribution in the home entertainment environment's systems and devices. As mentioned earlier and in Chapter 6, 4C Entity's CPPM and CPRM technologies, which fall under the CPSA, help to define a framework that enables the integration of major existing content protection technologies including watermarking for disc-based content. Also 5C Entity's DTCP, under the DTLA, is responsible for the technology that protects audio and video entertainment content on the digital network. DTCP is designed to extend protection to content that originates from approved and compliant devices or protection schemes such as CSS for DVDs. 'Essentially the 4C Entity emphasises secure storage, while the 5C Entity emphasises secure transmission' (Larose 2004). The 4C Entity http://www.4centity.com and 5C Entity http://www.dtcp.com/ websites contain more information.

Copy Protection Technical Working Group (CPTWG)

CPTWG is an ad hoc and voluntary group that was formed in 1996 by technology and entertainment companies to evaluate content-protection technologies aimed at the home entertainment environment. This group acts as an arbitration mechanism for resolving major content industry issues, such as copy protection, by inviting submissions from the stakeholders of potential solutions, which are evaluated based on a set of criteria and from which a final recommendation is made for adoption by the industry. Technologies that have passed through the CPTWG process include: DVD-CSS, DTCP, HDCP, CPRM, CPPM and the American 'Broadcast Flag' for digital TV copy protection. The CPTWG website http://www.cptwg.org/ has further information.

TV-Anytime Forum

According to their website this organisation:

> is an association of organizations which seeks to develop specifications to enable audio-visual and other services based on mass-market high volume digital storage in consumer platforms (TV-Anytime 2005)

The TV-Anytime specification is intended to ensure that content can be stored securely in a consumer device and still be interoperable with other compliant devices in the home. Members of the TV-Anytime Forum include major broadcasters (e.g. BBC, BSkyB, RTL and Fuji Television), equipment makers (e.g. Philips and Sony Corporation, JVC, Toshiba, Matsushita and Sanyo), telephone operators (e.g. British Telecom, France Telecom), mobile phone makers (Motorola, Nokia and Sagem) as well as software and content-protection companies such as Microsoft, ContentGuard and NDS. The European Telecommunications Standards Institute (ETSI) adopted and published TV-Anytime's specifications (Phases 1 and 2) as ETSI Technical Specifications. The website http://www.tv-anytime.org/ has further information.

Other related standards organisations

OASIS

According to its website OASIS was founded in 1993 and 'is a not-for-profit international consortium that drives the development, convergence, and adoption of e-business standards' (OASIS 2006). It has been responsible for numerous WS standards as well as various standards for security, ebusiness and other application-specific markets including DRM. OASIS has also adopted an open, transparent governance and operating model, with members driving the agenda and consensus-based decision-making process. The consortium also operates two major information portals on XML and WS (i.e. http://www.xml.org and http://xml.coverpages.org). The OASIS website at http://www.oasis-open.org has further information.

IETF

This is a large open international community of individuals and organisations that are concerned with the evolution of the internet architecture and the smooth operation of the internet. IETF works via several working groups, which are organised by topic into several areas (e.g. routing, transport, security etc.). Within IETF, the Internet Architecture Board (IAB) is a sub-group that has been chartered by the Internet Society (ISOC) to oversee the architecture of the internet. Also under the mandate of ISOC, the Internet Assigned Numbers Authority (IANA) performs the role of central coordinator for the assignment of unique parameter values for internet protocols. The IETF website at http://www.ietf.org/ has further information.

W3C

This is an international consortium with over 400 member organisations around the globe. It is responsible for developing and promoting technology standards for the web, such as HTML, XML and Cascading Style Sheets. XML has developed to become one of the foremost technologies used by DRM systems for managing digital content in the online environment. It is used in the basic structure for XrML and ODRL, which are the foundations of standards such as the MPEG REL, the OMA REL, the MPEG Digital Item Declaration and many other standards and proprietary technologies. W3C membership is open to any organisation that is willing to sign its membership agreement and it adopts a rigorous process through which all proposals must pass before getting its seal of approval. The W3C website at http://www.w3.org has more information.

ISO

This is the ultimate international standards organisation and it is described on its website as:

> a global network that identifies what International Standards are required by business, government and society, develops them in partnership with the sectors that will put them to use, adopts them by transparent procedures based on national input and delivers them to be implemented worldwide (ISO 2006b)

ISO was set up as a federation of the national standards bodies of over 150 countries around the world and it has a total of some 16,077 standards in its portfolio as of August 2006. The ISO website at http://www.iso.org has further information.

European Committee for Standardisation (CEN/ISSS)

CEN is one of three formal European Standards Organisations within which the Information Society Standardisation System (ISSS) operates as the department responsible for standards activity in information and communications technologies (ICTs). In 2003 the CEN/ISSS DRM Group undertook and published an overview report on DRM standardisation, at the behest of the European Commission, in order to identify the status of DRM usage and to ensure effective implementation of DRM in the marketplace. This report is available at http://www.cen.eu/ along with further information about CEN.

SmartRight

Based on the SmartRight technology originally developed by Thomson, the eponymous SmartRight organisation is a consortium of mostly European companies that supports a smartcard-based 'copy protection system for digital home networks'. Licensing is handled by the SmartRight Licensing Authority, which licenses the intellectual property to anyone wishing to implement the SmartRight technology. The SmartRight website http://www.smartright.org/ is a source of further information.

The International Group for Electronic Commerce in the Book and Serials Sectors (EDItEUR)

EDItEUR is the international group responsible for coordinating the development of the standards infrastructure for electronic commerce in the book and serials industries. It is composed of about 90 members from 17 countries and acts as the umbrella body for many national electronic data interchange (EDI) groups in the publishing industry. EDItEUR is managed by the London-based Book Industry Communication (BIC) group and it provides several services to its international membership including research, standards and guidance in areas such as: EDI and other ecommerce standards for book and serial transactions; bibliographic and product information; the standards infrastructure for digital publishing; radio-frequency identification (RFID) tags; and the trading and management of rights. The EDItEUR website http://www.editeur.org/ has further information.

SMPTE

This society was founded in 1916 as an international professional association of motion picture engineers. It is a very active standards developing organisation and has over 400 standards, recommended practices and engineering guidelines for television, motion pictures, digital cinema, audio and medical imaging. Membership is open to any interested individual or organisation in the field. Some significant SMPTE standards include: all film and television transmission formats and media, including digital; physical interfaces for transmission of television signals and related data (such as SMPTE time code and the Serial Digital Interface); the SMPTE Color Bar Test Pattern and other diagnostic tools; and the Material eXchange Format (MXF). See http://www.smpte.org/ for information regarding these and other areas.

Creative Commons

CC is a worldwide organisation that offers copyright alternatives to content developers and owners for use in licensing their works anywhere in the world (see Chapter 3). See http://creativecommons.org.uk for more information.

Liberty Alliance

This alliance led by Sun Microsystems has adopted the mission to establish an open standard for federated network identity through open technical specifications. It facilitates the creation of federated network identity solutions with inbuilt interoperability among multiple identity databases. It is also designed to appeal to the consumer's privacy concerns by not relying on a single central repository of user information, but instead using the federation of linked systems to build a complete profile as required. See http://www.projectliberty.org/ for further information.

Windows Live ID (also Microsoft .NET Passport)

Microsoft's proprietary online identification standard delivers online identity services that are independent of individual websites, services and devices. It ties together Windows XP licence, MSN ID, Hotmail, etc. It was originally designed as a single (logical) database of identities but this was heavily criticised by privacy advocates as a security risk. The .NET Passport and Live ID solutions can also be used within the enterprise where individual privacy is not such a difficult issue. The Live ID homepage at https://accountservices.passport.net/ or http://get.live.com has more information.

CISAC

CISAC is a non-governmental, non-profit organisation that was founded in 1926 with the express goal of working towards increased recognition and protection of creators' rights. It is made up of numerous societies of authors and composers around the world (e.g. members included some 217 societies from 114 countries as of June 2006). Authors may not join CISAC directly; instead they are represented by their societies, which cover creators within all of the artistic repertoires: music, drama, literature, audiovisual works, graphic and visual arts. CISAC developed the Common Information System (CIS) with the aim of implementing a worldwide DRM system based on standardised identification of creative works and linked networks of information between the CISAC societies. The CISAC website http://www.cisac.org/ has more information.

Music Industry Integrated Identifier Project (MI3P)

CISAC and BIEM (an international mechanical rights society body that represents some 45 national mechanical rights societies in over 40 countries, see http://www.biem.org) launched the MI3P initiative to develop a global identification scheme for digital musical content in cooperation with RIAA and IFPI. MI3P was intended to design a system for identifying transactions involving sound recordings in an electronic environment, enabling the delivery of online music to consumers and the management of the associated rights. This system, which would cater for the end-users' desire for content anywhere, anytime and on any device, was to be based on a unique identifier that permanently associates the recording with its rights information. It was also meant to be interoperable with existing identification systems such as CISAC's ISWC and ISRC as well as CIS. The MI3P delivered a global infrastructure for the music industry based on a system of standardised and efficient data exchange between all of the players (music rights societies, record labels and digital service providers (DSPs)). Apart from the unique identifiers the standard also included support for messaging and reporting functionality, which is vital for every stage of music ecommerce. The main identifiers and messages are listed in Table 7.2.

TABLE 7.2   *MI3P identifiers and messages*

Name	Type	Description
MWLI – Musical Work License Identifiers	Identifier	Identifies the licences issued by the music rights societies under which musical works are being exploited
GRid – Global Release Identifiers	Identifier	Identifies the sound recordings that are released and distributed (also described above)
ELM – European Licensing Message	Message	This message is used to complete the full licensing of online rights in Europe

(continued)

TABLE 7.2 *(continued)*

Name	Type	Description
DSR – DSP Sales Report	Message	This is the message that specifies how sales must be reported by a DSP to a licensor
ERN – Electronic Release Notification	Message	These are the messages exchanged between record labels and DSPs to notify the availability of new releases

Digital Data Exchange (DDEX)

The DDEX was launched in 2005 with the objective of implementing the MI3P standards for music exchange and ecommerce. It is seen as the most effective way to achieve cross-industry adoption and implementation of MI3P and its charter members consist of music rights societies, record labels and DSPs including The American Society of Composers, Authors and Publishers (ASCAP), the Harry Fox Agency Inc. (HFA), The MCPS–PRS Alliance, Sociedad General de Autores y Editores (SGAE), EMI Music, SonyBMG Music Entertainment, Warner Music Group, Universal Music Group, as well as music service providers (i.e. Apple, Microsoft and RealNetworks). The MI3P founding organisations (i.e. CISAC, BIEM, IFPI and RIAA) have licensed their IPRs in MI3P to DDEX in order to better enable it to implement and deliver the business objectives of their standards. However, it is important to note the disclaimer on their website:

> DDEX is not involved in the standardisation of copy or content protections schemes, copyright protections schemes, codecs or other supporting technology. Similarly, DDEX is not involved in the standardisation of any aspect of the licensing of media content and rights (DDEX 2006)

The DDEX websites at http://www.digitaldataexchange.com and http://ddex.net/ have more information.

CONCLUSION

In this chapter we have been able to provide an overview of the various standards and organisations that have evolved in this area and which relate either directly or indirectly to DRM. We have looked at the different types of standards and their position in the standards hierarchy and examined their characteristics as well as the benefits and issues they bring to the table, including the major problem of DRM interoperability or lack thereof. This was followed by an examination of some example standards in the three DRM-related areas of identification, metadata and rights standards, followed by other types of relevant standards. Finally, we have briefly looked at some of the various standards bodies and initiatives in this space, including industry-led efforts such as MI3P and EDItEUR. Perhaps the obvious conclusion to be drawn from all of this is that there are far too many standards and not enough real effort is being focused on the wider picture of the core consumer requirement of content anywhere, anytime and on any device. However, and as observed earlier, this only confirms the difficulty in trying to marshal the dynamic forces that exist in a rapidly evolving sphere of activity such as online digital content creation, distribution and protection. The standards are themselves evolving just as rapidly as the various aspects of DRM that they are tying to influence; therefore we may not see any stabilisation until the inevitable consolidation and rationalisation of DRM technologies and products occur in the not too distant future.

8 DRM Products and Vendors

This chapter was initially intended to present in some detail the numerous companies and organisations that offer DRM products and services; however, since the main objective of this book is to serve as an introduction to the field of DRM and given the fact that this is a rapidly evolving field, it seemed more sensible to highlight only some of the representative operators and products in this field instead. Therefore the approach adopted is basically to list the main DRM players in broad categories and to very briefly describe their products and their organisational profile where appropriate. It is necessary to point out that the information presented here has been gathered from different sources and at different times, therefore it may not provide a complete picture nor indeed cover the very latest developments such as mergers and acquisitions or brand new products and updates; however, every attempt has been made to include a link to the product or vendor website for more detailed and up-to-date information.

This also serves as a health warning that the product and vendor list in this chapter will be of more value as a historical snapshot of the DRM product and vendor landscape (circa mid-2000s). This is due to the rapid evolution of the content consumer market and especially the events that look set to occur within the latter half of the decade, which, in this author's opinion, will make or break (or at least completely alter) DRM as we know it.

Finally, the focus of this chapter is very much on DRM systems as described in the earlier chapter on DRM technology. This is necessary in order to limit the number and scope of products covered and to maintain a consistent view of the topic. Also because this book is predominantly about DRM in the consumer content environment, we focus mostly on media DRM products and companies in this chapter and dedicate the next chapter to the enterprise market.

DRM VENDORS AND PRODUCTS

The following products and vendors are listed and grouped according to their main areas of operations, that is, PC media DRM, mobile DRM, ebooks, removable media (DVD, CD etc.) or other technologies. This is just a convenient grouping and certainly not an exclusive or rigid differentiator, as the same vendor will often have products that cut across multiple areas. The initial source of information for these companies and products came from two major websites: the Worldwide Review of DRM Companies (http://www.digital-rights-management-review.com/) and the UK DRM library website (http://www.drm.uk.com/Digital_Rights_ Management_Companies.htm), which is part of the WWW Virtual Library (http://vlib.org). From these starting points, the additional information was gathered from publicly available company and product websites, brochures and other information sources.

Major media DRM product vendors

This section looks at the main players in the media DRM content space. They also represent and have built their products around protecting the major media file and delivery formats in use by consumers such as the Apple AAC format, Windows Media Format (WMF), RealMedia streaming formats and MP3 files.

Apple FairPlay DRM

- **Company name** – Apple Computer, Inc.
- **Company location** – United States of America
- **Company website** – http://www.apple.com
- **DRM product** – FairPlay DRM

Apple's FairPlay DRM technology is used by its flagship digital media products: iTunes (online media store) and the iPod (media player device). Apple uses MPEG's Advanced Audio Codec (MPEG-AAC) specification to encode the music files sold from its iTunes music store and it encrypts these .AAC format files with FairPlay DRM's proprietary encryption algorithm to ensure that they can only be played on authorised computers. According to Apple's website FAQ page, the FairPlay DRM was designed to be fair to the artistes, the record company and the consumer, and it specifies the entitlements provided to the user as follows:

> your FairPlay agreement entitles you to play your music on up to five computers (and enjoy unlimited synching with iPods), allows unlimited burning for individual songs and lets you burn playlists up to 7 times each (Apple 2006)

One of the main criticisms of FairPlay DRM is the lack of interoperability support and this may have contributed to the many circumvention or workaround tools and methods that have sprung up since the early days of the iTunes store. These exploits are usually addressed by regular updates to the iTunes and iPod software, but that does not seem to stop the hacks from occurring. In 2006 Jon Lech Johansen again claimed to have reverse-engineered FairPlay DRM to allow other content providers to play their own protected content on the iPod thus enabling or enforcing interoperability.

Further developments in support of the above criticism and perhaps also in response to public backlash against DRM included the open letter by Apple's CEO, Steve Jobs, in which he positioned their use of FairPlay DRM as the result of conditions set by the dominant 'big four' recording companies who 'required Apple to protect their music from being illegally copied' (Jobs 2007). Strong media coverage and reaction to this letter included accusations that Apple was trying to hijack the perceptible shift in sentiment by some in the recording industry towards DRM-free content models.

Microsoft Windows Media DRM

- **Company name** – Microsoft Corporation
- **Company location** – United States of America
- **Company website** – http://www.microsoft.com
- **DRM products:**
  - Windows Media DRM (WMDRM) Platform
  - Microsoft Windows Vista
  - Microsoft PlayReady

WMDRM

> This is a platform for developing Windows based DRM applications and solutions that are used to protect and ensure secure delivery of digital media content on computers, portable and network devices (MSDN 2005)

It uses strong encryption algorithms, and is made up of the following components:

- **Windows Media Rights Manager SDK.** This helps to create tools for the content provider (e.g. labels and studios) to encrypt, package and license the content. It is also used to create the licences issued by the licensing service provider to unlock content on the device and to collect content usage and tracking information.
- **Windows Media Server or Web Server.** This is used by online shops and content service providers to host and distribute the packaged digital media content.
- **Windows Media Format SDK.** This component may be used by application developers to create players for the WMDRM-protected digital media.
- **Windows Media DRM 10 for Portable Devices.** This is used by hardware developers to create applications and portable devices (e.g. media players and mobile phones) that can transfer and play WMDRM-protected content.

- **Windows Media DRM 10 for Network Devices.** This is used by device manufacturers to create applications and devices that can play protected content from a remote server (e.g. STBs, DVD players and digital media receivers).
- **Windows Media Data Session Toolkit.** This is used by content providers to protect digital media distributed or transferred via physical media (e.g. CDs and DVDs).

The online VOD provider CinemaNow uses WMDRM to protect its content. Its platform Patchbay adapts and extends WMDRM by integrating with geo-location applications such as NetAcuity, which help to enforce territorial rights. Several tools have been created to circumvent WMDRM including 'FairUse4WM', which can apparently strip DRM from media files. However, these exploits are quickly patched, but they do tend to reappear and need to be patched yet again in an unending cycle.

Microsoft Windows Vista Content Protection

Windows Vista aims to provide end-to-end content protection in a Trusted Computing Platform model. It consists of several technologies that help to create a comprehensive protection environment for 'premium content' (e.g. HD audio and video) including:

- **BitLocker Drive Encryption.** This works with Intel's Trusted Platform Module (TPM) to ensure that the encrypted disc drive will only work on its originating system. The TPM chip located on the motherboard holds the BitLocker decryption keys that allow access to the encrypted drive.
- **Output Protection Management (OPM).** This comprises several technologies (e.g. Protected Video Path (PVP)) that extend DRM protection to computer hardware. PVP authenticates all of the hardware components that process and play protected content and will degrade or disable playback of premium content if any of the components do not meet the required criteria. According to a *Computerworld* article, PVP eliminates the 'analogue hole' security gap by

> enabling a series of DRM measures that keep a high-resolution content stream encrypted, and in theory completely protected, from its source media all the way to the display used to watch it (McKenzie 2006)

These protection measures help to ensure that Microsoft is well positioned to take advantage of the protected HD content that is likely to dominate in the near future. Some sceptics including Professor Gutmann suggest that Windows Vista will cause frustration to some users when their 'legally-purchased content would not play on a legally-purchased player because the content protection got in the way' (Gutmann 2007) and this, he reckons, will be a motivating factor for hackers to try and break it.

Microsoft PlayReady

Microsoft's mobile DRM solution was announced at the 3GSM World Congress in February 2007 and, according to their press release, it

> features support for many content types and formats including music (AAC, AAC+, and HE-AAC, in addition to WM Audio), video (H.264, WM Video), games, ring tones, and images (Arzani 2007)

PlayReady also supports several business models including subscription, rental, superdistribution and pay-per-view and is backward compatible with Windows Media DRM 10 for Portable Devices (Microsoft 2007).

RealNetworks Helix DRM

- **Company name** – RealNetworks, Inc.
- **Company location** – United States of America
- **Company website** – http://www.realnetworks.com/
- **DRM product** – Helix DRM

Helix DRM is a multi-format DRM platform and a core component of RealNetwork's Helix Media Delivery System. It boasts an impressive list of supported file and device formats including AAC, RealAudio, RealVideo, MP3, MPEG-4, 3GPP (streaming mobile content), H263, AMR (Adaptive Multi-Rate), WAV (Wave form Audio), AVI (Audio-Video Interleared), GIF (Graphic Interchange Format), JPEG and PNG (Portable Network Graphic). The Helix DRM architecture is made up of the familiar three main components as follows:

- **Helix DRM Packager.** This component uses strong encryption to package and secure digital media content for distribution and delivery. The business rules and usage rights for the content are stored separately in order to enable the application of multiple business rules on the same content. Also it can be used in conjunction with the Real Producer streaming platform to provide on-the-fly DRM protection for live or non-live streamed content.
- **Helix DRM License Server.** This component provides licensing services including licence request verification, issuing, usage tracking and audit information for royalty calculations and payments etc.

- **Helix DRM Client.** This enables the consumption of secure streamed or downloaded content on the consumer device by enabling the customised media-rendering application to display the content in a secure environment. The multi-platform RealPlayer client is one such client.

In June 2004 the introduction of RealNetwork's Harmony Technology, which enabled the transfer and use of music purchased from their RealRhapsody music store to various portable devices (including Apple's iPod), meant that users were not limited to using a specific device to listen to their purchased content. This move was regarded by some as a positive step towards DRM interoperability and by others as a necessary step for RealNetworks who have no native OS platform (unlike Apple or Microsoft) or a hardware media player device (such as Apple's iPod, Microsoft's Zune or Creative's Zen). In any case this step has helped to highlight one of the major plights faced by the DRM industry as a whole, which is the lack of any one single interoperability standard, but it also allows a glimpse of the potential benefits of DRM translation interfaces and systems such as Harmony, which can extend rights protection from one DRM system to another. This can only be a good thing because, as observed in a law and technology journal,

> the consumer's choice of DRM-protected music is no longer restricted to the type of player they'll use to play it (George and Chandak 2006)

Mobile DRM product vendors

The following DRM products and vendors are positioned towards the mobile content delivery markets and they typically implement the OMA DRM standard in their mobile media protection offerings.

CoreMedia DRM

- **Company name** – CoreMedia AG
- **Company location** – Germany
- **Company website** – http://www.coremedia.com
- **DRM product** – CoreMedia DRM 2005 Product Suite

According to a CMS Watch article:

> CoreMedia AG, which has long been known as a Content Management System (CMS) product vendor, appears to have shifted its focus more towards DRM; this is supported by the fact that DRM accounts for 50% of their revenue (Boye 2006)

The CoreMedia DRM offering consists of an OMA DRM-compliant product suite that includes the following components:

- **CoreMedia DRM Platform.** This core component in the CoreMedia DRM product suite provides DRM packaging for digital content and supports multiple DRM implementations (e.g.: OMA DRM v1.0 and v2.0 as well as Windows Media DRM).
- **CoreMedia DRM Client.** CoreMedia's DRM client implements the CMLA's trust model, which enables it to provide users with the ability to access their protected content across device domains (in this case between mobiles and Windows PC environments).
- **CoreMedia DRM OEM Components.** CoreMedia also offers individual components of its product suite for use in building sophisticated content service delivery platforms (SDPs).
- **CoreMedia DRM IOP Test Server.** CoreMedia's interoperability test server can be used by mobile equipment manufacturers to verify their products.

Overall CoreMedia is regarded as a leading mobile DRM vendor with major clients that include global mobile phone operators. CoreMedia DRM also supports content sharing via superdistribution and it champions interoperability for DRM with its positioning as a multi-platform solution provider in this space.

Beep Science DRM

- **Company name** – Beep Science AS
- **Company location** – Norway
- **Company website** – http://www.beepscience.com
- **DRM products:**
  - Beep Science DRM for Mobile Music and Video
  - Beep Science DRM for Native Mobile Gaming

The Beep Science DRM solution works for mobile music and video content as well as native gaming applications and is fully compliant with the OMA v2.0 DRM standard. It is based on client-server architecture with downloadable client component and server components.

- **The DRM Server.** This provides on-the-fly content packaging and encryption using hybrid symmetric and asymmetric encryption algorithms for the content and the encryption keys respectively. The server is also responsible for key, licence and policy management, and is designed to work with existing CMSs.
- **The DRM Client.** This is in the form of downloadable software, which according to Beep Science's website:

> can be customised and integrated with existing music/media player and media manager components, or it can be deployed with generic and customisable manager and player components as necessary (Beep Science 2004)

The DRM Client is small and works via a core DRM agent, which implements the authentication and authorisation framework ensuring secure content access:

> It integrates with a media manager and a trusted media player (including trusted media codecs) to form a complete DRM-enabled media centre for protected content (Beep Science 2004)

DRM service providers and operators

In this section we cover some other organisations that provide various DRM-related services and solutions. We include operators with alternative business models such as outsourced DRM services, licensing, watermarking and analogue protection vendors as well as DRM intellectual property holding companies.

EZDRM

- **Company name** – EZDRM.com (StrikeTheSet LLC)
- **Company location** – United States of America
- **Company website** – http://www.ezdrm.com/html/drm.asp
- **DRM product** – DRM Licensing Service Provider (WMDRM)

EZDRM.com is a provider of DRM services to various content service providers and other organisations. It specialises in Windows Media 10 DRM and functions as a DRM licence services provider. As described in the 'DRM reference architecture' section of Chapter 6, DRM-protected content requires a licence to access and use it and EZDRM fulfils this role for its clients.

OD2 (Loudeye)

- **Company name** – On Demand Distribution Limited (OD2)
- **Company location** – United Kingdom
- **Company website** – http://www.ondemanddistribution.com
- **DRM product** – B2B Digital Media Distribution Service Provider

Founded in 1999, OD2 is a provider of several online music services including online delivery, content protection, catalogue management, ecommerce enablement and other white label services to many different music and media content organisations. The digital music distribution and protection functionality are based on Windows Media DRM, which may be added on-the-fly as part of its encoding services. It also provides an online royalty management service that issues an electronic licence for every track sold online, and in addition there is a system available for content owners to track sales and to manage royalty distribution. OD2 also offers a client-side interface that allows users to stream, download, burn and transfer music content. These and other services form its extensive stable of offerings to its impressive client list, which includes many EU-based online portals such as MSN, NTL, Tiscali, Mycokemusic, MTV, Oxfam Big Noise Music and CD WOW. In 2004 OD2 was acquired by Loudeye Corporation, which was itself bought by Nokia (http://www.nokia.com/) in October 2006.

Audible Magic

- **Company name** – Audible Magic Corporation
- **Company location** – United States of America
- **Company website** – http://www.audiblemagic.com/index.asp
- **DRM products:**
  - Audio Fingerprinting
  - Network Content Protection (P2P networks)

Audible Magic provides a registration service to owners of music, which offers some level of protection from piracy over P2P networks or illegal mass CD duplication. This is achieved by using Audible Magic's patented media fingerprinting process to register the work along with other relevant details onto their database, which provides the basis for various anti-piracy services and solutions. This database contains registration data on over 4 million sound recordings and is arguably one of the largest collections of fingerprinted audio works in the world. Audible Magic's products and services include the following:

- **CopySense Network Appliance.** This product provides control over the access and use of illegal content from P2P networks on the network. It selectively filters out illegal copies of content on the P2P network but allows legitimate P2P activities to proceed.
- **RepliCheck.** This is a copyright identification and anti-piracy information service offered by Audible Magic to CD replicators. It uses Audible Magic's CopySense product to identify audio tracks that are intended for replication in order to confirm they are indeed cleared and eligible for duplication before manufacturing starts.

Technologies such as fingerprinting and watermarking look set to blossom in the wake of any public backlash against the use of draconian and non-interoperable DRM solutions, and as a result companies with these products will benefit tremendously in the long run. Furthermore in 2006

Audible Magic licensed a video fingerprinting technology called Motional Media ID with which they can offer video identification capabilities.

Digital World Services (DWS)

- **Company name** – Digital World Services (DWS) AG
- **Company location** – Switzerland
- **Company website** – http://www.dwsco.com/
- **DRM product** – ADORA

DWS offers a comprehensive DRM-enabled content delivery platform technology solution that focuses on music and video delivery for multi-platform consumption. It provides support for multiple media (music, video and games), DRM (SDC, Microsoft and Adobe), format (WMA, AAC, MP3 and MPEG-4), channels (online, mobile and cable) and service delivery platforms (OD2 and ADORA). Their main products include the following:

- **ADORA.** This is the main distribution platform and enables the creation, protection and delivery of digital and mixed-media products. It supports multiple platforms and devices (e.g. mobile phones, MP3 players, PDAs, PCs and STBs). The main components include:
  - **Rights Locker** – manages the licensing information for user rights on content;
  - **DRM Abstraction Layer** – enables integration and support for multiple DRM systems, thus catering for their client's diverse DRM requirements and investments;
  - **CMS** – ADORA features an inbuilt CMS;
  - **Reporting** – for usage monitoring and tracking as well as royalty collection data.
- **FutureShop.** This is the ecommerce front-end for ADORA that enables the end-user to purchase content and interact with the content provider.

Secure Digital Container (SDC)

- **Company name** – Secure Digital Container (SDC) AG
- **Company location** – Switzerland
- **Company website** – http://www.digicont.com/
- **DRM product** – SDC Java DRM

SDC AG holds the first patent on music DRM in USA and Europe. It was founded in 1994, some five years earlier than sister company DWS. SDC's DRM is based on the Java digital container, which is conceptualised as a 'digital multimedia object'. The system packages the content, metadata, rights and code into the container which is then distributed to be rendered on any Java-enabled device. It supports the OMA standard and ensures content security with a 128-bit key encryption algorithm. In January 2007 SDC AG was acquired by US-based PacketVideo Corporation.

Aegis DRM

- **Company name** – AegisDRM Limited
- **Company location** – United Kingdom
- **Company website** – http://www.aegisdrm.com
- **DRM products:**
  - AegisDRM Protector
  - AegisDRM RightsServer
  - AegisDRM LicenseMaster
  - AegisDRM PaM

AegisDRM Ltd is a private company based in the UK that specialises in providing DRM services for protecting documents, software, digital media (audio and video) and physical media (CD, DVD etc.). They have developed a suite of services based on their DRM product, which consists of the following components:

- **AegisDRM Protector.** This is the packaging component that applies DRM to the content and makes it secure for delivery.
- **AegisDRM RightsServer.** This component manages the rights and licence aspects of DRM and controls the access to documents, files, spreadsheets, web pages and media content over multiple channels.
- **AegisDRM LicenseMaster.** This component enables software vendors to protect their software and provide a secure (25-digit) product-activation service that allows the software to run only after it has been activated. It also allows for a time-limited trial of software before mandatory activation.
- **AegisDRM PaM.** This is the AegisDRM Protector add-in for Microsoft Office (PaM) and it works with the AedisDRM RightsServer component to provide fine-grained control of the activities a recipient can carry out on a document that has been protected with PaM. This is particularly useful for secure collaboration and other sensitive information scenarios.

AegisDRM products appear to be based around Microsoft Windows DRM and the company operates at different levels as a DRM product vendor, service provider or underlying technology provider in this field.

ContentGuard

- **Company name** – ContentGuard Inc.
- **Company location** – United States of America
- **Company website** – http://www.contentguard.com
- **DRM product** – DRM intellectual property

This company was formed in 2000 as a spin-off entity from Xerox PARC's Rights Management Division, which owned a large amount of DRM intellectual property based on Dr Mark Stefik's earlier work on DPRL (discussed in Chapter 5). ContentGuard controls over 119 issued patents and over 300 applications pending worldwide. The portfolio is wide-ranging and covers important areas such as security and trust models, content protection, rights and RELs (e.g. XrML) and DRM architectures. Their view of DRM covers the five primary elements of content source, content destination, digital asset, licence (with established content ID, rights and conditions) and a trust model that covers all elements (Van Tassel 2006). The three primary shareholders in ContentGuard are Microsoft, Thomson and Time Warner.

Intertrust

- **Company name** – Intertrust Technologies Corporation
- **Company location** – United States of America
- **Company website** – http://www.intertrust.com/
- **DRM products** – DRM intellectual property and technologies

Just like ContentGuard, Intertrust is a major holder of DRM intellectual property with over 50 US patents and around 100 pending applications worldwide. Between 2001 and 2003 Intertrust successfully sued Microsoft for patent violation and won a settlement of over US$400 million, which also provided Microsoft with a blanket licence to the DRM patents. Intertrust is jointly owned by Sony and Philips. Intertrust is now into its second-generation, Java-enabled DRM platform called Rights | System, which is aimed at the high-end content provider organisation and features desirable characteristics such as flexibility, renewable and updateable usage rights information and superdistribution. Intertrust is also a champion of DRM interoperability and is very active in the two standardisation bodies Coral Consortium and Marlin (discussed in Chapter 7). Intertrust is also currently working on various enabling DRM technology environments for the consumer media industry and to this end have created two reference technologies as follows:

- **NEMO.** This is their reference technology for interoperability between different DRM systems.
- **Octopus.** This is a toolkit for building DRM engines. It is intended to provide an alternative to the locked-in, 'black-box' DRM implementations of today and offers developers and users the ability to build their own DRM systems for a given application using most available and open components.

Further developments include the announcement in February 2007 of an Intertrust licensing program for OMA and Marlin DRM services. This framework is intended to facilitate the implementation of the OMA 2.0 and Marlin standards by mobile content operators. Its scope includes 'All Intertrust, Philips and Sony patents for OMA and/or Marlin DRM services' (Intertrust 2007).

DRM-related technology solution vendors

Digimarc

- **Company name** – Digimarc Corporation
- **Company location** – United States of America
- **Company website** – http://www.digimarc.com
- **DRM products** – Watermarking technologies

Digimarc Corporation is a supplier of secure identity and media management solutions based mostly on their patented watermarking technology. According to their website Digimarc has some 275 US patents and over 500 pending applications for patents in digital watermarking, personal identification and related technologies. Some of the many applications of Digimarc's watermarking technologies include the following:

- **DRM.** This can be better enabled by watermarking because it adds another level of persistent rights management information within the content.
- **Media identification and management.** It can be used in this context for communicating copyright information to media consumers, persistent asset tags and to enable remote functionality to be triggered at the consumer's location.
- **Counterfeit and piracy deterrence.** This area includes usage tracking and monitoring, copy protection, content taxonomy and filtering, and anti-counterfeiting mechanisms.
- **Authentication.** It can be used for authentication and integrity, as well as ID authentication.
- **Monitoring.** It can also be applied for broadcast and internet monitoring.
- **Mobile commerce.** Finally it finds applications in ecommerce and linking, authentication and integrity.

Digimarc partners with many companies who license its watermarking technologies for use in their products. They include organisations in various sectors such as documents and imaging (e.g. Adobe, Corel, Jasc Software and Ulead), video (e.g. Cinea, Nielsen Media Research and Philips), audio (e.g. MSI, Philips, Thomson and Verance) and mobile telephony (e.g. Mediagrid). In 2001 Digimarc, along with several other companies such as Sony, Adobe, Macrovision, Philips, Pioneer, Hitachi and NEC, formed the Video Watermarking Group (VWM) to create watermarking solutions that combat video piracy and to address thorny issues such as the 'analogue hole'. Digimarc is also a member of the Digital

Watermarking Alliance (DWA), an industry alliance formed to further the adoption of watermarking (more information on the DWA can be found at http://www.digitalwatermarkingalliance.org/).

Verance

- **Company name** – Verance
- **Company location** – United States of America
- **Company website** – http://www.verance.com
- **DRM products** – Audio watermarking technologies

Verance was formed in 1999 and specialises in content management and audio watermarking technologies for which it holds a significant patent portfolio. Verance's technology was adopted by the SDMI and is also the worldwide industry standard for copy-protected DVD audio. The technology works by enabling content providers to easily embed rights management information into the waveform of their audio, audiovisual or multimedia products, which can then be detected by special software when it is distributed and played via a variety of transport and player mechanisms.

Macrovision

- **Company name** – Macrovision Corporation
- **Company location** – United States of America
- **Company website** – http://www.macrovision.com
- **DRM products:**
  - ACP
  - Ripguard
  - Hawkeye

Macrovision was founded in 1983 and developed its leading analogue copy protection technology, which is used to protect against 'analogue hole' exploits. According to sales director Patrick Fleming speaking at the IP-Trends 2006 European Summit in Monaco, Macrovision owns an impressive DRM-related intellectual property portfolio with some 710 patents and over 470 pending applications worldwide. Its main media content protection products are used to address the three major holes in content distribution (i.e. analogue, digital and network) as listed below:

- **ACP.** This protects media content from being copied in analogue format.
- **Ripguard.** This prevents the digital copying or 'ripping' of DVD media content, which helps to reduce propagation via P2P networks.
- **Hawkeye.** This provides content protection and an avenue to advertise and promote the legitimate content on P2P networks. It works by flooding the network with spoof content that serves to frustrate the freeloader and also guide them to purchase legitimate content from the website of the content owner or retailer.

Microsoft licensed Macrovision's intellectual property in 2005 and made a ten-year commitment to enable interoperability and compatibility with the Windows Media DRM 10 Ecosystem.

Other media DRM product vendors

This section lists some of the other vendors and providers of DRM technologies, products and services. It is not an exhaustive list, but it shows the breadth of operators in this space.

DigitalContainers

- **Company name** – DigitalContainers, LLC
- **Company location** – United States of America
- **Company website** – http://www.digitalcontainers.com/
- **DRM product** – Digital Container (wrapper technology)

This company specialises in protecting any digital content through P2P networks using its patented token-based symmetric-key technology. Their main product is the Digital Container, which features file protection and encryption, tracking, authentication and ecommerce support. The Digital Containers are based on Java technology and work by wrapping the file in a secure digital shell that can only be opened with a key. This protects the file on the internet and also provides the owner with the ability to track, control and audit its movement and use. Digital Containers do not require software on the client as they run on the supported Java Virtual Machines (JVM) on the client device.

DivX

- **Company name** – DivXNetworks, Inc.
- **Company location** – United States of America
- **Company website** – http://www.divx.com/
- **DRM product** – DivX DRM

This company, which began in 2000, specialises in protecting video content. Its core product is a video compression technology, which uses the DivX codec to reduce the size of digital video files to a fraction of what they would be in other formats. DivX has several programs including a DRM solution. DivX DRM enables secure digital distribution of DivX video for playback on PCs and other DivX certified consumer electronics products.

LiquidAudio

- **Company name** – Geneva Media LLC
- **Company location** – United States of America
- **Company website** – http://www.liquidaudio.com
- **DRM product** – Liquid Digital Media Services

One of the earliest digital music companies, LiquidAudio was formed in 1996 to deliver secure music content on the internet. The company was acquired in 2003 by Geneva Media LLC an affiliate of Anderson Merchandisers and they offer several digital media-related services to their clients. Their WMDRM-based services include DRM encryption, metadata management, content hosting and storage, distribution and fulfilment, reporting and WMDRM licensing.

IPR Systems

- **Company name** – IPR Systems Pty Limited
- **Company location** – Australia
- **Company website** – http://www.iprsystems.com/
- **DRM products** – ebook protection and ecommerce systems

This company was founded in 1999 and has been very active in the field of ebook-related DRM solutions. For example, one of their (now former) employees Dr Renato Ianella (http://renato.iannella.it/) created the ODRL REL, which is the basis of OMA DRM. Their DRM products include: the Digital Box eXchange (DBX), an ASP-based ebooks delivery system; the Learning Object Xchange (LOX), an ODRL-based system for the exchange of educational material among educational institutions; and RightsCopy, a system for managing content rights (print, copy, transfer etc.).

Musicrypt

- **Company name** – Musicrypt Inc.
- **Company location** – Canada
- **Company website** – http://www.musicrypt.com/
- **DRM product** – Digital Media Distribution System (DMDS)

Musicrypt has patented DMDS, which is a secure delivery solution used by the music industry. It works by incorporating biometrics, high-value encryption and watermarking to ensure safe and secure distribution of high-value content. The technologies used include the BioPassword, which is a keystroke biometric verification software that validates users through a profile created from their individual typing rhythm.

SafeNet

- **Company name** – SafeNet, Inc.
- **Company location** – United States of America
- **Company website** – http://www.safenet-inc.com/
- **DRM product** – DRMFusion

Safenet was founded in 1983 and developed as a network protection solutions provider with products that ensured security over networks and virtual private networks (VPNs). In 2005 Safenet acquired DMDSecure BV, a DRM repackager and reseller along with their product DRMFusion. The technology provides secure rights management for the delivery of on-demand or live digital protected content over mediums such as IP-based networks and devices.

Trymedia

- **Company name** – Trymedia Systems (a division of Macrovision Corporation)
- **Company location** – United States of America
- **Company website** – http://www.trymedia.com
- **DRM product** – ActiveMARK Content Protection

Trymedia Systems Inc. a digital games delivery solution provider was acquired by Macrovision in 2005 to become the foundation for its games division. Trymedia's ActiveMARK DRM provides protection by enabling an optional revert-to-trial mode on any copies and it works on both physical and downloaded versions of game content. In this way the new recipient can try it out before deciding whether to purchase the full rights to the game.

CONCLUSION

It can be seen from the above DRM products, vendors and service providers that the same DRM reference architecture as given in Chapter 6 holds true for most of them, but that they differ somewhat in exactly how they are implemented. Also as stated earlier this is by no means a complete list, but it should give an indication of the types of DRM solutions that may be found in the market at this particular point in time. One interesting point is that some of these vendors also offer other relevant products in the DRM ecosystem (e.g. content management or CRM), which work very closely with their DRM products to enhance and extend the functionality. This is not a coincidence and as observed in a study commissioned by a German Government program '*Innovationspotenziale der Informationstechnik*' (roughly translated as the Innovative Potential of Information Technology) in 2005:

> DRM systems collect much more information than is needed to perform their function, and that the operators tend to use this information to improve their customer service (Grimm 2005)

However, it also advised that this data collection should be carried out in a transparent manner so that the customer is aware of what information is being collected about them and to what use it would be put (e.g. for service improvement or personalisation). The fact that DRM is already perceived by some consumers to be synonymous with the invasion of their personal privacy means that the above advice really ought to become best practice if the industry wants to gain and maintain the trust of their customers.

Finally, in this chapter we have kept the discussion firmly focused on the topic of media DRM systems, but there exists a category of enterprise document and information control solutions that fall under the classification of ERM systems and this is the subject of discussion in the next chapter.

9 Enterprise DRM

This chapter discusses the field of enterprise digital rights management, which may also be referred to as enterprise DRM or enterprise rights management (ERM). For our purposes, however, these terms are used interchangeably. ERM is directly related to information management and its many facets including the full information lifecycle and the rights and privileges granted for its use in the corporate ecosystem. In this chapter we focus on presenting a complete overview of the topic and provide a definition of ERM, identify the main drivers behind its use and examine the main differences between ERM and media DRM systems. We also provide a view of how ERM fits within the enterprise systems landscape and describe the operational and functional scope of ERM, as well as how it delivers the extended enterprise information control capability. Finally, in the last part of the chapter we provide a quick overview of some of the major vendors in this field and comment on the state of the market as well as the possible future state of affairs in this sector. One quick point of disclosure: the author's interest in ERM as a field of study was sparked off in 2004 by a JupiterMedia Web Seminar on the subject. This was followed by a spate of international conference activity over a period of two years including various roles as event coordinator, speaker or moderator on several expert panel sessions around this topic. This chapter is based on the observations, take-outs such as product descriptions and diagrams, and points of view expressed by many of the participants and attendees at these events. The overall intention is to present a flavour of this interesting off-shoot of DRM and enterprise information security, and perhaps to spark off the interest of others to explore further and follow the path of its evolution, which has recently taken a rather interesting turn.

WHAT IS ENTERPRISE DRM?

> The application of Digital Rights Management technologies to the Enterprise really started to emerge as a distinct market in its own right (i.e. outside of media DRM) around 2003–2004 (Rosenblatt 2004b)

This was in the early years immediately after the infamous 'Dot Com' bubble burst and ended what is now sometimes referred to as the 'Web 1.0' era. It was also just after the accounting scandals and subsequent collapse of huge companies such as Enron and Worldcom unleashed the tide of regulatory compliance requirements across the financial world and other industry sectors. These factors all played some part in the rise of the nascent ERM technology market as a solution to the questions they raised. It is therefore important to understand just what the term ERM means to the industry and how it helps to address the main areas of concern to them.

Definition and overview

According to a 2005 Forrester report, the definition of 'Enterprise Rights Management' may be presented as follows:

> ERM technology allows organisations to establish and enforce policies regarding who can do what (e.g., open, copy, share, email, forward, or print) with electronic messages and enterprise content, both inside and outside an organisation. ERM is the application of digital rights management (DRM) technology to business content (e.g. emails and electronic documents like spreadsheets, word processing documents, drawings and models, and forms) (Erica 2005)

The above definition also describes the scope of ERM and its use in organisational information security and content protection. According to a SANS Institute (http://www.sans.org) paper in 2005, the approach taken by security conscious organisations towards their network perimeter security is one of 'defence in depth' and this may include implementing several layers of security mechanisms such as firewalls, intrusion detection systems, VPNs, secure router configurations and robust network policies that cover things such anti-virus, anti-spam, patch management and configuration management (Biller 2005).

The addition of DRM technology to this mix of enterprise information and content security systems serves to further enhance the security of the organisation by enabling it to provide persistent protection and post-delivery control of their content and information, even after it has left the traditional boundaries of the organisation. It is this particular quality that differentiates ERM from other enterprise information security and protection mechanisms and which also makes it complementary to those systems. Consequently various predictions were made in the early stages that the ERM market would undergo a period of consolidation where most of the vendors would be taken over by larger organisations in the information management field (Rosenblatt 2004b), and this clearly started to happen with the takeover in 2006 of two dedicated ERM vendors, Authentica and SealedMedia by EMC and Stellent respectively (Oracle Corporation subsequently acquired Stellent in late 2006). The main features and benefits of ERM include the following:

- post-delivery protection for enterprise documents (e.g. email, office and PDF documents);

- prevent redistribution of content (according to what the rights policy enforces);

- confidential handling of mergers and acquisitions (through virtual deal rooms);

- dealing with change of trust (with respect to employees, partners or suppliers);

- enforcing classification of information (to comply with standards such as ISO 1799);

- improving productivity (by encouraging revision and version control).

Figure 9.1 illustrates the additional persistent protection offered by ERM in comparison with the traditional corporate perimeter defences deployed by many organisations.

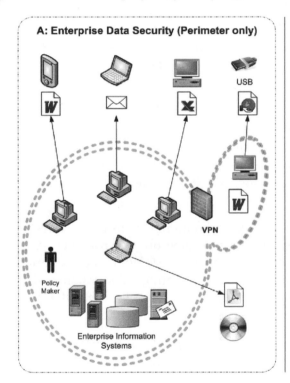 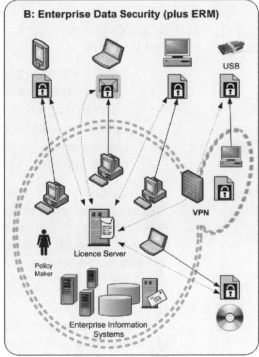

FIGURE 9.1 *Enterprise rights management*

Business drivers for ERM

The market for ERM has become more visible as companies and organisation in various sectors are increasingly looking to try and find solutions that address the information security issues specific to their particular industry. Some of the business drivers for the adoption of ERM by the enterprise are described in the following sections, starting with the major driver of compliance with government or industry regulations.

Regulatory compliance

Several regulations enacted by various governments in the late 20th and early 21st century require organisations to better protect their business records and to maintain the privacy of their customer information. Some of these regulations are summarised as follows.

UK Data Protection Act (United Kingdom, 1998)

According to the website of the UK Office of Public Sector Information (OPSI), the 1998 Data Protection Act is:

> An Act to make new provision for the regulation of the processing of information relating to individuals, including the obtaining, holding, use or disclosure of such information (OPSI 1998)

It includes some specific provisions for the rights of data subjects in Part II such as:

- right of access to personal data;
- right to prevent processing likely to cause damage or distress;
- rights in relation to automated decision-taking;
- right to prevent processing for purposes of direct marketing;
- compensation for failure to comply with certain requirements;
- rectification, blocking, erasure and destruction.

Sarbanes–Oxley (USA, 2002)

Also known as the Public Company Accounting Reform and Investor Protection Act, this regulation came into force on 15 November 2004. Sarbanes–Oxley is a piece of US compliance legislation that is aimed squarely at addressing the integrity of accounting information and it has global implications for companies that do business in or with the USA.

HIPAA (USA, 1996)

This US regulation relates to maintaining the privacy and confidentiality of patient information between organisations that provide healthcare-related services.

Gramm–Leach–Bliley (USA, 1999)

In a similar way to the UK's Data Protection Act, the Gramm–Leach–Bliley (GLB) Financial Modernisation Act of 1999 is aimed at protecting the privacy of consumer information, but in this case it applies mainly to US 'financial institutions'. According to the US Federal Trade Commission's (FTC) website

> The GLB Act requires companies to give consumers privacy notices that explain the institutions' information-sharing practices. In turn, consumers have the right to limit some – but not all – sharing of their information (FTC 2002)

It also governs how other institutions can use or disclose non-public information about the data subject.

NASD 2711: Research Analysts and Research Reports (USA, 2002)

This particular piece of US Securities Firm regulation governs the communication between the investment banking and research departments within a financial firm. For example it enforces rules that make it mandatory for any written communication between investment bankers and analysts to be witnessed by a compliance officer.

ISO 17799 (International, 2000–02)

Also known as ISO/IEC 17799:2005 this is an international code of practice for information security management, which provides best practice for enterprise information security. It essentially establishes guidelines and general principles for initiating, implementing, maintaining and improving information security management in an organisation. This standard addresses the following areas:

- security policy;
- organisation of information security;
- asset management;
- human resources security;
- physical and environmental security;
- communications and operations management;
- access control;
- information systems acquisition, development and maintenance;
- information security incident management;
- business continuity management;
- compliance.

Basel II (International, ongoing since 2001)

The Basel II Framework is an international standard established for managing capital risk, which is then implemented at national levels among its member countries. In addition it encourages banks to identify the risks they may face, today and in the future, and to develop or improve their ability to manage those risks.

It is important to note that some of these regulations, which originate in one specific country, may also affect and influence other organisations outside that country that do business in the originating country. A prime example of this is the US Sarbanes–Oxley Act, which also affects foreign companies that operate or trade to some extent in the USA. Another interesting point about regulatory compliance as a business driver for ERM is that although it appears quite high up on the list of priorities for various organisations in heavily regulated industries, it is still not quite enough of a justification on its own for implementing ERM in the organisation. This is because several other factors also come into play when making that decision, such as ROI and other 'bottom-line' focused considerations. It was concluded during a panel session on ERM and financial services in the 2004 DRMStrategies conference, that it might take some major compliance-related lawsuits to inspire many 'wait-and-see' organisations to implement ERM solutions.

Legal risk management

Misappropriation of customer information by companies may lead to lawsuits by their customers. The information may include customer address details, national insurance numbers and other identifying data that could be stolen, lost or sold by employees or ex-employees of the organisation. The risk of legal action is particularly relevant to situations where the information is then used for unsolicited marketing, emails (spam) or even identity theft.

Intellectual property and competitive advantage

The loss or leakage of proprietary intellectual property is a particular problem for specific industries and sectors that rely on their intellectual property for competitive advantage. These companies are exposed to all sorts of threats from their competitors and internal saboteurs through direct means or corporate espionage. Any technologies such as ERM that can help manage and mitigate this risk will be of immediate interest to companies that operate in those industries such as the financial services, pharmaceuticals, manufacturing, automotive, software, luxury goods and fashion, perfumes, toys, sports apparel, aircraft and consumer electronics makers.

Export controlled information

Some countries such as the US do not allow the export of certain technologies or information related to things such as encryption, supercomputers or military technologies, and will severely punish any organisation and their executives that violate the USA Export Administration Regulations.

ERM versus DRM

How do you distinguish between ERM and media DRM? This is one of the first questions that people who are more familiar with media DRM normally ask ERM vendors and this section briefly describes some of the distinguishing features of ERM in comparison with media DRM as follows.

Stronger authentication

By default ERM tends to employ stronger authentication as a rule and this may be attributable to the existence of enterprise authentication mechanisms within the corporate environment. Rigorous enterprise authentication is normally featured as part of enterprise security systems and it may include several identification and authentication systems such as LDAP or other directory access mechanisms and protocols, the use of security tokens and other remote authentication tools and SSO implementations.

Policy management

This is very important in the enterprise because it defines and directs how corporate rules and governance may be applied across the organisation even at an individual level. Policies are a fundamental requirement and core component necessary for the implementation and operation of ERM solutions. A brief overview of the concept of policy management is provided in a separate section below.

Changeable rights

A core requirement for ERM systems is that they must provide support for the changing nature of individual roles and responsibilities found within the enterprise world. In the media DRM world this is not such an issue because the rights are usually negotiated and paid for by the individual, but in the enterprise space the individuals are granted rights and privileges according to their position of responsibility, which may change when they get promoted, transferred or sacked. Also after an organisation publishes certain information such as their year-end results, then the rights attached to the hitherto internal document may need to be opened up in order to allow access by others.

Usage tracking

In the enterprise environment the tracking and monitoring of the usage of corporate information and content is more a necessity than a desire to spy on employees. This may be due to a variety of factors such as regulatory compliance and corporate accountability requirements. In the world of media DRM consumers may consider this to be a gross invasion of their rights to personal privacy especially if they were not made aware of this in the first place.

Ecommerce integration

This is not usually necessary in the enterprise context, because there is no need for employees to purchase the rights to the information or content that they require to perform their jobs.

Copyrights and fair use or fair dealing

Again this is not really an issue in the corporate environment because of the above point and also because the organisation will mostly own the information and content they use and produce anyway.

Integration

In the enterprise environment, ERM may be integrated with systems such as the CMS and workflow packages, while the media DRM solution may need to integrate and work with various devices in the HEN.

Ease of use

This feature is more of a desirable option than a cast iron necessity for ERM systems. The audience are already captive and do not have much of a say in which system the company decides to standardise, much like with the choice of hardware or other software they use. This is not strictly true, however, because if users find the system unbearably difficult or unintuitive to use then they will probably try and find ways around it, thereby defeating the purpose.

Policy management

As stated earlier this is at the heart of the enterprise information and content management efforts. Basically most organisations run their businesses according to a set of formal and informal rules that are applicable to most aspects of the organisational operations such as the quality of provided services and products, the security and safety of the people, systems and data, as well as in the management of employee, customer and supplier relationships. These rules are usually embodied in the many policies of the organisation and they influence, affect and apply to various entities in the enterprise. For example, the policies that govern information security in the enterprise will probably cover the following entities: the content and metadata, the users, their role and their rights and privileges over the content. This is illustrated in Figure 9.2, which has been adapted from a presentation by Rosenblatt (2004b).

The entities in Figure 9.2 are described as follows:

- **Users.** This entity refers to those who that make use of the enterprise content and information. This entity relates to the identity of the user, which may be a person or a device used by that person.
- **Roles.** This refers to the organisational hierarchy and to the position occupied by the user in the organisation. The role also helps to specify the information rights and privileges required by that individual to carry out their job function or role.

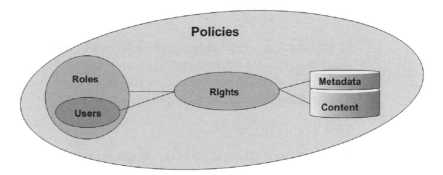

FIGURE 9.2   *Policy management concept (source: adapted from Rosenblatt (2004b))*

- **Rights.** These specify the applicable permissions, conditions and privileges that may be granted to a user over the content and information (e.g. the rights to read, create, modify, delete, print and distribute enterprise content).
- **Content.** This covers various forms of enterprise content including documents, email and the data or information they contain (e.g. text, images, audio, video etc.).
- **Metadata.** This refers to the information about the content and may include the rights and conditions as well as usage statistics, originator or creator, modification history etc.
- **Policies.** The policy ties all of the above entities together and specifies how information may be used within and outside the enterprise. Enterprise policies are very much like the business models of media DRM but apply only to enterprise content.

Another use of enterprise policy is in the area of security and a good security policy is a vital component in an enterprise security system. According to a 2005 SANS Institute paper: 'The Enterprise Security Policy is used to govern the application of protective and security measures throughout the organisation' (Biller 2005). Some of the qualities required of a good security policy include:

- **clarity and simplicity** – must be comprehensible to all users;
- **realistic** – achievable policies are easier to implement;
- **consistent** – no exceptions, in order to avoid confusion;
- **enforceable** – must be easy to enforce and police throughout the enterprise;
- **communicated** – must be communicated to each and every member of the organisation;
- **regular review and updates** – must be created and maintained as a living document.

ARCHITECTURE AND APPLICATIONS OF ERM

In this section we provide a high-level overview of ERM, along with an example of its application and implementation. The main focus is on the differences that exist above and beyond the core DRM reference architecture, which we covered in Chapter 6.

ERM Architecture

The core architecture of ERM is composed of the very same three components we came across in the DRM reference architecture (see Figure 6.6), as well as providing support for additional features such as secure messaging, each of which is described briefly as follows.

The content packager

As in the reference architecture this component packages and encrypts (where necessary) the content to be protected. It also applies the defined terms and conditions or default usage rights that are applicable to the content. The content packager may be implemented as a user desktop- or server-based function.

The licence server

This component generates the licence and credentials that enable the user to exercise their rights to carry out a specific activity with or on the content. The licence as well as the permissions they contain will typically depend on and be built around the user identity, their role in the organisation and the file rights and enterprise policies. This component is usually implemented to work with the relevant enterprise directory or identification services (e.g. LDAP or other mechanisms).

The ERM controller (client)

This component controls the user's access to the enterprise content. It reads and interprets the licence attached to it and also decrypts the content for rendering via native or dedicated client applications on the user's device. These clients may include the usual enterprise productivity tools such as word processors, spreadsheet programs, presentation and other dedicated document application such Adobe's Acrobat Reader. The ERM controller may be integrated into these application clients on the user's device or machine environment in one of two ways as follows.

- **Application level.** This is typically implemented via a plug-in mechanism that hooks onto the native authoring and viewing applications and takes over their whole or specific functionality such as open, save, print, copy, paste etc. This enables the system to use most of the application's features (e.g. annotation in Word or Acrobat). However, the downside is that this may be complex to implement and needs a plug-in to be written for every target application, which might make it difficult to maintain and may not work well with all applications.

- **OS level.** This method traps the systems input/output (I/O) calls and checks the credentials of the originating instruction for appropriate permissions. This is a much cleaner and simpler integration method and it works with any applications on the system. However, it does not discriminate and traps all I/O calls in the system. It may also have unpredictable effects on some end-user machines.

Secure messaging

ERM systems also need to provide and support secure messaging functionality for the enterprise. One of the ways it can do this is via the use of encrypted containers to secure the information for transmission, which can then be decrypted at the other end via the ERM controller. This is referred to as basic secure messaging. A more advanced form of secure messaging involves securing the end-to-end messaging process of creation, transmission channel and consumption applications. This may be accomplished via a dedicated messaging platform or through add-ons to the normal email system.

Application of ERM

There are many uses for ERM in the enterprise and some of these have already been mentioned under the ERM business drivers described earlier in this chapter. This section basically presents some of the considerations to be made before implementing an ERM solution as well as providing a generic example of an application of ERM in the financial services industry.

Implementation considerations

In order to establish whether ERM would benefit an organisation the following generalised steps derived from Rosenblatt (2004b) may be applied to determine the relevance for this type of solution:

(i)   Collect the existing information usage rules (or new ones as appropriate).

(ii) Break them down into specific rules and ensure the appropriate entities (e.g. role, user, rights, content and metadata) are assigned for each rule. If this is not possible then ERM may not be applicable for it or the rule may be badly formed.

(iii) From the resulting list remove the rules that are covered by existing security mechanisms systems (e.g. firewall, LDAP, content filtering tools etc.).

(iv) Of the remaining rules identify specific ones that can benefit from ERM such as any rule that could be enforced better by features such as persistent protection (e.g. time-sensitive information).

(v) Next quantify the business risk associated with these rules prefer-ably using financial quantification (e.g. the cost associated with compliance failures such as fines and legal penalties).

(vi) Compare the resulting figure with the cost of implementing an ERM solution.

(vii) If the financial exposure to the above risk is higher than the cost of implementing the ERM then it should qualify as a good investment for the organisation.

Example ERM applications in financial services

There are several applications for ERM in the financial services industry and indeed in most other industry verticals, but the two examples presented here are chosen to show their immediate relevance and justification for implementation.

Virtual data rooms

Virtual data rooms (or virtual deal rooms) are used for transactions where the vendor wishes to disclose a large amount of confidential information to the bidders during a due diligence process such as in mergers and acquisitions. Traditionally this was based on a physically secure and con-stantly monitored room located in the premises of the vendor or their advisers with elaborate protocols to ensure that security and confidential-ity of the information was maintained. However, this can be slow and very expensive for both parties, especially when it involves a large deal with many parties to cater for; therefore the emergence of an electronic equiva-lent or virtual deal environment is perceived as a positive step forward. This usually involves a secure extranet that is accessible by invitation only to the prospective bidders and with provisions for managing and tracking their activities throughout the process usually via an ERM system. The use of ERM technologies to create virtual data rooms is now a preferred and significantly cost-effective option for the vendor and bidders in these trans-actions. It provides significant savings in time, money and effort for the various parties, and provides benefits that are commensurate if not surpassing of its physical deal room counterpart.

NASD 2711

Another example of ERM use in financial services is in the enforcement of the NASD 2711 regulation in a financial institution. This regulation broadly holds that certain controls must be implemented to control and monitor the communication between an investment banker and the research analyst of the same firm. The policy can be roughly broken down into the following rules:

- the banker cannot modify an unpublished research report (easy to enforce without ERM);

- the banker may only read unpublished report to check facts (not easy to enforce either way);
- all banker and analyst communications must be witnessed by a compliance officer (easy to enforce with ERM but not so otherwise).

The above results shows that ERM can help to enforce two out of the three policies, compared with just one out of three policies without ERM. The financial cost of non-compliance with NASD 2711, which includes the prospect of hefty fines, loss of licence and possible scandal, would be far greater than the cost of implementing ERM in this situation.

Issues and limitations of ERM

Two major issues that need to be addressed in ERM are listed below:

- **Interoperability.** Different ERM systems implemented by different organisations may not work with each other. This is an issue that affects the whole area of DRM and one that is discussed in Chapter 7.
- **Secure key storage.** The encryption keys used by DRM systems need to be stored safely; otherwise the whole system could be easily defeated by hacking the client device and applications. This is more feasible than actually attempting to crack the encryption, which is currently either virtually impossible or extremely difficult to do.

ERM PRODUCTS AND VENDORS

The purpose of this section is to provide a brief overview of some ERM vendors and products in the market and to comment on the state of the market especially with respect to the ongoing consolidation in this space. This is not an exhaustive list of vendors and products, but it should be sufficient to give a perspective on the types of organisations and products in this market.

Major ERM vendors

The following sections present some of the major players and dedicated vendors of ERM products and solutions.

Adobe Systems Inc.

- **Company name** – Adobe Systems Inc.
- **Company location** – United States of America
- **Company website** – http://www.adobe.com
- **DRM product** – Adobe LiveCycle Policy Server

After discontinuing support for their original Adobe Content Server 3 product in 2004, Adobe came up with the LiveCycle suite of document management products, which is designed to provide comprehensive document management and security for the enterprise. The protection offered is not only applicable to documents in the PDF format, but can be extended to some other office documents such as Microsoft Word and Excel. The major steps in the LiveCycle ERM document protection process include the following:

(i) Create the document that contains the sensitive information or convert existing documents to Adobe PDF format.

(ii) Select a predefined security policy, or create a new one, and apply it to the PDF, Word or Excel document; then save the document.

(iii) Distribute the protected file through any channel (e.g. email, online, CD, DVD etc.).

(iv) When the user attempts to open the protected file, the client will contact the policy server to check for the current usage and access rights. The policy server then authenticates the user before granting the appropriate usage rights to the document.

(v) The LiveCycle policy server also captures an audit trail of all activities carried out on the document by the user (including opening and printing) in order to provide usage monitoring information for management audit or compliance purposes.

The above process can also be applied to automatically generated documents using other components of the Adobe LiveCycle suite such as the workflow management services product (LiveCycle Process Management Services), which works in concert with the policy server to generate and protect the document as appropriate.

Microsoft Rights Management Server

- **Company name** – Microsoft Corporation
- **Company location** – United States of America
- **Company website** – http://www.microsoft.com
- **DRM product** – Microsoft Windows Rights Management Services (RMS) for Windows Server 2003

RMS is Microsoft's ERM technology that works with RMS-enabled applications and browsers to provide persistent protection for enterprise digital content and information. It combines features of Windows Server 2003, developer tools, security technologies, XrML, licences and authentication to provide protection. According to Microsoft's 2005 RMS white paper, the main components of RMS technology include the following:

- **Windows RMS server software.** This is a web service that handles the certification of trusted entities (using XrML), the licensing of rights-protected information, the enrolment of servers and users, as well as other administration functions.

- **Windows Rights Management client software.** This is a group of Windows application programming interfaces (APIs) that facilitate the machine activation process and which allow RMS-enabled applications to work with the RMS server to provide appropriate licences.

- **SDKs.** These include a set of tools, documentation and sample code that enable software developers to customise their Windows RMS server environment and to create RMS-enabled applications (Microsoft 2005).

RMS enables users to specify trusted entities (e.g. individuals, groups, computers or even applications). It provides the ability to assign rights to files and incorporate them into a licence. Once the rights have been set and the content encrypted by RMS, the author can publish it safely. Microsoft's approach to ERM leverages their extensive software infrastructure and the internet to provide a well-rounded offering. Furthermore, the SDK makes it easier for developers and other ERM vendors to extend the product and apply RMS protection to other applications as well.

SealedMedia (Stellent)

- **Company name** – SealedMedia
- **Company location** – United States of America
- **Company website** – http://www.stellent.com/en/products/irm/
- **DRM product** – SealedMedia E-DRM

SealedMedia was founded in 1996 in the UK and has since made a name in the ERM market. According to SealedMedia's technology specifications their core E-DRM product is made up of the following components (SealedMedia 2006):

- **SealedMedia License Server.** This is a core component that administers the licences and usage permissions on protected content.

- **SealedMedia Management Website.** This web application delivers the rights model and provisioning as well as online status reporting, help and tutorials etc.

- **SealedMedia Management Console.** This provides rights administration functionality for use by the appropriate enterprise business policy maker.

- **SealedMedia Desktop.** This component integrates the sealing (or packaging) functionality into Windows Explorer, Office and Outlook. It also incorporates the decryption module (formerly known as SealedMedia Unsealer).

- **SealedMedia eRoom.** This is a secure data room service that primarily enables secure web-based collaboration on projects involving confidential and sensitive information.

SealedMedia E-DRM provides core or extended support for various file formats such as email (Microsoft Outlook and Lotus Notes), Microsoft Word, Microsoft Excel, Microsoft PowerPoint, Adobe PDF, HTML, GIF, JPEG, PNG, MP3, Apple QuickTime, MPEG-1 and MPEG-4 in the Microsoft Windows environment. It uses strong AES and RSA encryption to provide protection for the sealed content. SealedMedia was acquired by Stellent (based in the USA) in 2006. In true market consolidation fashion Stellent was itself subsequently acquired by Oracle Corporation, which at the time of writing was in the process of integrating Stellent (and SealedMedia) into the Oracle Fusion Middleware family of products under the Content Management category.

Authentica (EMC)

- **Company name** – EMC Corporation
- **Company location** – United States of America
- **Company website** – http://www.authentica.com
- **DRM products:**
  - Active Rights Management (ARM) Platform
  - Secure Mail and Secure Mobile Mail
  - Secure Document

Authentica specialises in enterprise document protection using its ARM product suite, which is built on the Microsoft Windows RMS infrastructure. Authentica's products are briefly described as follows:

- **Secure email.** This can be deployed on individual desktops via a plug-in that works with the user's native email client. It may also be deployed via the Authentica Secure Gateway, which provides automatic email protection using pre-set enterprise policies at the email server. A secure web interface is also provided by the Authentica Content Security Server, which enables the application of full ERM functionality outside the enterprise. Secure Mobile Mail extends ERM protection to emails on handheld devices such as the Blackberry.
- **Secure Document.** This product provides protection for two main document formats, Adobe Acrobat and Microsoft Office documents. It may be deployed via plug-ins to Adobe Acrobat or Microsoft Office or via the web interface using the Content Security Server.

EMC Corporation acquired Authentica in 2006 and with its core storage business, alongside other information lifecycle security and management acquisitions (such as RSA and Documentum), EMC looks set to take on the heavyweights like Microsoft, Adobe and Oracle in the near future.

Liquid Machines

- **Company name** – Liquid Machines
- **Company location** – United States of America
- **Company website** – http://www.liquidmachines.com
- **DRM products:**
  - Liquid Machines Document Control
  - Liquid Machines Email Control
  - Liquid Machines For Windows RMS
  - Liquid Machines Gateways for: Blackberry, Documentum, Google Mini and Fileshare

Liquid Machines products deliver persistent protection for enterprise content using auto-integration technology, which enables the protection to operate at a machine application code level. Liquid Machines technology and approach are policy based and its 'Policy Droplet' control provides a consistent view of the policies that govern content over various applications. The products are briefly described as follows:

- **Liquid Machines Document Control.** This enables the creation of policies at various user, author or enterprise levels, which are applied to documents as they are created.
- **Liquid Machines Email Control.** This provides secure messaging by enabling the creation of email policies that can be automatically applied to sensitive messages according to a predefined (by author, administrator or enterprise) policy or template.
- **Liquid Machines for Windows RMS.** This extends Windows RMS policies to work on other applications and enforces appropriate controls on content usage:

> It also enhances RMS by providing server-side policy enforcement that can automatically apply protection based on corporate guidelines at the email server gateway (Liquid Machines and Microsoft 2005).

- **Liquid Machines Gateways.** Liquid Machines provides several gateway applications that enable the provision of ERM protection to content created on other platforms and applications such as Blackberry, Documentum and Google. This means that users can apply enterprise policies on information and documents using devices and applications other than the typical authoring platforms and products.

Other ERM product vendors

In this section we look at the some of the other players in the field of ERM. They include companies that have been around for a long time as well as newer players with distinct products and services in this area.

RightsMarket

- **Company name** – RightsMarket Ltd
- **Company location** – Canada
- **Company website** – http://www.rightsmarket.com/
- **DRM product** – RightsEnforcer

According to the RightsMarket website, 'RightsEnforcer is a Document Distribution Security and Control System' and one that provides all of the features and capabilities of fully fledged ERM systems: post-delivery revocation, policy-based packaging and permissions as well as usage tracking mechanisms. RightsEnforcer works by 'wrapping' files before or at the time of sending and creating a usage or permissions (policy) record on the RightsEnforcer Server.

Avoco Secure

- **Company name** – Avoco Secure
- **Company location** – United Kingdom and United States of America
- **Company website** – http://www.avocosecure.com
- **DRM product** – Secure2Trust (S2T)

The S2T solution is based on a P2P architecture and philosophy, and can be implemented to use a central source of enterprise security classification templates (e.g. confidential, top secret, controlled, public etc.) that can be automatically applied to documents as they are created. It uses Microsoft's Active Directory for authentication and supports file sharing both within and between companies with a common trust domain. This latter capability is achieved by minimising the dependence on a central licence server and by supporting several methods of authentication such as anyone, certificate, group member (secure team), owner only, password and active directory. Also the content packaging may be done by the S2T client or 'peer' without having to contact a licence server; in fact server contact is minimal and only required when necessary to perform processes such as synchronise times, check active directory or certificates for authentication. S2T also enhances its security proposition by using low-level kernel device drivers and swap file protection to deter hacking.

FileOpen

- **Company name** – FileOpen Systems, Inc.
- **Company location** – United States of America
- **Company website** – http://www.fileopen.com
- **DRM products:**
  - Publisher3
  - WebPublisher3

This US company specialises in PDF document protection via their solution, which consists of an encryption engine, permission server and client. There are two flavours of the product, which work in slightly different ways:

- **FileOpen Publisher3** – encrypts files and manages the permissions via an interface with a hosted PermissionServer;
- **FileOpen WebPublisher3** – files and manages the permissions via custom scripts on a local server.

The client (used with either system) is a plug-in called FileOpen.api, which has to be present on the client machine to access the protected PDF document.

DRM ONE

- **Company name** – Fasoo.com
- **Company location** – Korea
- **Company website** – http://www.drmone.com/
- **DRM product** – DRM ONE

This Korean company provides a suite of ERM products on the Windows platform including the following:

- **DRM ONE for Server.** This is an integrated ERM solution that works with various corporate systems like Enterprise Relationship Planning (ERP) or ECM to apply corporate policy.
- **DRM ONE for File-Server.** This product is designed to protect files stored in corporate file servers.
- **DRM ONE For Web.** This is a web-based solution for online protection of web-based content. It uses an embedded script and downloadable ActiveX control to provide the ERM control over the web page.
- **DRM ONE For PC.** This provides automatic DRM protection for files created on a PC via pre-set controls that govern the use of the file. The DRM server provides policy management and usage tracking functionality for administrators.

Fasoo also provide an ASP service called DRM ONE for P2P. This service enables users to send secure email messages from Fasoo's website and provides ERM functionality that allows the revocation of messages even after delivery.

Digilox

- **Company name** – Digilox
- **Company location** – India
- **Company website** – http://www.digilox.com

- **DRM products:**
  - PDFLox
  - CDLox
  - JavaLox
  - Secure Messaging

India-based Digilox specialises in protecting software, documents, ebooks and CDs, as well as providing secure messaging solutions to industry clients in banking and publishing. Their products include: Secure Instant Messaging (SIM) for secure, non-repudiable, communication of sensitive information; CDLox for CD-based content protection of private documents, software upgrades and sensitive information; PDFLox, which is a web-based PDF content protection service; and JavaLox, which provides protection for Java applications by encrypting and wrapping the Java files.

LockLizard

- **Company name** – LockLizard
- **Company location** – United Kingdom
- **Company website** – http://www.locklizard.com
- **DRM products:**
  - Lizard Safeguard
  - Lizard Protector
  - Lizard Guardian

This UK company (based in Scotland) has three main Enterprise DRM solutions as follows:

- **Lizard Safeguard.** This provides protection for PDF files using strong 256-bit AES encryption for packaging and a web-based licensing component for centralised control of the rights and licences.
- **Lizard Protector.** This protects web page content with DRM techniques that enforce appropriate usage rules.
- **Lizard Guardian.** This provides protection for software via real-time web-based licensing and ecommerce integration.

CONCLUSION

In this chapter we have explored the field of ERM as an interesting offshoot of DRM; we defined the term ERM and described its scope, boundaries and business drivers such as regulatory compliance. We then went on to examine the concept of policy management as part of the distinguishing factors between ERM and DRM, followed by a brief look at the architecture and client integration as well as ERM application and justification steps, examples and pressing issues. Finally, we gave a presentation of the different vendors and products in this space.

In the next chapter we look at the possible future trends in the field of DRM as a whole and provide a glimpse of the direction most likely to be taken by this fascinating topic in the near to medium term.

10 Future Trends in DRM

Predicting the future is always a bit of a gamble and certainly more so for any predictions on trends related to the internet. The rate of change has been so rapid in this area that the phrase 'internet time' has been coined to describe the seemingly instant uptake (and obsolescence in some cases) of many internet-based services and innovations in recent years. In writing this chapter, this author is fully aware of this risk but cannot resist an attempt at calling some of the likely trends that may occur in future, based on the topics covered in the previous chapters. However, it is vital to include a major disclaimer to the effect that all future trends discussed are based on simple, non-expert observations and may not manifest in the manner described, if at all. For the above reasons this chapter is kept necessarily brief; also, because we are dealing with internet time, the trends discussed may have already become obsolete by the time that this chapter is read.

STAKEHOLDER TRENDS

This section has been divided into the five familiar segments of stakeholder interests and covers some of the major trends in the various areas related to DRM.

Technology trends

The major trends in computing, internet technology and consumer devices have been fairly predictable and they take the shape of smaller, faster, cheaper and in many cases better incarnations of existing technology (i.e. the hardware and software components). The major trend in consumer technology is related to convergence. This is evident in the multiple functions now found on a single device (e.g. telephony, video, audio and internet connectivity). PC technology looks set to continue in this path with more powerful multiple functionality in smaller devices. The trend in connectivity (e.g. broadband, wireless and mobile) indicates an impending ubiquity of access to content from different sources, formats and media that can be rendered on many devices. This is of course heavily dependent on the success and interoperability of technologies such as authentication, content management, security (including DRM) and other enabler components of tomorrow's communication and information infrastructure.

Authentication and identity management are a big part of the enabling technology for the many future services and solutions that will deliver flexible and dynamic permissions and rights assignment, usage tracking, payment and fulfilment functionality in a seamless and near-invisible manner. When coupled with the application of intelligent negotiation and scheduling agents on the user device, the possibilities are endless and point the way to an enhanced user experience of the marvels of connectedness that await us in the near future. An example scenario could be the ability to access relevant information and content in a dynamic and context sensitive manner; for example, a traveller on their way to the station or airport may be informed of the sudden availability of an alternative, better or cheaper option to their destination by their personal communications device, which then offers to replan, reschedule or reroute the itinerary and handle the requisite payments, cancellations etc. to achieve this. The technology required to make this work is certainly available today, but the inter-enterprise trust models needed to make it a reality do not yet exist across the various corporate entities that would need to collaborate and deliver this service. These same trust models are required on an individual scale to make DRM successful in enabling the flexible, dynamic content businesses of the future.

Legal trends

The legal and legislative trends are especially relevant to copyright and the global intellectual property system. The ultimate goal of intellectual property is both to protect creative ideas and to enable the realisation of economic benefits from creative effort as an incentive for more creativity. This has always been a slow and steady process, but perhaps the time has come for the international IPR system to be modified and geared more towards promoting the 'incentive' side of the intellectual property objective instead of focusing far too much on the 'protective' aspects; however, it could be argued that they are both sides of the same coin.

The legislative and legal stakeholders may further help this process by becoming less reactive and more proactive in their regulatory initiatives and legal positioning on matters that concern new technology and intellectual property. This does not imply that an army of techno–legal whizz-kids is required (although it could help), but it does mean that the international legal and legislative communities must try and keep up to date with the new developments that they are required to make judgements about. The aim would be to develop a more forward-looking perspective on technological progress and perhaps rely a little bit less on historical precedents in order to help make decisions on the impact of new applications of technology to both the established and emergent content businesses.

Commercial trends

The main trends here focus on the emerging rights-enabled business models of the future. The commercial stakeholder is usually interested in implementing, managing and maintaining a truly sustainable and profitable business. The extra benefits that DRM can help provide are in bringing the added dimensions of dynamism and flexibility to the business-to-consumer interface. These qualities are becoming an increasing necessity in the connected world of today (and will probably become routine in tomorrow's world) and when delivered alongside robust user feedback mechanisms, as well as timely (or near instant) response to customer issues, it makes for a winning proposition in almost any content business model. The content businesses of tomorrow will likely show more aspiration towards becoming lifecycle content providers that can follow their customers from the cradle to the grave and adapt to their changing tastes in all stages in between. The ever-constant premise here is that any sensible business strategy must work in harmony with its users and be responsive to their needs even when it means re-engineering the business itself to meet that objective. In this way it becomes virtually impossible to remain static in a rigid and entrenched model that may be liable to obsolescence.

The implication of applying this strategy to content businesses on internet time is that their models may have to change quite rapidly, radically and constantly. This was described in a 2006 *Fortune Magazine* article entitled 'Managing in chaos' (Colvin 2006) with examples from the current crop of internet supermodels such as Google. Unfortunately, this vision also presents a huge challenge to the established content businesses, which are torn, on the one hand, by their responsibility to deliver shareholder value today and, on the other hand, their need to create the dynamic, flexible and profitable company of tomorrow. This may have led to the 2007 lawsuit by Viacom against Google's YouTube for copyright infringement, even though they would be quite happy to take advantage of any successful and profitable online channel-to-market for their content (whether 'user generated' or not). Also the recording industry, under pressure about their draconian use of DRM, have undergone a slight shift in position and according to a *MusicWeek* article, they have indicated 'that a softening of the stance must come sooner rather than later' (Talbot 2007). It is now obvious that the issue was with the way in which the industry chose to apply DRM and not with DRM technology.

Both examples provide a scenario where DRM-related technologies (e.g. watermarking and fingerprinting) could prove to be a great enabler. By working behind the scenes to provide usage tracking and other vital data, DRM technologies can greatly enhance the cross-enterprise accounting, royalty calculation and settlements activities in an automated and transparent manner. Imagine a world where users are able to post content online without worrying about the implications, because the system understands the source and destination of all payments required to meet the more coherent and streamlined intellectual property obligations of tomorrow. We live in hope.

Trends in creativity

The trend here is mainly influenced by the relative ease with which high-quality content can now be produced using the technologies that are available and affordable by most people. This can be traced in the music industry by the virtual studio technologies that have made it possible to create complex productions on nothing more complex than a good laptop and sound card. This is as a result of the earlier stated evolutionary leaps in the technologies and components that power the versatile hardware and software components in these personal systems. The most anyone can expect from the technology is the facilitation of increased output from the creative industry. This does not equate to better quality content as a matter of course and in fact there may be a lag before the industry can make the best use of the various means of content consumption available to the user. Judging from the number of 'reality' format shows on TV today, this may be an indication that the content industry is struggling to fill the excess bandwidth created by these extra channels to the user.

Furthermore the reality of multichannel content consumption (and the technologies for creating them) also means that creators can repurpose their content for multiple formats and channels far easier than before and this may influence them to focus more on making reusable content that can be adapted to those channels now and in the future. It is no longer enough to simply research, write and publish a book (including the normal movie option, TV tie-in, public appearance and lectures where applicable), but one must also explore the use of tools such as weblogs, podcasts, websites and collaborative wikis to both develop and help market the book before, during and after publication, and beyond (even to the distant 'long tail' niche market of its later years). In fact the book entitled *The Long Tail: Why the Future of Business is Selling Less of More* by Anderson (2006) was developed along these very lines.

The role of DRM and related technologies in this context is to enable the collaborative creation, use and reuse of content by a highly connected user group that spans the globe. Also it can be used to track and monitor who created what content or its component piece and how that has been used or modified in its entire lifecycle and not necessarily for purposes of rights enforcement.

Consumer trends

This is probably the most difficult to predict out of the five stakeholder groupings, mostly because users can be fickle and liable to change at any time. However, it is this same quality that makes them the most interesting group, along with the fact consumers are the ultimate arbiters of success or failure of any technology, business model, legal statute or creative effort. As pointed out by this author in a Capgemini white paper on the new music business, 'The consumers or end-users are in fact the most important stakeholder group' (Umeh 2005).

The biggest of the current trends within the consumer group is the so-called user-generated content, which can be found in various community-based social networking websites or popular web destinations such as MySpace.com, Flickr.com and YouTube.com. The challenge faced by rights holders is how or whether to enforce their rights in this environment where it may actually be to their advantage to have content. Based on the continued success of online advertising via popular web destinations such as Google, the trend looks set to continue until some major legal challenge such as Viacom versus YouTube forces the sites to become too restrictive, in which case the users will simply move on.

Users, especially the young, tend to be among the first to experiment and discover new ways to use and create content. They dictate the trends in usage that content businesses, legislation and creators have to address, but they can be influenced by the new technologies that enable these trends. This usually means that the users are often those to fall foul of established rules and usage dictates that govern how content is used. Research findings on consumer behaviour regarding digital music from two different sources show that:

- 'Users are often not aware of the restrictions applicable to content' (Wichmann 2005);
- and even if they were 'the prevailing motivational factors of cost, convenience and practicality will sway their decision' (Fetscherin 2005).

This is something that content businesses and other stakeholders need to take into account if they want to compete effectively for a share of the consumer's wallet. The well-publicised struggle for the mindshare, walletshare and timeshare of the content consumer shows that users are subject to high demands on their time for content consumption through channels such as mobile phones, TV, internet, gaming and other connected devices. The activities supported by these channels include shopping, gaming and work, as well as the education, communication, information and entertainment activities. This will make it even more challenging to capture and retain users in the near future.

DRM TRENDS

This section focuses on the future headline trends that will probably dominate the DRM space. It includes the ongoing and sometimes intractable issues that we have touched on in earlier chapters, as well as other general and overarching situations that influence the whole of DRM, copyright and the IPR philosophy.

Interoperability – 'one size fits most'

Standards need to be developed that enable interoperability and inter-working of the various components in the DRM space, this includes fundamental aspects such as identity management, authentication, cryptography, rights management and RELs, as well as standard and consistent interfaces to asset systems and CMSs and other collaborative enablers such as messaging and metadata. However, the entrenched interests of the various parties involved make this a daunting task with a remote chance of success; therefore a pragmatic look at this particular issue would indicate that as in most things of this nature an uneasy balance should eventually emerge. This would probably be in the form of real or *de facto* standards that would cater for the needs of the majority in a 'one size fits most' type of middle ground. However, because this is a dynamic environment, this balance will shift from time to time as new developments occur that move the landscape in favour of one party or another, but always as a response to the shifts. Extensible XML-based standards are a good step in this direction because they incorporate the requisite flexibility in their specification language that is necessary to help adapt them in most circumstances.

Usability – 'DRM becomes invisible to the end-user'

This is the holy grail of usability for the simple reason that if DRM does not intrude too much on the user experience then they are less likely to notice and complain about it. However, this perceived 'intrusion' in the user experience probably has more to do with the erroneous impression of early internet users that most of the content on the internet is fair game, that is, 'if it is there, then it must be OK to use it'. It goes without saying that the rights owners especially in the content industry do not agree with this viewpoint. More to the point though, the intrusive impact of DRM is probably felt more by legitimate users who become all too aware of the presence of DRM when they are unable to render their legally purchased content on other devices, for example. This can be very annoying and as discussed in Chapters 6 and 8 may encourage them to try and find ways around the protection much to the chagrin of the supporters of anti-circumvention regulations. When legitimate users are driven to these lengths it becomes very clear that the product, service, business model and enforcement measures may be flawed. In order to make DRM 'invisible', it would require some painful sacrifices on the part of the commercial stakeholders to adopt a more user-orientated approach and business growth strategies, which would be more beneficial to everyone in the long run, based on the presumption that that the old models as we know them are well and truly dead in the water.

Digital rights: 'management or enablement?'

A change of name and focus may be required for the remaining aspects of DRM that are perceptible to the user and which are manifested in the sophisticated business models of tomorrow. For example, any image change initiative for DRM must be appreciative of the following factors:

- First of all, the three letter acronym 'DRM' may be misleading in what it represents to each of the stakeholders and this would be a major detraction from its alternative use or objective as an enabler of rights management in relation to content.
- Secondly it may be far better and certainly more positive and accurate to refer to DRM as digital rights enablement (DRE) technology because this is the motivation for most of the technologies that collectively form DRM and on which it can certainly deliver. It also builds on a realigned view of DRM as an 'enabler' as opposed to an 'enforcer' of content rights within and outside the digital space.
- Finally, as with any other tool the improper application of DRM (or its new and cleansed identity) will only lead right back to the very issues observed in the past, which have been highlighted in previous chapters.

IPDRAMA – 'ongoing and relentless'

The ever-present tension in the interconnected areas of intellectual property and digital rights and asset management (IPDRAMA) is patently manifest in the divide between content and rights owners and the consumers. This may be exacerbated by the use of legal instruments by certain entrenched parties and the economic system of IPRs to maintain the status quo. However, this may actually be a good thing because as long as there is demand for content produced by whichever means, there will always be a market for it as well as business strategies to capitalise on it. This is an area most closely aligned with the evolutionary paradigm of

> survival of the fittest and only the strategies that are flexible and can adapt to various environments and circumstances are most likely to survive (Umeh 2006)

It also affords an opportunity for strategies in content technology, business and usage to evolve new and different ways to flourish in their prevailing markets. This implies that the current state of events and the resulting tensions are really the normal course of evolution and that what is perceived as bad practice today may become the best practice of tomorrow; however, this can be very difficult to accept for the vested interests of today. Figure 10.1 illustrates this with the infamous 'DVD' Jon Lech Johansen shown in his roles as both hero and villain depending on which side of the fence you sit. However, and to stretch a metaphor, although it may be uncomfortable to sit on the above fence this may prove to be the best strategy in the long run because it is perfectly rational to take advantage of the lessons learned by others and use this to innovate your own business (without breaking the law) before it gets too difficult to compete in the changing landscape.

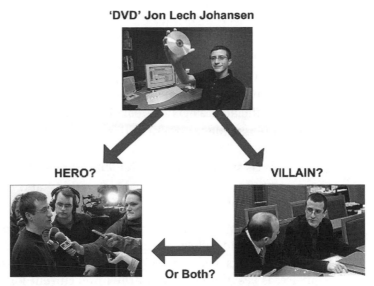

FIGURE 10.1 *'DVD' Jon Lech Johansen (source: adapted from Clubic.com (2003), SG.hu (2003) and SJJF (2000))*

CONCLUSIONS

This book has taken us on a journey through the various aspects of the technology innovations that influence and make up the field of DRM. We have looked at the evolution of communication and legal construct such as intellectual property and copyright. We have also examined the stakeholder and industry issues, as well as several of the rights-enabled business models that drive the creation of DRM and related products. We explored the various technologies that actually combine to provide DRM capabilities, as well as the standards, organisations and companies that are involved in making DRM products and technologies. Finally, we looked at the related field of ERM and its consolidation with other enterprise content and security management products and organisations. In this chapter we have then attempted, based on the previous chapters, to make some general predictions on the future trends in this space. This author strongly believes that DRM is an enabler technology that will help to realise the increasingly obvious role to be played by technological innovation in our cultural evolution as a species.

All of this would seem to point to a future where technologies such as DRM or its offspring (i.e. DRE or DRM 2.0) will help to enable a flexible, dynamic and well-connected techno–information continuum that surrounds the user, anticipating their every content need and fulfilling them (including handling any necessary negotiations on permissions and price) without the direct intervention of the user. This may seem a slightly utopian (or dystopian) fantasy, reflective of an impending technological singularity as espoused by some futurists, but the reality is that the technology components necessary to make this happen are already in place and readily available today. They include:

- ubiquitous connectivity (the internet and broadband access);
- real-life business and rights modelling capability (information rights management);
- artificial intelligence (learning programmes and algorithms);
- identity management and trust management (e.g. trusted computing);
- mass storage (cheaper, reliable storage is key);
- community-based social networking and search (MySpace.com, YouTube.com, Flickr.com, Google.com etc.).

The main question is whether DRM will survive and deliver on its promises to the stakeholders (e.g. content creators, rights owners, IPR organisations and consumers) considering the amount of flak it currently generates. The answer is yes, but not necessarily in its current form. Therefore like it or not, DRM technology (in this or another guise) is here to stay and although it will take considerable effort and compromise from all stakeholders to make it work as it ought to, eventually it must fulfil its potential as one of the core enablers of the digital lifestyle of tomorrow.

List of abbreviations

3D	Three-Dimensional
3DES	Triple Digital Encryption Standard
AAC	Advanced Audio Coding
AACS	Advanced Access Content System
ACAP	Automated Content Access Protocol
ACP	Analogue Copy Protection
AEBR	Advanced eBook Processor
AES	Advanced Encryption Standard
AMR	Adaptive Multi-Rate
API	Application Programming Interface
ARM	Active Rights Management
ARPANET	ARPA Network
ASP	Application Service Provider
AVI	Audio-Video Interleaved
BSD	Berkeley Software Distribution
CA	Conditional Access
CASE	Computer-Aided Software Engineering
CATV	Community Access Television
CCD	Charge Coupled Device
CD	Compact Disc
CD-R	Compact Disc Recordable
CD-ROM	Compact Disc Read Only Memory
CD-RW	Compact Disc Re-Writable
CEL	Contract Expression Language
CF	Compact Flash
CGMS	Copy Generation Management Systems

CGMS-A	Copy Generation Management Systems – Analogue
CGMS-D	Copy Generation Management Systems – Digital
cID	Content Identifier
CIS	Common Information System
CMLA	Content Management License Administrator
CMS	Content Management System
CPPM	Copy Control for Pre-Recorded Media
CPRM	Copy Control for Recorded Media
CPSA	Content Protection Security Architecture
CPU	Central Processing Unit
CRID	Content Reference Identifier
CRM	Customer Relationship Management
CSS	Content Scrambling System
DAM	Digital Asset Management
DAT	Digital Audio Tape
DBX	Digital Box eXchange
DCE	Distributed Computing Environment
DCPS	Digital Copy Protection System
DeCSS	Content Scrambling System Decryption
DES	Digital Encryption Standard
DITA	Darwin Information Typing Architectures
DMDS	Digital Medial Distribution System
DMM	Digital Media Management
DNS	Domain Name System
DOI	Digital Object Identifier
DPRL	Digital Property Rights Language
DRM	Digital Rights Management
DSA	Digital Secure Algorithm
DSL	Digital Subscriber Line
DSP	Digital Service Providers
DSR	Digital Service Providers Sales Report

DSS	Digital Signature Standard
DTCP	Digital Transmission Content Protection
DTH	Direct To Home
DTV	Digital Television
DVB	Digital Video Broadcast
DVD	Digital Versatile Disc
DVD-R	Digital Versatile Disc Recordable
DVD-ROM	Digital Versatile Disc Read Only Memory
DVD-RW	Digital Versatile Disc Re-Writable
ECC	Elliptical Curve Cryptography
ECM	Enterprise Content Management
EDI	Electronic Data Interchange
ELM	European Licensing Message
EPG	Electronic Program Guide
ERM	Employee Relationship Management
ERM or E-DRM	Enterprise Rights Management or Enterprise DRM
ERN	Electronic Release Notification
ERP	Enterprise Relationship Planning
ExCCI	Extended Copy Control Instruction
FAQ	Frequently Asked Questions
FM	Frequency-Modulated
FTP	File Transfer Protocol
GB	Gigabyte
GIF	Graphic Interchange Format
GPL	General Public License
GRid	Global Release Identifier
GSM	Global System for Mobile
GUID	Globally Unique Identifier
HD	High-Definition
HDCP	High-Bandwidth Digital Content Protection
HDD	Hard Disk Drive

HDTV	High-Definition Television
HEN	Home Entertainment Network
HTML	HyperText Markup Language
HTTP	HyperText Transfer Protocol
I/O	Input/Output
IBM	International Business Machines
ICANN	Internet Corporation for Assigned Numbers
ICT	Information and Communications Technologies
IDEA	International Data Encryption Algorithm
IDM	Identity Management
INDECS	Interoperability of Data in Ecommerce Systems
IP	Internet Protocol
IPDRAMA	Intellectual Property and Digital Rights and Asset Management
IPMP	Intellectual Property Management Protocol
IPR	Intellectual Property Rights
IPTV	Internet Protocol TV
ISAN	International Standard Audiovisual Number
ISBN	International Standard Book Number
ISRC	International Standard Recording Code
ISSN	International Standard Serial Number
ISWC	International Standard Work Code
ISP	Internet Service Provider
ITU	International Telecommunications Union
JANET	Joint Academic Network
JPEG	Joint Photographic Experts Group
JVM	Java Virtual Machines
LAMP	Linux, Apache, MySQL and PHP
LDAP	Lightweight Directory Access Protocol
LGPL	Lesser General Public License
LOM	Learning Objects Metadata

LOX	Learning Object Xchange
LV	Laser Vision
MAC	Media Access Control
MAM	Media Asset Management
MD2	Message Digest 2
MD4	Message Digest 4
MD5	Message Digest 5
MIPv4	Mobility for IPv4
MIT	Massachusetts Institute of Technology
MP3	MPEG-3
MPEG	Moving Picture Experts Group
MWLI	Musical Work License Identifiers
MXF	Material eXchange Format
NEMO	Networked Environment for Media Orchestration
NewsML	News Markup Language
NNTP	Network News Transfer Protocol
NVRAM	Non-Volatile Random Access Memory
OAI-PMH	Open Archives Initiative Protocol for Metadata Harvesting
OASIS	Organization for the Advancement of Structured Information Standards
OCF	Open eBooks Container Format
ODRL	Open Digital Rights Language
OMA	Open Mobile Alliance
ONIX	Online Information eXchange
OPM	Output Protection Management
OS	Operating System
P2P	Peer-2-Peer
PC	Personal Computer
PDA	Personal Digital Assistant
PGP	Pretty Good Privacy
PKI	Public Key Infrastructure

PNG	Portable Network Graphic
PRISM	Publishing Requirements for Industry Standard Metadata
PRL	PRISM Rights Language
PRM	Partner Relationship Management
PSTN	Public Switched Telephone Network
PVP	Protected Video Path
PVR	Personal Video Recorder
RAM	Random Access Memory
RC4	Rivest Cipher 4
RC5	Rivest Cipher 5
RDD	Rights Data Dictionary
REL	Rights Expression Languages
RFC	Request For Comments
RMS	Rights Management Services
ROAP	Rights Object Access Protocol
ROI	Return On Investment
RoMEO	Rights Metadata for Open Archiving
RPC	Regional Protection Control
RSA	Rivest, Shamir and Adelman
RSS	Really Simple Syndication
S2T	Secure2Trust
SAML	Security Assertion Markup Language
SCMS	Serial Copy Management System
SD	Secure Digital
SDK	Software Development Kit
SDMI	Secure Digital Music Initiative
SDP	Service Delivery Platforms
SHA-1	Secure Hash Algorithm
SIM	Secure Instant Messaging
SMS	Short Message Service

SMTP	Simple Mail Transfer Protocol
SOAP	Simple Object Access Protocol
SPC	Supplementary Protection Certificate
SPD	Self-Protecting Documents
SRM	Suppler Relationship Management
SSO	Single Sign On
STB	Set-Top Box
SVP	Secure Video Processor
TB	Terabyte
TCP	Transmission Control Protocol
TFT	Thin-Film Transistor
TPM	Trusted Platform Module
TRU	Traditional Rights Usages
TTP	Trusted Third Party
UKPO	UK Patent Office
UMID	Unique Material Identifier
UUID	Universally Unique Identifier
URI	Universal Resource Identifier
URL	Uniform Resource Locator
URN	Uniform Resource Name
VCD	Video CD
VCR	Video Cassette Recorder
VHS	Video Home Systems
VOD	Video-on-Demand
VOIP	Voice Over IP
VPN	Virtual Private Network
VTR	Video Tape Recorder
WAV	Waveform Audio
WCM	Web Content Management
Wi-Fi	Wireless Fidelity
WIPO	World Intellectual Property Organisation

WMDRM	Windows Media DRM
WMF	Windows Media Format
WORM	Write Once, Read Many
WS	Web Services
XACML	eXtensible Access Control Markup Language
XCP	Extended Copy Protection
XML	eXtensible Markup Language
XMCL	eXtensible Media Commerce Language
XrML	eXtensible Rights Markup Language

References

4C Entity (2000) Content Protection System Architecture (revision 0.81). http://www.4centity.com

Anderson, C. (2006). *The Long Tail: Why the Future of Business is Selling Less of More*, Hyperion, New York.

APIG (2006) Digital Rights Management: Report of an Inquiry by the All Party Internet Group. http://www.apig.org.uk/current-activities/apig-inquiry-into-digital-rights-management/DRMreport.pdf

Apple (2006) Authorization. http://www.apple.com/lu/support/itunes/authorization.html (available at http://www.hackingnetflix.com/2005/10/apple_licenses_.html)

Arzani, A. (2007) *3GSM Roundup: Earthquakes Shake Mobile DRM World*. DRM Watch. http://www.drmwatch.com/drmtech/article.php/3661311

Beep Science (2004) *DRM for Mobile Music & Video*. Beep Science, Oslo, Norway. http://www.beepscience.com

Berners-Lee, T. (2005) Universal Resource Identifiers (URI): generic syntax. *Request for Comments 3986*. The Network Working Group. http://www.gbiv.com/protocols/uri/rfc/rfc3986.html

Biller R. S. (2005) *Regaining Control over your Mobile Users* (version 1.4c). SANS Institute, Bethesda, MD.

Black, T. (2002) *Special Report: Intellectual Property in the Digital Era*. Sweet & Maxwell, London.

Boye, J. (2006) *Is German CoreMedia Still a CMS Company?* CMS Watch. http://www.cmswatch.com/Trends/747-Is-German-CoreMedia-still-a-CMS-company?

Byrne, T. (2006) Web content management systems: architectures and products. In *Proceedings of the Gilbane San Francisco 2006 Conference*, San Francisco, CA, 24 April.

CARET (2005) Intellectual property and copyright in the digital environment. Centre for Applied Research in Educational Technologies, University of Cambridge. http://www.caret.cam.ac.uk/copyright/page171.html#topic180

CEN/ISSS (2003) Digital Rights Management Final Report. http://www.cen. eu/cenorm/businessdomains/businessdomains/isss/activity/drm_fg.asp

Chiariglione, L. (2006) ISO/IEC JTC1/SC29/WG11, *Coding of Moving Pictures and Audio*. http://www.chiariglione.org/mpeg/standards/ mpeg-21/mpeg-21.htm

Choate, P. (2005) *Hot Property: The Stealing of Ideas in an Age of Globalization*. Knopf, New York.

Clubic.com (2003). *Lech Johansen gagne son procès face à la MPAA*. http://www.clubic.com/actualite-10659-lech-johansen-gagne-son- proces-face-a-la-mpaa.html

Cobb, C. (2004) *Cryptography For Dummies*. John Wiley & Sons, Indianapolis, IN.

Colvin, G. (2006) Managing in chaos. *Fortune Magazine*, 154(6), 26–32.

Connected Earth (2006) Developing the telephone. http://www.connected- earth.com/galleries/telecommunicationsage/thetelephone/

Cornthwaite, J. (2006) On-line infringement of musical copyright: the UK legal perspective. In *Presentation to the British Computer Society Seminar on IT's Music Industry*, 18 October.

Coyle. K. (2003) The technology of rights: digital rights management. http://www.kcoyle.net/drm_basics.html

Crawford, S. (2005) History of telephony. http://scrawford.blogware.com/ blog/_archives/2005/6/30/986539.html

Datamonitor (2004) *Emerging Identity Management Prospects*. Datamonitor, London.

DDEX (2006) *Welcome to DDEX*. The Digital Data Exchange. http:// ddex.net/

Deloitte (2006) *Turn on to Digital: Getting Prepared for Digital Content Creation and Distribution in 2012*. Deloitte, London.

DPC (2002) Media and formats. http://www.dpconline.org/graphics/ medfor/media.html

eMarketer (2006) Worldwide online access: 2004–2010. http://www. emarketer.com/Report.aspx?bband_world_jun06

Erica, R. (2005) *Mitigate Content-Related Risk with Enterprise Rights Management*. Forrester Research, Cambridge , MA.

Fetscherin, M. (2005) Consumer acceptance of digital rights management. In *Proceedings of the DRM Strategies Conference*, New York, 27–28 July.

Filmsite.org (2006) Timeline of greatest film milestones and important turning points in film history. http://www.filmsite.org/

Fish, R. (2006) *The Record Industry is Dead, Long Live the Music Industry!* FishTank, London.

Fisher, K. (2005) DVD audio encryption scheme defeated. http://arstechnica.com/news.ars/post/20050706-5065.html

Fisher, W. F. (2004) *Promises to Keep*. Stanford University Press, Stanford, CA.

Flake, G. (2006) Innovation. *Fortune Magazine (Europe Edition)*, 154(1), 10 July.

Fox, S., Anderson, J. Q. and Raine, L. (2005) *The Future of the Internet*. Pew Internet & American Life Project, Washington, DC.

FTC (2002) In brief: the financial privacy requirements of the Gramm–Leach–Bliley Act. *Facts for Business*. Federal Trade Commission, Washington, DC. http://www.ftc.gov/bcp/conline/pubs/buspubs/glbshort.shtm

Gantz, J. and Rochester, J. B. (2005) *Pirates of The Digital Millennium*. Prentice-Hall, Englewood Cliffs, NJ.

Garnett, N. and Sander, T. (2002) Fair use by design. In *Proceedings of the 12th Conference on Computers, Freedom and Privacy*, San Francisco, CA, 16–19 April.

George, C. and Chandak, N. (2006) Issues and challenges in securing interoperability of DRM systems in the digital music market. *Int. Rev. Law Comput. Technol.*, 20(3), 271–285.

Goldstein, P. (2003) *Copyright's Highway* (revised edition). Stanford University Press, Stanford, CA.

Gowers (2006) *Gowers Review of Intellectual Property*. The Stationary Office, London.

Grimm, R. (2005) *Privacy for Digital Rights Management Products and their Business Cases*. University Koblenz and Fraunhofer Institute for Digital Media Technology.

Gunther, M. (2006) Fox the day after tomorrow. *Fortune Magazine*, 153(9), 29 May.

Gutmann, P. (2007) *A Cost Analysis of Windows Vista Content Protection*. Department of Computer Science, University of Auckland. http://www.cs.auckland.ac.nz/~pgut001/pubs/vista_cost.html

H2G2 (2004) The history of magnetic recording. British Broadcasting Corporation, London. http://www.bbc.co.uk/dna/h2g2/A3224936

Harlow, J. (2006) Booming porn faces backlash. *The Sunday Times*, 29 October.

IETF (2006) ISO/IEC JTC1/SC29/WG11, *Coding of Moving Pictures and Audio*. https://www.ietf.org/IESG/LIAISON/ITU-1834.txt

IETF (2007) Mobility for IPv4. http://www.ietf.org/html.charters/mip4-charter.html

IFLA (2000) Optical media. International Federation of Library Associations. http://www.ifla.org/VI/6/dswmedia/en/txt_opti.htm

IFPI (2006) What is ISRC? *The International Standard Recording Code.* International Federation of the Phonographic Industry. http://www.ifpi.org/content/section_resources/isrc.html

Internet Systems Consortium (2007) Internet domain survey host count. http://www.isc.org/index.pl

Intertrust (2007) OMA/Marlin Services Licensing Program. http://www.intertrust.com/main/licensing/oma_marlin.html

ISO (2006a) About the MPEG-21 standard (ISO/IEC 21000). http://iso21000-6.net/about_m21.html

ISO (2006b) International standards for a sustainable world. In *ISO in Brief.* International Organization for Standardization. http://www.iso.org/iso/en/aboutiso/isoinbrief/isoinbrief.html

Jaguar (2004) System 7 Builds Intellectual Property Supply Chains. http://www.jaguartc.com/news/jn06222004.asp#item1

Janjicek, R. (2001) *CRM Architecture for Enterprise Relationship Marketing in the New Millennium.* Hewlett-Packard, Palo Alto, CA.

Jobs, S. (2007) *Thoughts on Music.* Apple Inc. http://www.apple.com/hotnews/thoughtsonmusic/

Johansen, J. L. (2006) DeAACS.com. [So Sue Me] Jon Lech Johansen's blog. http://nanocrew.net/2006/01/08/deaacscom/

Larose, G. (2004) DRM standards and standards-related groups. http://www.info-mech.com/drm_standards.html

Legat, M. (2002) *An Author's Guide to Publishing* (3rd revised edn). BCA, London.

Liquid Machines and Microsoft (2005) *Liquid Machines and Microsoft Windows Rights Management Services (RMS): End-to-end Rights Management for the Enterprise.* Liquid Machines and Microsoft.

Lyman, P. and Varian, H. R. (2003) How much information? 2003. UC Berkeley, Berkeley, CA. http://www.sims.berkeley.edu/research/projects/how-much-info-2003/printable_report.pdf

Madhavan, M. (2006) Intellectual property rights overview. http://www.jisclegal.ac.uk/ipr/intellectualproperty.htm

McGill, L. (2005) *Steganography: The Right Way*. SANS Institute, Bethesda, MD. http://www.sans.org/reading_room/whitepapers/stenganography/1584.php

McKenzie, M. (2006) Vista and more: piecing together Microsoft's DRM puzzle. *Computerworld*, 15 November. http://www.computerworld.com/action/article.do?command=printArticleBasic&articleId=9005047

Microsoft, (2005) *Microsoft® Windows® Rights Management Services for Windows Server(TM) 2003*. Microsoft Corporation, Redmond, WA.

Microsoft (2007) *Microsoft Announces Breakthrough Technology Enabling Simple Access to Broad Set of Digital Content, Including Music, Games, Video, Ring Tones and Pictures*. Microsoft Corporation, Redmond, WA. http://www.microsoft.com/presspass/press/2007/feb07/02-123GSMNewTechnologyPR.mspx

Morgan Stanley (2003) *Media Adoption Curve*. Morgan Stanley, New York.

MSDN (2005) Understanding how Windows Media Rights Manager works. http://msdn2.microsoft.com/en-us/library/ms984883.aspx

OASIS (2006) OASIS advancing e-business standards since 1993. http://www.oasis-open.org

OeBF (2003) *OeBF Rights Grammar Requirements: Required Rights Features for Digital Books*. Rights and Rules Working Group, Open eBook Forum.http://www.idpf.org/specifications/rrwgcoordinated.htm

OFCOM (2006) *The Communications Market*. Office of Communications, London.

OMA (2006) OMA-AD-DRM-V2_0-20060303-A, *DRM Architecture* (approved version 2.0). Open Mobile Alliance.

Oppliger, R. (2005) *Contemporary Cryptography*. Artech House, Norwood, MA.

OPSI (1998) *Data Protection Act 1998*. Office of Public Sector Information, London. http://www.opsi.gov.uk/

Postalheritage (2006) History. http://postalheritage.org.uk/history/

Radcliffe, J., Kirkby, J. and Thompson, E. (2001) *The Eight Building Blocks of CRM*. Gartner Research, Stamford, CT.

Reimer, J. (2006) Royalty agreement reached for UK digital music downloads. http://arstechnia.com/news.ars/post/20060928-7861.html

Rogers, E. M. (1995) *Diffusion of Innovations* (4th edn). Free Press, New York.

Rosenblatt, B. (2004a) Digital rights management tutorial and overview. In *Proceedings of the JupiterMedia DRM Strategies 2004 Conference*, Los Angeles, CA, October. GiantSteps MTS.

Rosenblatt, B. (2004b) Digital rights management for the enterprise. *JupiterWebinars*, February. JupiterMedia, New York.

Rosenblatt, B. (2006a) French legal body sets back copyright bill. http://www.drmwatch.com/legal/article.php/3624376

Rosenblatt, B. (2006b) UK's APIG issues DRM Report. http://www.drmwatch.com/legal/article.php/3611951

Rosenblatt, B. and Dykstra, G. (2003) *Integrating Content Management with Digital Rights Management*. Giantsteps Media Technology Strategies and Dykstra Research.

Rosenblatt, B., Trippe, B. and Mooney S. (2002) *Digital Rights Management Business and Technology*. M&T Books, New York.

RSA Lab (2000) *RSA Laboratories' Frequently Asked Questions About Today's Cryptography* (version 4.1). RSA Security Inc., Bedford, MA.

Russinovich, M. (2005) Sony, rootkits and digital rights management gone too far. http://blogs.technet.com/markrussinovich/archive/2005/10/31/sony-rootkits-and-digital-rights-management-gone-too-far.aspx

Samtani, R. (2005) DRM interoperability. In *Proceedings of the Jupiter DRM Strategies 2005 Conference*, New York, 27–28 July.

Schneier, B. (1996) *Applied Cryptography* (2nd edn). John Wiley & Sons, New York. http://www.schneier.com/book-applied.html

SealedMedia (2006) *Technology Specifications SealedMedia 5.0 E-DRM Technology Characteristics*. SealedMedia, Los Gatos, CA.

SG.hu (2003) *"DVD Jon" nem tartja törvénytelennek az iTunes törését*. http://www.sg.hu/cikkek/30058/_dvd_jon_nem_tartja_torvenytelennek_az_itunes_toreset

SJJF (2000) The Save Jon Johansen Foundation. http://sjjf.zerblatt.org/english/pictures.php

SMPTE (2003) *Final Report R30 Technical Committee Study Group on Content Identifier Harmonisation*. Society for Motion Picture and Television Engineers. http://www.lac-bac.gc.ca/iso/tc46sc9/wg1/wg1n200.pdf

Stefik, M. (1996) Letting loose the light. In *Internet Dreams: Archetypes, Myths, and Metaphors*. MIT Press, Cambridge, MA.

Sterling, J. A. L. (2003) *World Copyright Law* (2nd edn). Sweet & Maxwell, London.

St Laurent, M. (2004) *Understanding Open Source and Free Software Licensing.* O'Reilly, Sebastopol, CA.

Talbot, M. (2007) Midem: time's up for DRM. *MusicWeek*, 3 February.

Talmo K. E. (2006) *The History of Copyright: A Critical Overview With Source Texts in Five Languages.* Nisus Publishing (forthcoming). http://www.copyrighthistory.com/donaldson.html

The Economist (1851) Imitation v inspiration. The Economist. http://www.economist.com/opinion/displayStory.cfm?story_id=1325360

THOCP (2006). The industrial era. The History of Computing Project. http://www.thocp.net/timeline/2005.htm

Thompson, B. (2006) The weblog of Bill Thompson technology critic and essayist. http://www.andfinally.com

Trippe, B. (2006) Success in standards-based content creation and delivery at global companies: understanding the rapid adoption of the Darwin Information Typing Architecture (DITA). In *The Gilbane Report.* Bluebill Advisors, Boston, MA.

Tunebite (2006) Tunebite Platinum. http://www.tunebite.com/website/v2/en/platinum.php

TV-Anytime (2005) About the TV-Anytime Forum. http://www.tv-anytime.org/about/

UKPO (2006) What is intellectual property? http://www.ipo.gov.uk/whatis.htm

Ulwick, A. (2002) *Outcome-Based Segmentation.* Strategyn, Aspen, CO.

Umeh, J. (2004) Digital rights management: an overview. In *Presentation for British Computer Society North London Branch Event on DRM.* BCS, London. http://nlondon.bcs.org/

Umeh, J. (2005) *Evolving the New Music Business.* Capgemini, London.

Umeh, J. (2006) *Rights Management and the Music Industry: Finding A Way.* Capgemini, London.

US Copyright Office (2006) Copyright Law of the United States of America. http://www.copyright.gov/title17/92chap1.html

Van Tassel, J. (2006) *Digital Rights Management Protecting and Monetizing Content.* Focal Press, Woburn, MA.

Wang, W. (2004) *Steal This File Sharing Book.* No Starch Press, San Francisco, CA.

Wichmann, T. (2005) INDICARE survey digital music usage and DRM. In *Proceedings of the DRM Strategies Conference*, New York, 27–28 July.

WIPO (2006a) What is intellectual property? World Intellectual Property Organisation. http://www.wipo.int/about-ip/en/

WIPO (2006b) What is WIPO? World Intellectual Property Organisation. http://www.wipo.int/about-wipo/en/what_is_wipo.html

XML Cover Pages (2006) Technology Report: Open Digital Rights Language (ODRL). http://xml.coverpages.org/odrl.html

Yates, B. L. (2004) Applying diffusion theory: adoption of media literacy programs in schools. *Studies in Media and Information Literacy Education,* 4(2). http://www.utpjournals.com/simile/issue14/issue14toc.html

Zakon, R. H. (2006) Hobbes' Internet Timeline v8.2. http://www.zakon.org/robert/internet/timeline

Further reading

Adobe Content Server3. http://www.adobe.com/products/conentserver/index.html

Bagehot, R. and Kanaar, N. (1998) *Music Business Agreements* (2nd edn). Sweet & Maxwell, London.

British Museum. http://www.thebritishmuseum.ac.uk

Craver, S. A., Wu, M., Liu, B., Stubblefield, A., Swartzlander, B., Wallach, D. S., Dean, D. and Felten, E. W. (2001) Reading between the lines: lessons from the SDMI challenge. In *Proceedings of the 10th USENIX Security Symposium*, Washington, DC, 13–17 August. USENIX Association: Berkeley, CA. http://www.usenix.org/events/sec01/craver.pdf

Data-room.org. http://www.data-room.org/contact_virtual_data_rooms.htm

Davis, S. and Laing, D. (2001) *The Guerrilla Guide to the Music Business*. Continuum, New York.

Eberhard, B., Buhse W., Günnewig, D. and Rump, N. (eds) (2004) *Digital Rights Management: Technological, Economic, Legal and Political Aspects* (1st edn). Springer, Berlin.

Europe4DRM. http://www.europe4drm.com/DRMexplained/metadata.htm

INDICARE (2006) Consumer's guide to digital rights management. http://www.indicare.org/consumer-guide/

International Federation of Library Associations and Institutions. http://www.ifla.org/

Microsoft. WMDRM. http://www.microsoft.com/windows/windowsmedia/forpros/drm/default.mspx

Mulholland, A., Thomas, C. and Kurchina, P. (2006) *Mashup Corporations: The End of Business as Usual*. Evolved Technologist Press, New York.

OASIS (2002) eXtensible Access Control Markup Language (XACML). Committee Specification 1.0 (Revision 1), 12 December. http://www.oasis-open.org/committees/xacml/repository/cs-xacml-specification-01-1.pdf

RealNetworks. http://www.realnetworks.com/products/media_delivery.html

SMPTE (2000) Excepts from SMPTE 330M-2000, *SMPTE Standard for Television – Unique Material identifier (UMID)*. http://www.smpte-ra.org/umidreg/s330mex.html

TechRepublic. Customer relationship management (CRM) resources. http://whitepapers.techrepublic.com.com/search.aspx?tags=Customer+relationship+management+%28CRM%29

Thinkquest. http://www.thinkquest.org

Tomlinson, S. (1998) History of writing. http://www.delmar.edu/engl/instruct/stomlin/1301int/lessons/language/history.htm

Wikipedia. http://en.wikipedia.org

Wong, P. W. (1998) A public-key watermark for image verification and authentication. In *Proceedings of the International Conference on Image Processing*, Chicago, IL, October.

Index

BCS Products and Services

Other products and services from the British Computer Society, which might be of interest to you include the following.

Publishing

BCS publications, including books, magazines and peer-review journals, provide readers with informed content on business, management, legal and emerging technological issues, supporting the professional, academic and practical needs of the IT community. Subjects covered include Business Process Management, IT law for managers and transition management. www.bcs.org/publications

BCS Professional Products and Services

BCS Group Membership Scheme. BCS offers a group membership scheme to organisations who wish to sign up their IT workforce as professional members (MBCS). By encouraging their IT professionals to join BCS through our group scheme organisations are ensuring that they create a path to Chartered Status with the post nominals CITP (Chartered IT Professional). www.bcs.org.uk/forms/group

BCS promotes the use of the **SFIAplus™** IT skills, training and development standard in a range of professional development products and services for employers leading to accreditation. These include **BCS IT Job Describer, BCS Skills Manager** and **BCS Career Developer**. www.bcs.org/products

Qualifications

Information Systems Examination Board (ISEB) qualifications are the industry standard both here and abroad, and with over 100,000 practitioners now qualified, it is proof of their popularity. They ensure that IT professionals develop the skills, knowledge and confidence to perform to their full potential. There is a huge range on offer covering all major areas of IT. In essence, ISEB qualifications are for forward-looking individuals and companies who want to stay ahead – who are serious about driving business forward. www.iseb.org.uk

BCS professional examinations are internationally recognised and essential qualifications for a career in computing and IT. At their highest level, the examinations are examined to the academic level of a UK university honours degree and acknowledge practical experience and academic ability. www.bcs.org/exams

European Computer Driving Licence™ (ECDL) is the internationally recognised computer skills qualification that enables people to demonstrate their competence in computer skills. ECDL is managed in the UK by the BCS. ECDL Advanced has been introduced to take computer skills certification to the next level and teaches extensive knowledge of particular computing tools. www.ecdl.co.uk

Networking and Events

BCS's Specialist Groups and Branches provide excellent professional networking opportunities by keeping members abreast of the latest developments, discussing topical issues and making useful contacts. www.bcs.org/bcs/groups

The Society's programme of social events, lectures, awards schemes and competitions provides more opportunities to network. www.bcs.org/events

Further Information

This information was correct at the time of publication, but could change in the future. For the latest information, please contact: The British Computer Society, First Floor, Block D, North Star House, North Star Avenue, Swindon, SN2 1FA, UK.
Telephone: 0845 300 4417 (UK only) or + 44 (0)1793 417 424 (overseas)
Email: customerservice@hq.bcs.org.uk
Web: www.bcs.org

Jude Umeh

The World Beyond Digital Rights Management
Jude Umeh

Digital content owners and commercial stakeholders face a
constant battle to protect their intellectual property and
commercial rights. Jude Umeh outlines the issues behind
this battle, current solutions to the problem and looks to the
future beyond digital rights management.

ISBN: 978-1-902505-87-9
Price: £34.95 Size: 246 x 172mm Paperback: 320pp
Published: Oct 2007 www.bcs.org/books/drm

IT Law An ISEB Foundation
Jon Fell (Editor)

IT professionals not only need to know the technology, they
should be aware of how the law applies to the technology.
This is a guide to the main aspects of law that an IT
professional is most likely to come up against. A textbook
for the 'ISEB Foundation Certificate in IT Law.'

ISBN: 978-1-902505-80-0
Price: £24.95 Size: 246 x 172mm Paperback: 320pp
Published: Oct 2007 www.bcs.org/books/isebITLaw

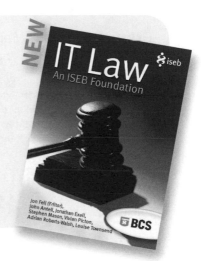

A Manager's Guide to IT Law
Jeremy Newton and Jeremy Holt (Editors)

This comprehensive guide to IT-related legal issues
explains, in plain English, the most relevant legal frameworks,
with examples from actual case law used to illustrate the most
common problems. Including: IT contracts; systems
procurement contracts; employment problems; instructing an
IT consultant; intellectual property law; escrow; outsourcing;
data protection.

ISBN: 978-1-902505-55-8
Price: £29.95 Size: 246 x 172mm Paperback: 180pp
Published: July 2004 www.bcs.org/books/itlaw

Data Protection & Compliance in Context
Stewart Room

This pragmatic guide provides practical advice on protecting data privacy under the Data Protection Act, human rights laws and freedom of information legislation; and gives a platform for building compliance strategies. Stewart Room, is the chair of the National Association of Data Protection and Freedom of Information Officers (NADPO).

ISBN: 978-1-902505-78-7
Price: £34.95 Size: 246 x 172mm Paperback: 304pp
Published: Oct 2006 www.bcs.org/books/dataprotection

Principles of Data Management
Facilitating Information Sharing
Keith Gordon

A practical guide to managing data – an increasingly valuble corporate asset in all organisations. Information is a key resource as important as equipment, assets, estate and capital. Invaluable for managing, marketing and IT directors and all business managers.

ISBN: 978-1-902505-84-8
Price: £29.95 Size 246 x 172 Paperback: 274pp
Published: Aug 2007 www.bcs.org/books/datamanagement

Practical Data Migration
John Morris

This guide contains techniques and strategies for ensuring data migration projects achieve maximum return on investment; ideas on rescuing ailing projects; and a model of best practice to be used for implementation of the methods. All blended with real life examples and clear definitions of commonly used jargon.

ISBN: 978-1-902505-71-8
Price: £29.95 Size: 246 x 172mm Paperback: 224pp
Published: May 2006 www.bcs.org/books/datamigration

World Class IT Service Delivery

Peter Wheatcroft

A manual on reaching and sustaining best practice in terms of performance, delivery and outlook in IT services to avoid customer dissatisfaction. Essential for IT service managers, IT directors, managers and procurement specialists.

ISBN: 978-1-902505-82-4
Price: £29.95 Size: 246 x 172 Paperback: 192pp
Published: May 2007 www.bcs.org/books/servicedelivery

Global Services
Moving to a Level Playing Field

Mark Kobayashi-Hillary and Dr Richard Sykes

Global Sourcing experts give an overview of how globalisation of the service industry is changing businesses and opening new opportunities to industries. A guide for managing, finance and IT directors and purchasing managers in all industries.

ISBN: 978-1-902505-83-1
Price: £29.95 Size: 246 x 172 Paperback: 192pp
Published: Apr 2007 www.bcs.org/books/globalservices

A Guide to Global Sourcing
Offshore outsourcing and other global delivery models

Elizabeth Anne Sparrow

The opportunities and obstacles associated with offshore outsourcing and other global delivery models. Country-by-country analysis of offshore services available.

ISBN: 978-1-902505-61-9
Price: £34.95 Size: 246 x 172mm Paperback: 196pp
Published: Nov 2004 www.bcs.org/books/globalsourcing

A Pragmatic Guide to
Business Process Modelling
Jon Holt

Explores all aspects of process modelling from process
analysis to process documentation by applying a standard
modelling notation, UML. Guidance for directors and
managers on business process modelling to improve
processes, productivity and profitability.

ISBN: 978-1-902505-66-4
Price: £29.95 Size: 246 x 172mm Paperback: 184pp
Published: Sept 2005 www.bcs.org/books/processmodelling

Business Process Management
A Rigorous Approach
Martyn A. Ould

A rigorous way of understanding the mass of concurrent,
collaborative activity that goes on within an organisation,
giving a solid basis for developing IT systems that
actually support a business' processes and improving
efficiency and profitability.

ISBN: 978-1-902505-60-2
Price: £34.95 Size: 246 x 172mm Paperback: 364pp
Published: Jan 2005 www.bcs.org/books/bpm

Business Analysis
Debra Paul and Donald Yeates (Editors)

A practical introductory guide for improving the effectiveness of IT
and its alignment with an organisation's business objectives.
Covers strategy analysis, modelling business systems/processes,
business case development, managing change, requirements
engineering and information resource management.

ISBN: 978-1-902505-70-1
Price: £29.95 Size: 246 x 172mm Paperback: 256pp
Published: Apr 2006 www.bcs.org/books/businessanalysis

Finance for IT Decision Makers
A practical handbook for buyers, sellers and managers (2nd Edition)

Michael Blackstaff

This covers aspects of finance relevant to professionals who make or influence decisions about IT. Written in plain language with practical examples, it explains: how to construct a financial case for IT projects; financing methods; current standards and legislation; cost/benefit analysis; investment evaluation methods; budgeting, costing and pricing; and more.

ISBN: 978-1-902505-73-2
Price: £34.95 Size: 246 x 172mm Paperback: 324pp
Published: July 2006 www.bcs.org/books/finance

Project Management in The Real World
Shortcuts to success

Elizabeth Harrin

This book provides a short cut to project management experience; it summarizes over 250 years of expertise from experienced project managers. It offers hints and tips on all aspects of project management including: managing project budgets; managing project scope; managing project teams; managing project plans; and managing yourself.

ISBN: 978-1-902505-81-7
Price: £24.95 Size: 246 x 172mm Paperback: 225pp
Published: Nov 2006 www.bcs.org/books/realworldPM

Project Management for IT-Related Projects
Textbook for the ISEB Foundation Certificate in IS Project Management

Bob Hughes (Editor)

The principles of IT-related project management, including project planning, monitoring and control, change management, risk management and communication between project stakeholders. Encompasses the entire syllabus of the 'ISEB Foundation Certificate in IS Project Management'.

ISBN: 978-1-902505-58-9
Price: £24.95 Size: 297 x 210mm Paperback: 148pp
Published: Aug 2004 www.bcs.org/books/projectmanagement

Software Testing An ISEB Foundation
Brian Hambling (Editor)

Providing a practical insight into the world of software testing, this book explains the basic steps of the testing process and how to perform effective tests. It supports the revised 'ISEB Foundation Certificate in Software Testing' and includes self-assessment exercises, worked examples and sample exam questions.

ISBN: 978-1-902505-79-4
Price: £24.95 Size: 246 x 172mm Paperback: 220pp
Published: Sept 2006 www.bcs.org/books/softwaretesting

Professional Issues in Information Technology
Frank Bott

This book explores the relationship between technological change, society and the law, and the powerful role that computers and computer professionals play in a technological society. Designed to accompany the BCS Professional Examination core Diploma module: 'Professional Issues in Information Systems Practice'.

ISBN: 978-1-902505-65-7
Price: £24.95 Size: 246 x 172mm Paperback: 248pp
Published: May 2005 www.bcs.org/books/professionalissues

Invisible Architecture
The benefits of aligning people, processes and technology

Jenny Ure & Gudrun Jaegersberg

The biggest problems faced in implementing computer systems, especially across different countries, are often not technical – they are 'socio-technical'. *Invisible Architecture* uses real examples to highlight the potential for harnessing 'soft' factors to competitive advantage.

ISBN: 978-1-902505-59-6
Price: £34.95 Size: 246 x 172mm Paperback: 104pp
Published: Mar 2005 www.bcs.org/books/invisiblearchitecture

⊞ BCS ORDER FORM

To order your book(s), please complete this form and send it to:
BCS Books, Turpin Distribution, Pegasus Drive, Stratton Business Park,
Biggleswade, Bedfordshire, SG18 8TQ, UK.
Fax: +44 (0)1767 601640 Tel: +44 (0)1767 604951
Enquiries to: Custserv@turpin-distribution.com
BCS Books are also available in all good bookshops.

	Price	Qty	BCS Member Price	Qty
The World Beyond Digital Rights Management	£34.95		£30	
IT Law: An ISEB Foundation	£24.95		£20	
A Manager's Guide to IT Law	£29.95		£20	
Data Protection and Compliance in Context	£34.95		£30	
Principles of Data Management	£29.95		£25	
Practical Data Migration	£29.95		£25	
World Class IT Service Delivery	£29.95		£20	
Global Services: Moving to a Level Playing Field	£29.95		£20	
A Guide To Global Sourcing	£34.95		£20	
A Pragmatic Guide to Business Process Modelling	£29.95		£25	
Business Process Management	£34.95		£30	
Business Analysis	£29.95		£20	
Finance for IT Decision Makers	£34.95		£25	
Project Management in the Real World	£24.95		£15	
Project Management for IT-Related Projects	£24.95		£15	
Software Testing	£24.95		£15	
Professional Issues in Information Technology	£24.95		£15	
Invisible Architecture	£34.95		£20	

P&P: UK £2.75 for the first book, plus 75p for any additional items.
Europe £5. Rest of world £12.

Postage: £ [ ]
Total: £ [ ]

Title: .... Initials: .... Surname: ....

Address: ....

BCS membership number (if applicable): ....

Telephone: .... Email: ....

I enclose a cheque [ ] made payable to **'The British Computer Society'** or please charge my:

[ ] **Visa** [ ] **Mastercard** [ ] **Switch/Maestro** [ ] **American Express** (please indicate)

Start date (Maestro/Switch only): .... Issue number (Maestro/Switch only): ....

Expiry date: .... Card number: ....

Name as it appears on card: ....

Signature: ....

*BooksUpdate service: please mark this box to receive occasional emails about new titles and
special offers on BCS publications (you can opt out from receiving these communications at any time).* [ ]